East Asian Business in the New World

ELSEVIER
ASIAN STUDIES SERIES
Series Editor: Professor Chris Rowley,
Cass Business School, City University, London, UK;
Institute of Hallyu Convergence Research, Korea University, Korea
Griffith Business School, Griffith University, Australia
(email: c.rowley@city.ac.uk)

Elsevier is pleased to publish this major Series of books entitled Asian Studies: Contemporary Issues and Trends. The Series Editor is Professor Chris Rowley of Cass Business School, City University, London, UK and Department of International Business and Asian Studies, Griffith University, Australia.

Asia has clearly undergone some major transformations in recent years and books in the Series examine this transformation from a number of perspectives: economic, management, social, political and cultural. We seek authors from a broad range of areas and disciplinary interests covering, for example, business/management, political science, social science, history, sociology, gender studies, ethnography, economics and international relations, etc.

Importantly, the Series examines both current developments and possible future trends. The Series is aimed at an international market of academics and professionals working in the area. The books have been specially commissioned from leading authors. The objective is to provide the reader with an authoritative view of current thinking.

New authors: we would be delighted to hear from you if you have an idea for a book. We are interested in both shorter, practically orientated publications (45,0001 words) and longer, theoretical monographs (75,000_100,000 words). Our books can be single, joint or multi-author volumes. If you have an idea for a book, please contact the publishers or Professor Chris Rowley, the Series Editor.

Dr Glyn Jones
Professor Chris Rowley
Email: g.jones.2@elsevier.com
Email: c.rowley@city.ac.uk

East Asian Business in the New World

in the New World

Helping Old Economies Revitalize

SHAOMIN LI

Old Dominion University

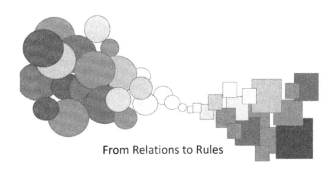

From Relations to Rules

ELSEVIER

AMSTERDAM • BOSTON • HEIDELBERG • LONDON
NEW YORK • OXFORD • PARIS • SAN DIEGO
SAN FRANCISCO • SINGAPORE • SYDNEY • TOKYO
Chandos Publishing is an imprint of Elsevier

CP

CHANDOS
PUBLISHING

Chandos Publishing is an imprint of Elsevier
50 Hampshire Street, 5th Floor, Cambridge, MA 02139, United States
The Boulevard, Langford Lane, Kidlington, OX5 1GB, United Kingdom

Notices
Knowledge and best practice in this field are constantly changing. As new research and
experience broaden our understanding, changes in research methods, professional practices,
or medical treatment may become necessary.

Practitioners and researchers must always rely on their own experience and knowledge
in evaluating and using any information, methods, compounds, or experiments described
herein. In using such information or methods they should be mindful of their own safety
and the safety of others, including parties for whom they have a professional responsibility.

To the fullest extent of the law, neither the Publisher nor the authors, contributors, or
editors, assume any liability for any injury and/or damage to persons or property as a
matter of products liability, negligence or otherwise, or from any use or operation of any
methods, products, instructions, or ideas contained in the material herein.

British Library Cataloguing-in-Publication Data
A catalogue record for this book is available from the British Library

Library of Congress Cataloging-in-Publication Data
A catalog record for this book is available from the Library of Congress

ISBN: 978-0-08-101283-3 (print)
ISBN: 978-0-08-101284-0 (online)

For information on all Chandos Publishing
visit our website at https://www.elsevier.com/

Working together
to grow libraries in
developing countries

www.elsevier.com • www.bookaid.org

Publisher: Glyn Jones
Acquisition Editor: George Knott
Editorial Project Manager: Tessa De Roo
Production Project Manager: Debasish Ghosh
Designer: Mark Rogers

Typeset by MPS Limited, Chennai, India

CONTENTS

About the Author   ix
Preface   xi

1. Introduction: East Asia in the Globalizing World   **1**
    1.1 East Asia at a Glance   1
    1.2 Globalization   3
    1.3 Globalization, East Asia, and the United States   7
    Questions   12
    References   12

2. Western Rules Versus Eastern Relations: A Fundamental Framework to Understand East Asia   **15**
    2.1 Some Puzzles   15
    2.2 What Made the "East Asian Economic Miracle"?   17
    2.3 Key to Understand East Asia: Rule-Based and Relation-Based Governance Systems   20
    2.4 How Do People Govern Transactions in a Relation-Based Society?   22
    2.5 The Costs and Benefits of a Relation-Based Governance System   25
    2.6 Caution: Rule-Based Versus Relation-Based Are Not Black and White   30
    Questions   31
    Endnotes   31
    References   31

3. Political and Economic Systems in East Asia   **33**
    3.1 The Interplay of the Political and Economic Systems   33
    3.2 The Political Economic Systems of Major Countries in East Asia   37
    3.3 East Versus West: Two Contrasting Legal Traditions   45
    3.4 The Role of the State: A Comparison of East Asia and the United States   49
    Questions   52
    Endnotes   52
    References   52

4. The Role of Culture in Economic Development: Does Culture Give East Asia an Edge Over America in Economic Competition?   **55**
    4.1 What Is Culture?   55
    4.2 Culture and Economic Performance   62
    4.3 Changing the Culture to Be More Productive   66
    Questions   69
    Endnotes   69
    References   69

5. Why Some East Asia Countries Thrive Despite Corruption   **71**

    5.1 Effect of Corruption on Economic Growth   71

    5.2 Why Do Some Economies Grow Fast Despite Corruption?   76

    Questions   83

    Endnote   83

    References   83

6. Information and Investment in East Asia: What We Need to Know When Investing in Relation-Based Societies   **85**

    6.1 Information in Relation-Based Societies   85

    6.2 Information Management by a Relation-Based Government   86

    6.3 Information Management by Firms   87

    6.4 Relation-Based Ways of Financing   89

    6.5 Why Foreign Investment Flows to Countries With Poor Legal Systems   89

    6.6 Direct Investment and Indirect (Portfolio) Investment   90

    6.7 Types of Investment and Modes of Governance   91

    6.8 Implications of Investment Type and Governance Mode   94

    Questions   95

    Endnotes   95

    References   95

7. The Currency Exchange Market in East Asia   **97**

    7.1 The Foreign Exchange Market   97

    7.2 Case 1: Japan Airlines   98

    7.3 Exchange-Rate Regimes in the World   99

    7.4 The Exchange-Rate Regimes of East Asia   101

    7.5 Case 2: Why Quantitative Easing Has Different Results in the United States and China?   102

    Questions   103

    Endnote   104

    References   104

8. Business Strategies in East Asia   **105**

    8.1 International Business Strategy   105

    8.2 Strategies in East Asian Countries   111

    8.3 The New Hybrid Strategy: Mass Customization   114

    8.4 Strategic Considerations   116

    Questions   117

    References   118

9. **Market Structures in East Asia: Why Selling to Some Countries Are So Difficult?**   **119**
    9.1   Customer Service Quality in Different Societies   119
    9.2   Salient Features of Relation-Based Market Structure   120
    9.3   Trade Flows Between Rule-Based and Relation-Based Countries   127
    9.4   Counterfeit Goods in East Asia   131
    Questions   132
    Endnote   132
    References   133

10. **Human Resource Management in East Asia: Should You Speak Out During Company Meetings?**   **135**
    10.1   Mafia Boss or CEO?   135
    10.2   The Relation-Based Organization Structure and Management Style 136
    10.3   When Rules Meet Relations in the Workplace: The Frictions Between the Two Systems   143
    Questions   150
    Endnotes   150
    References   150

11. **Technology and Innovation: Will East Asia Surpass the United States in Innovation?**   **153**
    11.1   The Use of ICT and Efficiency   154
    11.2   The Internet and the Relation-Based Societies   155
    11.3   The Interface Between Governance and ICT in Relation-Based Organizations 158
    11.4   Innovation and Creativity in East Asia   163
    Questions   167
    Endnotes   167
    References   168

12. **The Transition From Relation-Based to Rule-Based Governance in East Asia**   **169**
    12.1   The Puzzle Solved: Together or Separate Checks?   169
    12.2   The Challenge Facing East Asia: The Transition From Relation-Based to Rule-Based Governance   171
    12.3   Opportunities and Challenges for Multinational Corporations Doing Business in East Asia During the Transition   181
    Questions   186
    Endnotes   186
    References   186

13. Conclusion: What Can We Learn From East Asia?   189

13.1 A Comparison Between East Asia and the United States   189

13.2 What Can We Learn From the Relation-Based Way?   191

13.3 What Can We Learn From East Asia?   194

13.4 Get Ready to Compete   196

Questions   197

Endnotes   197

References   197

Index   199

ABOUT THE AUTHOR

Shaomin Li is Eminent Scholar and Professor of International Business at Old Dominion University, Norfolk, Virginia. He studies the global environment of business, political economy, strategy, and e-business. His writings have appeared in such journals as the *Harvard Business Review, Journal of International Business Studies*, and *California Management Review*. His research on rule-based and relation-based governance has been featured by *The Economist* twice. Dr. Li's commentaries have appeared in the *Wall Street Journal, Financial Times*, and *New York Times*. In 2008 he was the recipient of the Outstanding Faculty Award granted by the Governor of Virginia. Professor Li graduated from Peking University in economics, received his Ph.D. in sociology from Princeton University, and was a postdoctoral fellow in East Asian studies at Harvard University.

PREFACE

This book discusses how to conduct business in East Asia. But this is not one of the many "doing business in [insert country name]" books; my main objective in writing this book is to help American workers and American businesses gain competitive advantages in the global marketplace, in which the emerging East Asian economies are rapidly becoming major players. So this book can be viewed as an America-centered book on understanding East Asian business.

The background and the motivation of writing this book is that the American economy appears to be on the decline, especially relative to the rapidly rising economies, such as China. To revitalize the American economy, we cannot only focus on understanding the American economy, but also must pay close attention to the economies with which America competes. The objective of this book is twofold: first, I will focus on the opportunities and the challenges of doing business in East Asia. This book will help readers understand Asian economies and business practices so that they can compete more successfully in East Asia. Second, I will discuss how the United States can *learn* from East Asia in revitalizing its economy. This is a feature of my book that will set it apart from the "doing business in [insert country name]" crowd. I will analyze the social institutions in major East Asian countries, including the political, economic, and cultural institutions, and compare them with the institutions in the United States, and identify the strengths and weaknesses of the US institutions, and provide strategic and policy recommendations that may help the US economy and firms to compete in the global marketplace.

The main features of this book include (1) discussing how America (or the "old economies") can learn from East Asia; (2) providing a theoretical framework of rule-based versus relation-based governance to help readers understand the differences in doing business in East Asia versus doing business in mature economies; (3) offering insights based on my business experience in East Asia; and (4) approaching the topic from a comparative perspective.

This book is for business people who conduct business or manage people in East Asia, or who work in multinational corporations doing business in East Asia. For those who are interested in understanding East Asia business and how to navigate in East Asia's environment. Readers who are concerned with the American economy and want to learn how to more effectively revitalize it will also find this book relevant.

This book can be used as a textbook for courses covering doing business in Asia. It can also be supplementary reading for courses on international business and on revitalizing one's home country economy. The level of these courses includes both upper level undergraduate and graduate (MBAs and doctoral students).

CHAPTER 1

Introduction: East Asia in the Globalizing World

1.1 EAST ASIA AT A GLANCE

East Asia is an important region in international business not only because of its political and economic power, but also because of its unique culture characteristics and history. The definition of East Asia varies substantially, with the most narrow definition including what I call the core countries of East Asia (China, Hong Kong, Japan, Macau, Mongolia, North Korea, South Korea, and Taiwan) to the most broad definition including the above-mentioned countries and the ASEAN (Association of Southeast Asian Nations) countries (Brunei, Indonesia, Malaysia, the Philippines, Singapore, Thailand, Vietnam, Laos, Myanmar, and Cambodia) (Wikipedia, 2015a, 2015b).

In this book, we include countries into East Asia from the doing business perspective, in the sense that these countries must share some major dimensions of business environment in common. This commonality in business environment among these countries is the result of their political and economic systems, geographic proximity, and a shared history and cultural tradition. Based on the above consideration, my coverage of East Asia is rather loose: it includes all the core countries of the narrow definition above and some of the ASEAN countries that have a similar business environment with the core countries, such as Singapore, Vietnam, Malaysia, and Indonesia. In the next chapter, we will show that one of the most common factors that distinguishes the business environment of East Asia from the West is how the business activities are governed: in the West, public rules, such as the rule of law, are the dominant means to govern business transactions, whereas in East Asia, it is the private relations that act as the backbones of conducting and protecting businesses (Li, 2009).

East Asia (the core East Asia countries and ASEAN) covers about 16,000,000 km^2 (6,300,000 miles^2), or about 37% of the Asian continent, about 60% bigger than the area of Europe and 65% bigger than the United States (Fig. 1.1).

Figure 1.1 Map of South East Asia (part). *Maps-World.net. (2004). Political map of Southern Asia—2004. http://www.maps-world.net/southern-asia.htm: Maps-World.ent (Maps-World.net, 2004).*

East Asia has a population of about 2.2 billion people, accounting for 53% of the total population of Asia. It has one of the world's highest population densities: 135 people/km^2 (344/mile^2), second only to Southern Asia. In comparison, the world average population density is 45/km^2, and the United States has a population density of 35/km^2 (Wikipedia, 2015a, 2015b).

Income per capita of East Asia varies widely, with \$91,000 in Macau, \$583 for North Korea, and \$4000 for ASEAN countries (Wikipedia, 2015a, 2015b).

East Asia has achieved impressive economic growth. After World War II, Japan quickly dug itself out of the war ruins and began to focus on

Table 1.1 GDP and GDP per capita, East Asian core countries

Country	GDP nominal millions of USD (2015)	GDP nominal per capita USD (2015)
China	11,384,763	8,280
Hong Kong	307,790	42,096
Japan	4,116,242	32,480
Macau	51,753	91,376
Mongolia	12,409	4,179
North Korea	11,516	583
South Korea	1,392,952	27,512
Taiwan	518,816	22,082
Vietnam	204,539	2,233

Source: World Bank (2015). *World development indicators.* Washington, DC: World Bank and Wikipedia. (2015b). *East Asia.* https://en.wikipedia.org/wiki/East_Asia.

economic development. It achieved high economic growth from the 1950s to the 1980s and is now one of the richest countries in the world. Later, in the 1960s, the economies of Hong Kong, Singapore, South Korea, and Taiwan began to take off and became newly industrialized states, earning them the name of the "four little dragons." In 1976, the communist dictator Mao Zedong died, which precipitated an economic liberalization that released tremendous energy from more than 1 billion people to propel its economy to grow at about 10% annually for the past three decades, making China an economic powerhouse second only to the United States (Table 1.1).

The rapid economic growth in East Asia, especially in China, provides vast opportunities as well as great challenges to the advanced economies in the West, especially the United States To assess these opportunities and challenges, we must understand globalization and how it moderates the interplay of East Asia and the United States.

1.2 GLOBALIZATION

Globalization refers to the shift toward a more integrated and interdependent world economy. The two most important dimensions of globalization are the **globalization of markets** and the **globalization of production** (Hill, 2005).

Figure 1.2 Ways to use an iPhone. *Photo collage by author.*

1.2.1 The Globalization of Markets

The **globalization of markets** is the trend in which markets of all countries, which historically were separate and distinct, are now merging together into a large continuous world market. National borders are losing their importance in shielding a country's market. Online stores such as Amazon.com make it easy for people to buy internationally. The globalization of the market nurtures a global consumer culture that transcends national borders. The attitude and preference of consumers from different countries converge: they share information and knowledge about new trends in consumption and purchase the same product that is hot worldwide.

The convergence of consumer behavior and attitude in the world can be clearly seen from the following picture collage about the use of the iPhone by people of all walks of life across various countries (Fig. 1.2).

Another good example of the globalization of markets is **Uber**, the new ride-hailing company. Uber is an application of the Internet to the passenger transportation market. As of 2015, 58 countries have Uber and the number is rapidly growing (Uber.com, 2015) (Fig. 1.3).

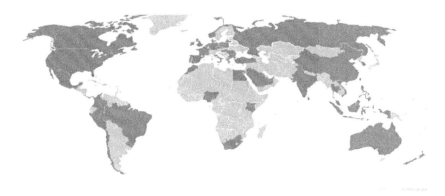

Figure 1.3 Uber's world map as of 2015. Dark green (dark gray in print versions) shows countries that have Uber. Light green (light gray in print versions) shows countries that do not yet have Uber. *Uber.com. (2015). Uber.com. Uber.com. https://www.uber.com/: Uber.com.*

1.2.2 The Globalization of Production

The globalization of production refers to the use of different locations globally to produce goods and services so that the total production process is optimal and efficient. The choices of locations are determined by the quality and cost of factors of production needed to produce the goods or service, such as labor, capital, land, or raw materials.

For example, **Apple** takes advantage of the globalization of production and strategically locates different value-adding stages of the iPhone production globally to best use resources from each location in order to make the iPhone with the highest quality and lowest costs. Its global chain of value creation spans from the United States (design, software development), Inner Mongolia of China (raw materials such as rare earth metals), Europe (the gyroscope used for tracking the smartphone's orientation), Korea, Taiwan, and Japan (LCD, chip), and China (assembly) (Financesonline.com, 2015).

1.2.3 Drivers of Globalization

Two main drivers responsible for the acceleration of globalization are the fall of trade and investment barriers and the advancements in technologies (Hill, 2005).

1.2.3.1 Falling Trade and Investment Barriers

Some 40 years ago, many countries were under communist rule and they did not participate in free trade and did not allow international investment (Fig. 1.4).

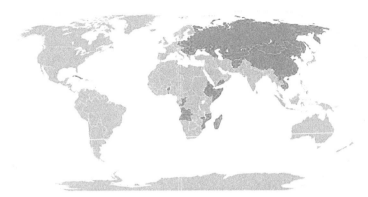

Figure 1.4 Map of communist countries, 1979–83. Red (dark gray in print versions) shows communist countries. *Wikipedia Commons. (2011, September 18). Communist countries 1979–1983. Wikipedia. https://commons.wikimedia.org/wiki/File:Communist_countries_1979-1983.png (Wikipedia Commons, 2011).*

The above map shows countries that declared themselves to be communist states under the Marxist–Leninist or Maoist definition between 1979 and 1983, the period that marked the greatest territorial extent of communist states.

Today, communism has been abandoned by most of these countries. The countries that restrict international trade based on communist/socialist ideology are few; the major ones include North Korea, Cuba (which is opening up), and Venezuela (practicing socialist economic policies).

1.2.3.2 Advancements in Technologies

There are two major technological advancements that have greatly facilitated globalization: (1) the advancement in transportation technology; and (2) the advancement in information and communication technology (ICT).

Mankind has greatly advanced transportation technologies in the past century, including the development of commercial aircrafts, containerization in shipping, and the emergence of supersized cargo ships. The advancement in communication technology is even more impressive. If the advancement in transportation technology has made the world smaller, the advancement in information and communication technology has made it flat. There are three great inventions in ICT that have drastically increased the ease and efficiency of conducting international business: **telecommunication technologies, microprocessors**, and most recently **the internet**, which has fundamentally changed the way we live and conduct business (Fig. 1.5).

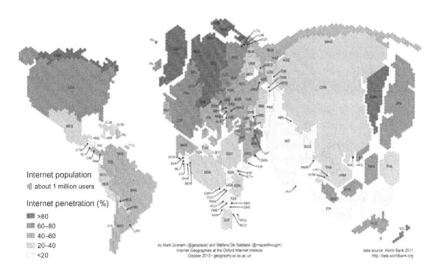

Figure 1.5 Internet population and penetration. *Oxford Internet Institute. (2015). Internet population and penetration. Information Geographics. http://geography.oii. ox.ac.uk/?page=*internet-population-and-penetration*: Oxford Internet Institute (Oxford Internet Institute, 2015).*

All these changes in the international political economy and in technologies have substantially changed the equation of political and economic power and the world order.

In the early 1960s, the US economy dominated the world, producing nearly 40% of the world's economic output, and China's share was 4%. By 2014, their shares of the world output had drastically changed to 22% and 13% for the United States and China, respectively (World Bank, 2015). A general consensus is that by 2026, China's GDP will surpass that of the United States (Holodny, 2015). The fundamental reason for China being able to rapidly catch up to the United States is China's economic reform and the opportunities provided by globalization.

1.3 GLOBALIZATION, EAST ASIA, AND THE UNITED STATES

1.3.1 The Globalization Debate: Who Gains and Who Loses in Globalization?

The effect of globalization varies not only from country to country, but also from segment to segment within a society. Below are some general observations.

For consumers: Globalization will increase competition and the supply of goods and services, therefore all consumers of such goods and services around the world will benefit from lower prices and more supplies.

For producers: Producers (such as manufacturing firms) that are less efficient and have higher production costs (such as due to higher wages) will see their markets taken away by firms that have lower production costs and are more efficient, resulting in their firms being driven out of business and their workers losing jobs. So, some producers (firms and workers) will benefit from and others will be hurt by globalization.

For the developed countries: Due to their high labor costs, many manufacturing firms cannot compete with their counterparts in developing countries. So they are forced to close and lay off their workers. However, due to the abundance of capital, investors from the developed countries flock to the developing countries to invest and earn higher returns. Furthermore, the importing of low-cost products from the developing countries increases the purchasing power of consumers (and the workers) in the developed countries. Overall, the increase in purchasing power outweighs the loss of wages by laid-off workers in developed countries. In addition, the moving out of polluting industries from these countries to the developing countries reduces pollution in the former. **For the developing countries**: in general, they gain more than they lose in globalization. More specifically, their gains and losses are opposite to those of the developed countries.

1.3.2 United States Must Embrace Globalization and Get Ready to Compete

While globalization benefits US consumers greatly by providing cheaper products and cheaper capital (eg, mortgages with low interest financed by countries with trade surplus such as China), it poses a serious threat to the manufacturing industry in the United States, as its labor cost is among the highest in the world. What is more worrisome is that the high labor cost is not the most vital weakness of the US economy; what seems to be more fundamental for America's weakness is in the social attitude toward work and education, which seems to be weaker than that of the emerging countries.

In the following example, we will see how serious Chinese is about education.

1.3.3 China's Maotanchang City: Largest Student College Test Preparation Facility

Maotanchang is a small city in Anhui Province, a less developed area of China, with a local population of 22,000. Now it is known for its unique industry: the production of students with a high Gaokao score by its nationally famous cram school.

Gaokao (high-level examination) is the Chinese equivalent of SAT. It is offered only once a year in early June and is the sole criterion to determine what college one can go to. Every year about 10 million college-bound high school graduates take Gaokao on the same day throughout China. Given the large number of Gaokao takers, their chance of getting into a top school is very slim.

The reason Gaokao is the sole determinant of college admission is that in a society with little public trust and high-level corruption and fraud, Gaokao is the most fair and objective criterion for college admission. In a society such as China that emphasizes elitism, brand name, educational achievement, having a college degree from a prestigious university is the most important achievement for a person, providing a necessary condition to be admitted into the professional and elite class. Thus Chinese parents and children take Gaokao very seriously. In order to get a high Gaokao score, parents send their children to cram schools. Maotanchang cram school is one of the best. It attracts tens of thousands of students, who, along with their parents or grandparents, are willing to pay high tuitions and living expenses to study here just for a chance to obtain a high Gaokao score and thus get into a good university (People.cn, 2015) (Figs. 1.6–1.9).

1.3.4 Are You Ready to Compete Globally?

A first question that came to my mind after reading the Maotanchang case is: are my students ready to compete with these Chinese students?

Like it or not, globalization is coming with an unprecedented speed, scale, and scope to all countries that are not entirely closed. Countries that embrace the challenge and are ready to complete will prosper, and countries that are ill-prepared will decline.

In this new global competition, East Asian countries such as China are thriving due to a number of factors in their institutions, which, as we will review in this book, may offer new perspectives for the United States to improve its competitiveness.

Figure 1.6 *Maotanchang cram school.* Students spend 17 hours studying every day, from 6:00 am to 10:50 pm. *Photo credit: Jiang, Y. (2014, June 5).* 座被高考魔化的城 *(A city demonized by the college entrance exam),* 搜狐大视野 > 新闻 > 《发现》. *http://pic.news. sohu.com/group-570015.shtml#0: Sohu.com (Jiang, 2014, June 5).*

Figure 1.7 *A classroom at Maotanchang.* There are 40 classrooms like this with 150 students in each. *Photo credit: Jiang, Y. (2014, June 5).* 座被高考魔化的城 *(A city demonized by the college entrance exam),* 搜狐大视野 > 新闻 > 《发现》. *http://pic.news.sohu. com/group-570015.shtml#0: Sohu.com.*

Figure 1.8 *Lunch break.* To save time, parents or grandparents bring lunch to the students. *Photo credit: Jiang, Y. (2014, June 5).* 座被高考魔化的城 *(A city demonized by the college entrance exam),* 搜狐大视野 > 新闻 > 《发现》. *http://pic.news.sohu.com/group-570015.shtml#0: Sohu.com.*

Figure 1.9 *The moment of truth: Gaokao day.* Maotanchang will send more than 100 buses to take students to take the exam. *Photo credit: Jiang, Y. (2014, June 5).* 座被高考魔化的城 *(A city demonized by the college entrance exam),* 搜狐大视野 > 新闻 > 《发现》. *http://pic.news.sohu.com/group-570015.shtml#0: Sohu.com.*

QUESTIONS

1. The Rise of Uber Globally

   Uber's new passenger transportation model poses a big challenge to the traditional taxi industry. Study Uber and discuss the following questions:

   a. Compared to the traditional taxi service, what are the competitive advantages of Uber? In other words, why do riders like Uber?

   b. Why is there strong opposition against Uber in some countries such as France?

   c. Facing the rapid rise of Uber, what should the government do to create fair competition in the passenger transportation industry?

   d. Facing strong opposition from some governments and the traditional taxi industry, what should Uber do to overcome these and continue its growth?

2. Globalization and the United States

   Is the United States a winner or a loser in globalization? Why?

3. Are You Ready to Compete?

   Based on "China's Maotanchang City," discuss the following questions:

   a. What are the most salient differences between the way these Chinese study and the way you study?

   b. Are you ready to compete with the Chinese? Why or why not?

   c. What should you do to improve your competitiveness?

REFERENCES

Business Insider. http://www.businessinsider.com/chinas-gdp-is-expected-to-surpass-the-us-in-11-years-2015-6.

Financesonline.com. (2015). How iPhone is made: The global assembly line. *Financesonline.com*. http://financesonline.com/hello-world-the-economics-of-iphone/.

Hill, C. (2005). *International business: Competing in the global marketplace* (5th ed.). New York, NY: McGraw-Hill.

Holodny, E. (2015, June 24). China's GDP is expected to surpass the US' in 11 years. *Business Insider*. www.businessinsider.com/chinas-gdp-is-expected-to-surpass-the-us-in-11-years-2015-6.

Jiang, Y. (2014, June 5). 座被高考魔化的城 (A city demonized by the college entrance exam). 搜狐大视野 > 新闻 > 《发现》. http://pic.news.sohu.com/group-570015.shtml#0: Sohu.com.

Li, S. (2009). *Rule-based versus relation-based governance: Together or separate checks?* New York, NY: Business Expert Press.

Maps-World.net. (2004). *Political map of Southern Asia—2004*. http://www.maps-world.net/southern-asia.htm: Maps-World.ent.

Oxford Internet Institute. (2015). Internet population and penetration. *Information Geographics*. http://geography.oii.ox.ac.uk/?page=internet-population-and-penetration: Oxford Internet Institute.

People.cn. (2015, August 7). "亚洲最大高考工厂"安徽毛坦厂中学毁誉参半. *People.cn*. http://edu.people.com.cn/n/2015/0807/c244541-27425136.html.

Uber.com. (2015). Uber.com. *Uber.com*. https://www.uber.com/: Uber.com

Wikipedia. (2015a). *Association of Southeast Asian Nations*. https://en.wikipedia.org/wiki/Association_of_Southeast_Asian_Nations.

Wikipedia. (2015b). *East Asia*. https://en.wikipedia.org/wiki/East_Asia.

Wikipedia Commons. (2011, September 18). Communist countries 1979–1983. *Wikipedia*. https://commons.wikimedia.org/wiki/File:Communist_countries_1979-1983.png.

World Bank (2015). *World development indicators*. Washington, DC: World Bank.

CHAPTER 2

Western Rules Versus Eastern Relations: A Fundamental Framework to Understand East Asia*

2.1 SOME PUZZLES

After a day-long meeting in New York, we—a group of Chinese businesspeople— went to a restaurant to eat. It was fun. "Together or separate checks?" The waitress asked us when we were almost done. "Together!" Someone shouted, and then a war broke out between us over who should pay. But if you think that we were trying to get someone else to pay, then you are wrong. Each of us competed for the bill (Fig. 2.1).[1]

Why do the Chinese always compete to pay while most Americans "go Dutch" when a group of people eat out? Does this mean that in general the Chinese are more generous than Americans? Similar puzzles abound. For example, why do strangers usually smile or nod at each other when they pass each other on streets in America while unrelated people don't acknowledge each other's existence when they pass each other in a narrow alley in China? Does this mean that Americans are friendlier than the Chinese? (Fig. 2.2).

What is the economic significance of all those differences? Are these differences due to culture? If they are, what is behind the culture? With rapid globalization and cultural interaction, will the Americans adopt the Chinese way, or vice versa? In general, how can we explain the differences between the East and West in social and economic interactions in their societies, and what do these differences mean when the East meets the West?

In search of answers to these puzzles, I have been studying different social systems for the past 15 years and, based on the findings by others and myself, have developed a theoretical perspective that can offer some not-so-obvious and yet consistent explanations to these puzzles.

---

* Adopted from Li, S. (2009). *Managing international business in relation-based versus rule-based countries.* New York, NY: Business Expert Press.

Figure 2.1 "Together!".

Figure 2.2 "Separate checks."

These solutions not only greatly satisfied my own intellectual curiosity but also helped others to understand these puzzles from a new perspective. During two decades of teaching international business, I have asked many of my students the above puzzles and have gotten all sorts of answers, ranging from a tautological explanation (eg, "This is just how things are") to a totally ridiculous response (eg, "Americans are dumb so that they greet everyone"). And most of the answers did not make logical and consistent sense. I would then offer them my simple but not-so-obvious answers that can consistently and logically explain the reasons behind these seemingly unrelated patterns, and I could see my bright students' eyes light up and they would exclaim, "Aha! Now I see it."

Their favorable reaction to my view on the patterns of social economic interactions across countries over the years eventually led me to write this book on the differences between the East and West in conducting business, in which I offer an unique and yet useful perspective to help business executives and students of international business understand business and society in East Asia.

Now, let's leave the "together or separate checks" and the "street encounter" puzzles for the time being and think about a more direct economic question: What made the "East Asian economic miracle" possible? The reader may wonder how such an economic question of considerable significance has anything to do with those puzzles. As I will show in the book, they are closely related.

2.2 WHAT MADE THE "EAST ASIAN ECONOMIC MIRACLE"?

The "East Asian economic miracle" usually refers to the sustained rapid economic growth achieved by the East Asian countries, including Japan after World War II, Hong Kong, Singapore, South Korea, and Taiwan between the 1960s and 1980s, and China from the late 1970s to the present. A common feature in the political economy[2] of these countries is that to various degrees they are (or have been) ruled by a government not subject to effective checks and balances and a legal system that lacks independence and is influenced by the ruler(s), undermining its ability to protect property rights. As a result of those shortcomings, these countries are characterized by a powerful state and a high level of corruption.

Thus the main puzzle about the "East Asia economic miracle" is how these countries achieved an economic miracle under political rule that seems detrimental to economic development.

A great deal of research and scholarship has been devoted to offering explanations of what made the "East Asian economic miracle" possible. Rich and expanding literature has been produced on this debate. A novice reader can easily be led into a jungle and get lost in the vast amount of articles and books offering complicated and often conflicting views. Here I attempt to offer a map to navigate in this jungle, and I provide a unique path for the reader to walk out of the jungle and see the puzzle differently.

Perhaps the best known theory to explain the "Asian miracle" is the political explanation. It has been argued that under a (benevolent) dictator or authoritarian ruler who is not too corrupt and is pro-business, a country's economy can be more effectively and efficiently developed.

While this argument seems to fit the political experience of some of the countries within the "Asian miracle" set, such as South Korea under the military dictator Park Chung Hee and Taiwan under the rule of Chiang Kai Shek and his son Chiang Chin Kuo, *it fails to explain what makes a dictator benevolent and not too corrupt.* For example, why is it that Park and the Chiangs were not interested in accumulating personal wealth, while their counterparts in the Philippines (Marcos) and Indonesia (Suharto) were busily transferring huge amounts of public funds into their Swiss bank accounts? In general, according to the study by Przeworski and associates, *The chance that a country will embark on a rapid economic development is the same under either dictatorship or democracy* (Przeworski, Alvarez, Cheibub, & Limongi, 2000).

Another dominant view on the "East Asian economic miracle" is offered by the cultural theorists, who try to explain the miracle from a cultural perspective (Harrison & Huntington, 2000). According to the cultural view, Asian countries are able to achieve high economic growth despite poor political systems (eg, lacking democracy and the rule of law) because of the deeply rooted Confucian values in their societies that emphasize long-term economic views (eg, save today for greater consumption value tomorrow; study hard today for a greater payoff in the future) and reciprocity in interpersonal relationships (eg, you give me one drop of water when I am in need and I will return with a water fountain in the future when I am able). While attributing the "East Asian economic miracle" to the Confucian culture may help us to see the link between a strong work ethic and economic growth, it only provides a partial explanation because there are still important questions left unanswered by culture. Even scholars who believe that culture makes almost all the difference in economic development admit that culture alone cannot consistently predict how an economy will develop. For example, *China has had the Confucian tradition for about 2000 years. Why hasn't its economic development always been positive? Why has it been on and off from time to time?* Moreover, this approach fails to answer what shapes a culture. How does culture interact with the political, legal, and economic institutions in a society to collectively affect economic development and business activities in the society?

Unsatisfied with either the authoritarianism argument or the cultural-deterministic view briefly described above, scholars of social sciences have been searching for more convincing answers from different perspectives. Increasingly, these efforts converge to one aspect that is very important for economic activities and yet has been overlooked by the mainstream scholars in addressing what made the "East Asian economic miracle": governance.

Governance can be defined as a mechanism people use to protect their interests in social and economic exchanges. For example, in a society with a fair, open, and effective legal system, people would resort to the courts or public arbitrations for a ruling if disputes arise. On the other hand, when the law is biased and judges are corrupt, then people may not choose the public rule as their means of settling disputes. Instead, they may look for a private way to solve it, which may include mediation or even violence (such as kidnaping). Interestingly, scholars observe that *what governance mechanism people or firms choose in a society is not entirely up to the individual or firm; it is primarily determined by the dominant governance environment of the society in which they live or conduct business.*

Governance environment refers to the set of political, legal, and social institutions that collectively facilitates or constrains the choice of governance mechanism the individual or firm has in a society. Scholars of social sciences have now come to a consensus that, broadly speaking, all societies can be grouped into two major camps in terms of governance environment: the ones that have good *public ordering*, or rule of law, and the ones that do not have good public ordering (Dixit, 2004). While readers from the West are familiar with the first type, they are unfamiliar with the latter, for some obvious reasons, which we will discuss in more detail in this book.

What do people rely on to protect their property rights and other interests in economic exchanges if the public laws are no good? Well, it really depends. If the public ordering (ie, public laws and government enforcement) is ineffective, the society must rely on some sort of private ordering in order to make certain (minimally) necessary economic activities feasible. But private ordering can have many forms. Some may be conducive to business and others may be hostile or even dangerous to conducting business. For instance, ordering can be based on a dictatorship imposed by a military strongman who monopolizes all business opportunities. Ordering can also be in a state of complete anarchy, in which bandits roam and rob people and make business activities based on free and voluntary exchange virtually impossible (Fig. 2.3).

Ordering can also be based on an extensive informal social network among businesses maintained by tradition or private enforcement, which may function effectively and efficiently under certain conditions. It is

Figure 2.3 Governance environment determines the choice of governance type.

this type of particular private ordering that has drawn increasing attention from social scientists. Among the efforts at studying private ordering, a new and useful approach is to compare the two major types of governance system to reveal not-so-obvious yet important patterns that may help us understand systematically how different countries conduct economic exchanges in their particular ways of interacting. This approach is called "rule-based versus relation-based governance."

2.3 KEY TO UNDERSTAND EAST ASIA: RULE-BASED AND RELATION-BASED GOVERNANCE SYSTEMS

The framework of rule-based and relation-based governance systems was first proposed by Shuhe Li and was expanded upon by others later on (Li, 1999). According to the framework, if we examine the governance environment at the societal level from political, legal, economic, and social perspectives, we can derive two contrasting systems, *rule-based* versus *relation-based*, in terms of how people protect their property rights and contracts.

In most developed societies, we observe that firms and individuals primarily rely on public rules—laws and government regulations—to resolve disputes and enforce rights and contracts. We call this reliance on public ordering a *rule-based governance system*. A rule-based governance environment must satisfy the following conditions: the public rules governing economic exchanges (such as laws, state policies, and regulations) are fairly made; the rule-making, rule-adjudication, and rule-enforcement are separate; rule-enforcement is fair and efficient; and public information infrastructure (such as accounting, auditing, and financial rating) is highly reliable and accurate. That the public information must be of high quality and trustworthy is vital for a rule-based economy to function smoothly and efficiently. Firms and people must be able to rely on publicly available information such as financial analyses and auditing reports in order to conduct business and make decisions, saving the cost of privately collecting information and investigating its quality for every potential business transaction. An important feature of relying on public information is that the information must be *explicit* and verifiable by a third party, otherwise it cannot be admitted in court if disputes arise. The court can only enforce the agreements between the parties that are publicly (third-party) verifiable; any implicit agreements privately made between them that cannot be verified by the court are not admissible to the court and thus cannot be enforced. As a result, business agreements in a rule-based society are usually formal and clearly written in explicit language. Because of the above conditions, citizens and organizations predominantly rely on public ordering in governing transactions.

The above features imply that rule-based societies tend to be mature democracies. For instance, for the laws and rules to be fair, a society must ensure fair participation of all interest groups in law making, which requires a representative democracy. For legal interpretation to be impartial, judges must be independent of political influence, which implies checks and balances between different branches of the government, and for the enforcement to be impartial and efficient, the executive branch has to be answerable to the constituents and be checked by the legislative and judiciary branches. This is why mature democracies share many commonalities, while nondemocracies may take many forms, ranging from monarchy, to military rule, to communist rule, to civil war and anarchy. Rule-based societies tend to have similar rules, yet nonrule-based societies may take different forms of private enforcement mechanisms to govern transactions (eg, community enforcement, private network enforcement, kinship enforcement, or mafia-dominated enforcement). In other words, while rule-based societies converge to the profile described above (eg, highly rule-based societies are all mature democracies), societies that lack a rule-based governance environment vary widely, ranging from warring states with complete chaos to tightly controlled societies under highly efficient authoritarian rules.

We observe that a specific group of nonrule-based societies that rely on private ordering (eg, the East Asian societies in general and the Chinese society in particular) are quite effective and efficient at governing the social exchanges that have been experiencing rapid economic growth. In addition to the absence of fair and efficient public rules due to the lack of any of the above-mentioned conditions necessary to a rule-based governance system, these societies have the following in common: They all have a governance environment based on private enforcement that can effectively and efficiently regulate markets and resolve disputes. This is what we call a *relation-based governance system.*

A relation-based society has the following characteristics: public rules (laws, government policies, and government regulations) are less fair because they are usually biased in favor of certain privileged groups (due to the lack of checks and balances); the executive branch of the government usually overshadows the legislative and judiciary branches and is likely to be controlled by a dictatorial ruling elite; courts and judges are controlled by the ruler(s); government operations are secretive and public information and press are controlled and censored by the government; industries and markets tend to be controlled by a small number of insiders (eg, people who have connections with the ruler) and are closed to outsiders; officials and business insiders are usually locked in a corruption-bribery relationship; and the informal network among the insiders in an industry is so closely knit and powerful that if one of the insiders is said to have broken the (unwritten) norms of the trade, the word of mouth by other insiders will effectively put him out of business.

For example, in Thailand, a relation-based society, there exists a class of powerful businessmen called *chao pho*, or godfathers. They "cultivate close links with local officialdom…to secure the licenses, permits, land deeds…to corner the lucrative government contracts." These godfathers also provide "some measure of security [and] justice…more speedily and more accessibly than officialdom." Also, "whenever these [ordinary] people have any problems they go to the *chao pho*" (Phongpaichit & Baker, 2000). Similar private social networks have also existed in Malaysia. Historically, because the government was unable to provide many public services, residents, especially the Chinese there, began to form a "sherh-hui-tarng," commonly known as a "secret society," to help each other in political, economic, and legal matters (Siaw, 1983). Vietnam, as a seasoned business writer summed up, relied on an "informal system of rule by people, rather than rule by law" (Hiebert, 1996).

2.4 HOW DO PEOPLE GOVERN TRANSACTIONS IN A RELATION-BASED SOCIETY?

Unlike a rule-based society, where public information is credible and heavily relied upon by citizens and businesses (making the protection of business transactions by public ordering feasible and efficient), public information in a relation-based society is usually untrustworthy. As a result, people and firms rely on private information to govern their transactions. There are several reasons why public information is not trusted. First, the government controls public information and the media in order to support its rule and agenda. For instance, it is well known that the governments in China and Vietnam (both are relation-based societies) tightly control the media and decide what news can be published (Kalathil & Boas, 2003). They even doctor news stories and time news releases in order to reinforce their rules. For instance, news of major scientific discoveries is often saved and released on major political holidays (eg, the National Day, the Communist Party's birthday). The practice of manipulating public information at the national level by the government does not help firms to report accurate information. As we will show later in the book, there is strong evidence that firms in relation-based societies such as China manipulate their income reports (Li, Selover, & Stein, 2011).

Another reason why public information is rarely useful as a means for firms to govern their transactions is the nature of these transactions. When the scale of the economy is small, and business people predominately deal with people they know, they rely on private information between the transacting parties, and they do not want to make their information available to a third party because the private business relationship is their most important asset. It is a small wonder that when researchers in Thailand interviewed successful business people about their political activities, few were willing to talk about it (Hewison & Thongyou, 2000). Similar patterns were also found among successful Chinese business people (Wu, 2008).

Such private relationships and information usually are *local* and *implicit*, and the agreement (eg, a handshake or a pat on the shoulder) is most often *informal* and cannot be verified by a third party such as a judge in a court. These practices, as we discussed earlier, are the opposite of rule-based governance, and as a result, business people must rely on private means to protect their transaction. Specifically, firms in a relation-based societies rely on three private monitoring mechanisms to govern their rights in transactions: These mechanisms are *ex ante* monitoring capability, *interim* (also called *ex nunc*) monitoring capability, and *ex post* monitoring capability.

Ex ante means "before the event" and is used in economic analysis to forecast the results of a particular action. Private *ex ante* monitoring capability refers to the effort invested by a transaction party *before* a business deal is made. In the absence of public information and enforcement, a firm must privately investigate its prospective transaction partner in terms of his or her track record and reputation. If the prospect has cheated, do not deal with him. If the prospective partner does not have a stable pool of business partners or clients, it implies that he may have a bad reputation and is avoided by other insiders. Such a prospect should be ruled out.

Interim monitoring is the ability of one party to obtain ongoing business and operational information about the other party, specifically whether the other party is on track with a project's schedule or whether the other party has any financial trouble or disputes. In a relation-based society, such information is not publicly available through credit investigating agencies. This is why news of financial insolvency of a firm in a relation-based society tends to cause large scale panic. Due to the lack of reliable public financial data, people do not know whether other firms may also be involved with the insolvent firm and are thus adversely affected. As a result, people stop lending to or withdraw deposits from firms likely to be involved with the insolvent firm (a snowball effect). Therefore one must invest in the capability of obtaining private and reliable information.

The third monitoring mechanism, private *ex post* capability, is the most important of the three. *Ex post*, Latin for "after the fact," is used here to refer to the ability to remedy or deter cheating or other opportunistic behaviors by the other party, in the absence of resorting to public regulators such as the courts (which tend to be corrupt, unfair, and inefficient in relation-based societies). In a relation-based society it is not uncommon for a promisee to resort to kidnaping in order to force a promisor to fulfill a promissory obligation (which may be an implicit, oral promise). For relation-based governance to work efficiently, private *ex post* monitoring must be effective and efficient. A *New York Times* report about informal, relation-based lending in China vividly describes such *ex post* monitoring (Bradsher, 2004).

> Borrowers default on nearly half the loans issued by the state-owned banks, but seldom do so here on money that is usually borrowed from relatives, neighbors or people in the same industry. Residents insist that the risk of ostracism for failing to repay a loan is penalty enough to ensure repayment of most loans…[As one lender puts it], "If it weren't a good friend, I wouldn't lend the money…" Violence is extremely rare, but the threat of it does exist as the ultimate guarantor that people make every effort to repay debts. "Someone can hire a killer who will chase you down, beat you up and maybe even kill you."

In Thailand, the powerful business people—godfathers—"built up networks of associates and gangs of subordinates." Because they took the law in their own hands, the areas in which they dominated "acquired a reputation for hired gunmen, sporadic violence, and regular newspaper reports of murders 'arising out of a business dispute'"(Phongpaichit & Baker, 2000).

In Vietnam, experienced business people all know that a formal contract is not very useful. "If the contract is not conducted satisfactorily," a successful Vietnamese entrepreneur commented, "we have the option to sue them, but that would be ridiculous. You know the legal system here" (Nguyen, Weinstein, & Meyer, 2005).

2.5 THE COSTS AND BENEFITS OF A RELATION-BASED GOVERNANCE SYSTEM

Since we observe that all advanced countries rely on public rules for governance, we may be tempted to rush to the conclusion that relation-based governance is categorically inefficient and thus detrimental to economic development. However, such a conclusion is premature. Relation-based governance systems are not all inefficient and thus hinder economic growth. Under certain conditions, relation-based governance can be quite effective and efficient due to its differing cost structure.

A well-functioning rule-based system is not free of cost to build and use. Imagine, for instance, the public ordering in the United States, one of the most advanced rule-based countries, and the infrastructure it must have in order for public ordering to function effectively and efficiently. In general, public ordering needs the establishment of the three-branch government. First of all, the country must build a legislative body, which in the United States means establishing and organizing the House and the Senate in Congress, the election system in all 50 states to select all the senators and representatives, and the infrastructure that supports the operations of legislation in Congress. Secondly, the country must build a court system ranging from the Supreme Court to local courts that are autonomous and well-funded. This infrastructure compels the society to invest in an education system that can train a sufficiently large number of judges who are professional, ethical, impartial, and well-paid. The society must also invest in training an army of lawyers and other legal workers with high professional and ethical standards. Last but not least, public ordering requires a credible and powerful law enforcement branch—the executive branch of the government, including a police force that must be well-trained, adequately paid, and thus uncorrupted.

Simply put, *a well-functioning rule-based system requires a large investment in legal infrastructure* that is costly and take a long time to build. From a cost accounting perspective, such an investment at the national level can be viewed as a *fixed cost* that does not vary regardless of how many people use it. Once the legal infrastructure is built and functioning, *the incremental cost of drafting and enforcing one more contract is relatively low*. In other words, whether the legal system enforces 1 contract or 1,000,000 contracts, the fixed, upfront investment for the legal infrastructure is the same (and *sunk* in the sense that it cannot be recovered), and the *marginal cost* (the incremental cost of enforcing an additional contract) is minimal.

Meanwhile, *in a relation-based society, business can thrive with minimal social order.* As long as crimes such as robberies are not out of control, business can be conducted and governed by well-functioning social-industrial networks maintained by private players (individuals or firms). In Thailand, where the public protection of business is not very effective or efficient, and the formal channel of financing (through banks) is expensive because of stringent rules, the Chinese Thai business community has resorted to informal financing among themselves. As one researcher observed, "Chinese [Thai] merchants…could inform themselves much more efficiently than branch offices of Bangkok banks about the credit status of other local Chinese… Their businesses were based on personal relationships…They arranged [private financing] to cut down fellow businessmen's transaction costs… Ultimately, they helped to increase the efficiency of Chinese business transactions and to redress a resource allocation distorted by economic regulation" (Ueda, 2000).

Another interesting difference in contract fulfillment and enforcement between the two systems is that, unlike public enforcement of contracts, which relies on third-party verifiable information that may be only part (the written part) of the general agreement between two parties, private enforcement is based on private information, which may not need to be verified by a third party. In this sense, private enforcement can be more complete than public enforcement, even including implicit agreements based on mutual understanding, the spirit of cooperation, or past practices.

In general, compared to the cost structure of the rule-based system, the relation-based governance system incurs few fixed costs (since it does not rely on a nationwide legal infrastructure). But *the marginal (incremental) cost of privately enforcing contracts increases as the scale and scope of one's business expands.* For example, if one only does business with his siblings, the marginal cost of the three types of monitoring (*ex ante*, interim, and *ex post*) is low, because he knows their reputation, their ability to deliver, and where their assets are (in case he needs to seize them). But when his business

grows and he runs out of family members, he may have to deal with people he does not know as well, such as neighbors or distant relatives, and
his marginal cost of monitoring increases. In general, the marginal (incremental) cost of establishing new relationships rises because cultivating new
relationships becomes more and more expensive and time-consuming
when one's private network expands from family members to strangers.
For this reason, in a relation-based society people first do business with
family members and then with friends and people they know. They try
to avoid dealing with strangers because it takes a long time to develop
close relationships, and the costs of private monitoring and enforcement
are high.

Therefore, *when the scale and scope of the economy are small, relation-based
governance may be effective and efficient,* as the society avoids costly investment
in developing and maintaining the legal infrastructures. People and firms
are constrained to and content with dealing with family members, friends,
and people in closely knit circles. As illustrated in Fig. 2.4, when the market is small, the average governance cost is lower in relation-based societies, giving them a comparative advantage during the take-off stage of their
economy.

However, when an economy expands from local to national and international scope, the relation-based governance becomes inefficient. The
average cost of finding and establishing new relationships rises and thus
the average cost of governance surpasses that of rule-based economies, as
illustrated at the turning point in Fig. 2.4. At this point, a relation-based
society begins to lose its comparative advantage in governance costs to a
rule-based society. It faces the pressure to evolve into a rule-based governance environment. A postponement of the transition caused by resistance
from people who are deeply entrenched and vested in the existing relational network hinders a country's economic development. This point will
be further elaborated later.

We now have a clearer idea regarding the question on the "East Asian
economic miracle": These countries have extensive informal social networks that enable them to rely on the relation-based system to govern
economic activities. This system has helped them to save the huge fixed
cost of building an effective public governance system. In other words,
they did not have to wait until they could build a vast, expensive legal
infrastructure for their economy to take off. These countries have relied
on private governance mechanisms maintained and enforced by family
members (Fig. 2.5), friends, cronies, and related people in high places

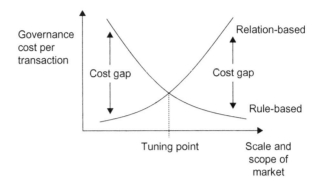

Figure 2.4 The governance cost of rule-based and relation-based systems.

Figure 2.5 The re-organization plan.

(possibly through bribery) to protect their business interests and operations. *The "East Asian economic miracle" has been achieved with the help of the relation-based governance system.*

Furthermore, we can now see that the Chinese heavily rely on *guanxi* (Chinese for connection and relation) in business activities not only because of their cultural heritage, but also, and more importantly, because the public rules are not effective and efficient in providing fair protection for their property rights and interests. *Relying on the relation-based way to conduct business activities is not merely a cultural phenomenon, it is fundamentally determined by the stage of political and economic development in a society.* Relying on private relations to settle business disputes is not unique to East Asian societies. Historically, feudal Europe and the United States were primarily relation–based societies (Li, 1999). Contemporarily, many

Table 2.1 Differences between relation-based and rule-based governance

Relation-based governance	Rule-based governance
Relying on private and local information	Relying on public information
Complete enforcement possible	Enforcing a subset of observable agreements
Implicit and nonverifiable agreements	Explicit and third-party verifiable agreements
Requiring minimum social order	Requiring well-developed legal infrastructure
Low fixed costs to set up the system	High fixed costs to set up the system
High and increasing marginal costs to maintain	Low and decreasing marginal costs to maintain
Effective in small and emerging economies	Effective in large and advanced economies

Source: Based on Li, S., Park, S. H., & Li, S. (2004). The great leap forward: The transition from relation-based governance to rule-based governance. *Organizational Dynamics, 33*(1), 63–78 (Li, Park, & Li, 2004).

Table 2.2 Types of governance and economic systems

Types of governance and economic systems		Degree to which a society relies on rule-based governance	
		Low	High
Degree to which a society relies on relation-based governance	Low	(Type D) Countries that have weak informal social networks, or live in chaos or civil wars (eg, Afghanistan, Iraq)	(Type A) Most mature market economies (United States, Western Europe)
	High	(Type B) Certain developing & transition economies that have strong extended informal social networks (eg, China, Vietnam, Thailand)	(Type C) Economies that mix rule-based system with strong relation-based culture (Taiwan, Hong Kong, Japan)

developing and transition economies such as Mexico, Mali, and Zambia are relation-based even though they do not have the Chinese or East Asian cultural heritage (Li, 2009).

Table 2.1 highlights the main contrasting features of the two systems we have discussed so far. We will discuss them in more detail in the book.

In Table 2.2, we examine the interface of the two systems. Based on the rule-based versus relation-based framework, we can make a typology of four types of societies: (A) societies that rely on rule-based governance system (most developed countries); (B) societies that lack fair and efficient public rules and rely on relation-based governance environment (developing countries with strong relation-based networks); (C) societies that are rule-based and yet have strong relation-based networks (such as Hong Kong); and (D) societies that lack fair and efficient public rules and do not have efficient and effective relation-based networks either (eg, countries in civil war or chaos).

2.6 CAUTION: RULE-BASED VERSUS RELATION-BASED ARE NOT BLACK AND WHITE

It should be noted that all human societies, including relation-based ones, have various degrees of formal rules. When we say a country is relation-based, it does not mean that this country has no formal laws. Even the most lawless country must have a set of published legal codes of some sort. But the state may not follow the laws and the ruler may simply ignore them. What distinguishes relation-based societies from rule-based ones is not who has the most comprehensive written laws, it is that people in relation-based societies tend to *circumvent* formal rules because the rules and the enforcement tend to be unfair, particularistic (depending on who has better relationship with people in power), and corrupt.

Another caveat is the distinction between a relation-based governance system and a relational business practice. By our definition, relying on a relation-based governance system is to use private means to fulfill the social function of protecting property rights, such as enforcing contracts, usually done by the government in societies where public ordering functions well. Thus, strictly speaking, relying on relation-based governance is to ignore the public law at best or violate it at worst, even though the law itself may be unfair or inefficient. In other words, resorting to the relation-based governance system implies that one must break an existing law in some way.

Relational business means conducting business though private relationships, such as knowing one's customers in person and matching an individual customer's need with a service uniquely tailored for the customer. It does not necessarily mean to circumvent the law. Thus the relation-based governance system, which is the main focus of this book, is different from relational business (such as relational marketing).

Throughout the book, we will show that the relation-based governance system is distinctive and yet intertwined with its counterpart, the rule-based system, and the relationship between the two is complicated. As the book unfolds, the reader will be able to see that the logic we use to explain the relationship is rather simple and powerful. Some economic phenomena that apparently contradict economic theories, such as why foreign investment pours into countries with a poor legal system, can be more logically and convincingly explained.

QUESTIONS

Based on the above framework of rule-based versus relation-based governance:
1. Is the relation-based governance way efficient in conducting business?
2. Is it ethical?
3. Will it fade away in East Asia?

ENDNOTES

1. This is a typical scene based on my extensive business experience with Chinese business people.
2. Political economy means the interplay of the political and economic forces that shape a society's overall development.

REFERENCES

Bradsher, R. (2004). Informal lenders in China pose risks to banking system. *New York Times.*
Dixit, A. (2004). *Lawlessness and economics: Alternative modes of governance.* Princeton, NJ: Princeton University Press.
Harrison, L. E., & Huntington, S. P. (Eds.), (2000). *Culture matters: How values shape human progress.* New York, NY: Basic Books.
Hewison, K., & Thongyou, M. (2000). Developing provincial capitalism: A profile of the economic and political roles of a new generation in Khon Kaen, Thailand. In R. McVey (Ed.), *Money and power in provincial Thailand* (pp. 195–220). Honolulu, HI: Hawaii University Press.
Hiebert, M. (1996). *Chasing the tigers: A portrait of the new Vietnam.* New York, NY: Kodansha International.
Kalathil, S., & Boas, T. (2003). *Open networks, closed regimes: The impact of the Internet on authoritarian rule.* Washington, DC: Carnegie Endowment for International Peace.
Li, S. (1999). Relation-based versus rule-based governance: An explanation of the East Asian miracle and Asian crisis. *Paper presented at the American Economic Association annual meeting in New York*, January. Listed on the Social Science Research Network (<http://papers.ssrn.com/paper.taf?abstract_id=200208>), 2000. Reprinted in *Review of International Economics*, 2003, *11*(4), 651–673. American Economic Association annual meeting in New York. New York.
Li, S. (2009). *Managing international business in relation-based versus rule-based countries.* New York, NY: Business Expert Press.

Li, S., Park, S. H., & Li, S. (2004). The great leap forward: The transition from relation-based governance to rule-based governance. *Organizational Dynamics, 33*(1), 63–78.

Li, S., Selover, D., & Stein, M. (2011). Keep silence, make money: The institutional pattern of earnings manipulation in China. *Journal of Asian Economics, 22*, 369–382.

Nguyen, T., Weinstein, M., & Meyer, A. D. (2005). Development of trust: A study of interfirm relationships in Vietnam. *Asia Pacific Journal of Management, 22*, 211–235.

Phongpaichit, P., & Baker, C. (2000). Chao Sua, Chao Pho, Chao Thi: Lords of Thailand's transition. In R. McVey (Ed.), *Money and power in provincial Thailand* (pp. 30–52). Honolulu, HI: University of Hawaii Press.

Przeworski, A., Alvarez, M., Cheibub, J., & Limongi, F. (2000). *Democracy and development: Political institutions and well-being in the world, 1950–1990.* Cambridge: Cambridge University Press.

Siaw, L. K. L. (1983). *Chinese society in rural Malaysia.* Oxford: Oxford University Press.

Ueda, Y. (2000). The entrepreneurs of Khorat. In R. McVey (Ed.), *Money and power in provincial Thailand* (pp. 154–194). Honolulu, HI: Hawaii University Press.

Wu, X. (2008). *China: The era of grabbing wealth: Business history, 1993–2008.* Taipei: Yuan Liu.

CHAPTER 3

Political and Economic Systems in East Asia

3.1 THE INTERPLAY OF THE POLITICAL AND ECONOMIC SYSTEMS

While distinctive and different, the political system and the economic system of a society (or a country, or nation) are closely linked in some systematic way. In other words, the two systems do not exist in a society completely independent of each other. This is why social scientists use the term **"political economy"** to describe the interplay of the political and the economic systems in a society and how they, interdependently, affect the social, political, and economic development of the society (Hill, 2005).

Broadly speaking, most of the political systems in the world that can be stable with a reasonably long duration (such as decades) can be divided into two types: **representative democracy** and **totalitarianism (dictatorship)**. Between the two types, we have transit political systems with various degree of chaos, such as anarchy, civil wars, or infant democracy.

Democracy is a political system in which the ultimate political power is in the hands of the people, who are represented by government officials who are elected by the people. As President Lincoln succinctly puts it, democracy is the "government of the people, by the people, for the people." Throughout the world, democracies vary widely in terms of the degree of maturity from infant democracies to mature democracies. Underdeveloped or infant democracies such as newly claimed democracies after the collapse of dictatorial regimes tend to be chaotic and do not function well. Mature democracies are the well-developed democracies that have a highly developed civil society with well-functioning elections, protection of human rights, and fair and efficient rule of law. Table 3.1 lists all the conditions necessary for a mature democracy, which is a useful tool to evaluate the degree of democratic development in a country.

Totalitarianism (dictatorship), the opposite of democracy, is a political system in which the ruler rules with absolute power. The ruler can be one person or family, one political party such as the communist party, or one

Table 3.1 Conditions necessary for mature representative democracies
Right to freedom of expression, opinion, and organization.
A free media.
Regular elections in which all eligible citizens are allowed to vote.
Universal adult suffrage.
Limited terms for elected representatives.
A fair and effective court system independent of the political system.
A nonpolitical state bureaucracy.
A nonpolitical police force and armed service.

Source: Li, S. (2015). International business operations–An online course (Li, 2015).

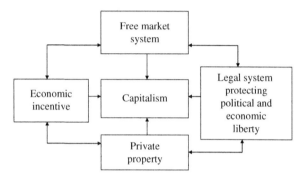

Figure 3.1 Essential elements of advanced capitalism. *Li, S. (2015). International business operations–An online course.*

small group of people such as a group of military strongmen. Its power is not derived from free and fair elections, rather, it is based on coercion backed by the armed force of the ruler.

Economically, there are two major systems: **market economy** and **nonmarket economy**. Market economy is also called **capitalism** or **free market**. It is based on private (or corporate) ownership of property and means of production; economic decisions are made by private or corporate entities based on the supply and demand through the signal of price in a free market.

Just like there are infant or pseudo democracies that do not work well, there are poorly developed capitalist economies that perform badly. For a capitalist economy (free market economy) to work efficiently and deliver prosperity, it must have four essential elements, as illustrated in Fig. 3.1.

All the four elements are fundamental building blocks of mature capitalist economies. Missing any one of them, the market system will not work well and will fail to deliver economic development and prosperity.

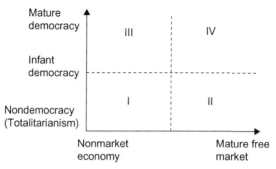

Figure 3.2 Combinations of the political and economic systems. *Li, S. (1987). The road to freedom: Can communist societies evolve into democracy? World Affairs, 150(3), 183–189 (Li, 1987).*

In a nonmarket economy such as a communist economy, capital goods and the means of production are controlled by the government; investment and production decisions are made by a government central planning body. Market exchange and market mechanism (price movement based on supply and demand) are banned or restricted.

The key question here is: what combination of the political and economic systems will best provide individual freedom, safety, and security to the society and citizens, and economic prosperity and equality?

Below are the four combinations of the two types of political system and the two types of the economic system (Fig. 3.2).

Countries in Quadrant I are mostly under totalitarian political rule and have government-controlled economies. People in these countries do not have much political freedom or many economic opportunities. Quadrant I is the least desirable position for a country. An example of such a country is a communist country, such as North Korea. Opposite to Quadrant I is Quadrant IV, which includes countries with mature democracy and free market. People in these countries enjoy great political rights and economic prosperity, and thus Quadrant IV is the most desirable position among all the Quadrants. Examples of these highly developed countries in East Asia are Japan, South Korea, and Taiwan.

Countries in Quadrant II have an interesting combination of the political and economic systems: politically, they are under totalitarian control, which means the state (the government) does not allow citizens to freely participate in political activities such as forming political parties or competing for offices; economically, the state permits or even supports a market-based economy, which allows private ownership, market exchanges, and profit making activities. A notable example of such countries in East Asia is China, which has achieved high economic growth in the past 30 years under a communist dictatorship. More interesting to note is that historically, several East Asian countries have achieved high economic growth under totalitarianism, such as South Korea and Taiwan. These cases have prompted some scholars of political economy (called neo-authoritarianism) to speculate that political dictatorship may be conducive, or even necessary, for a poor country to quickly develop its economy (Huntington & Nelson, 1976; Wang, 2014). However, critics are quick to point out that counterexamples abound: Indonesia under dictator Suharto (ruled 1967–98) and the Philippines under dictator Ferdinand Marcos (1965–86) did not achieve high economic growth (Przeworski, Alvarez, Cheibub, & Limongi, 2000). So it seems, the neo-authoritarianism scholars argue, in order for economies under dictatorship to grow, the dictator must not be too corrupt and yet pro-business, in other words, he/she must be a "benevolent dictator," such as the Chiangs (Chiang Kai-shek ruled 1948–75 and Chiang Ching-kuo ruled 1978–88) in Taiwan or Park Chung-hee (ruled 1962–79) in South Korea. But how can a country choose a benevolent dictator? The neo-authoritarianism scholars did not say.

More importantly and most pertinent to the case of China, how can the country under a dictator transform to democracy? So far the political scientists have failed to give any useful guidance.

In theory, Quadrant III should include countries that have a mature democratic political system with no free market. In reality, no countries have such a combination in the world. The reason is that under mature democracy, people have full and free political rights to choose the economic system, and they overwhelmingly choose to have the right to own property and embrace the free market system, and reject the total control of the economy by the state.

To summarize the above discussion about the types of political and economic systems and their combinations, we have the following observations. First, the nonmarket system cannot deliver economic development and prosperity, and it is always coupled with a nondemocratic system such as dictatorship (Quadrant I). Second, the market system can go with either democracy (Quadrant IV) or dictatorship (Quadrant II). When it goes with dictatorship, some economies grow fast (such as China), some failed to do so (the Philippines under Marcos and Indonesia under

Suharto). Third, mature democracies always go hand-in-hand with mature free markets, and they have best protection of human rights and freedom, and highest economic prosperity. Lastly, the commonly recognized goal of political economic development for less developed countries is to reach Quadrant IV. That Quadrant IV is most desirable is hardly debated, what is hotly debated, and the least known, is *how* to get there (Li, 2014).

3.2 THE POLITICAL ECONOMIC SYSTEMS OF MAJOR COUNTRIES IN EAST ASIA

Below, in a rough order of political economic development level, we briefly review the political economy of the major countries in East Asia. To provide a summarized view of the political economy of each country, we list the Political Freedom Index developed by Freedom House (2015) and the Economic Freedom Index developed by the Heritage Foundation (2015).

3.2.1 Japan

2015 Political Freedom Index (1 = best, 7 = worst): 1 (free).

2015 Economic Freedom Index (100 = best, 0 = worst): 73 (mostly free).

Japan is the most developed country in East Asia with a mature democracy and a free market system. At the same time, the relation-based way of doing business is still deeply rooted in Japan. Japan's political and economic achievement can be traced back to two major reforms. The first one is the Meiji Restoration in 1868, which centralized power and modernized Japan, and the democratization reform led by the United States occupation after the World War II in the late 1940s. After World War II, Japan adopted the modern, representative democracy in which the parliament and prime minister are elected and the emperor, which is hereditary, remains as the symbolic head of the state. Such an arrangement is called "**constitutional monarchy**."

The lack of natural resources and geographic limitation has made the Japanese people develop a hard-working culture. After the defeat in World War II, Japan quickly dug itself out of the ruins and began economic development. From the 1960s to the early 1990s, Japan enjoyed high economic growth, which made it a leader in applying technologies in consumer products.

A key feature of the Japanese way of doing business is that it has been highly relation-based (Li, 1999). Well-connected individuals and firms form zaibatsu (財閥), which means "financial cliques." These zaibatsu are very big and highly diversified financial business conglomerates that dominated the major sectors of the Japanese economy from the Meiji period until the end of World War II. Today, the relation-based way of doing business is reflected in the interlocking relationships among manufacturers, suppliers, and distributors, which is known as keiretsu (系列). Another feature of the Japanese economy is lifetime employment (CIA, 2015), although it has begun to decline (Yuasa, 2008).

3.2.2 South Korea and Taiwan

From the perspective of political and economic development, South Korea and Taiwan share some major similarities: both were split from the communist half, both were ruled by a right-wing dictatorial regime that banned citizens' right of political participation, but allowed the market economy to develop, and both have completed the democratization process, in which the pressure to democratize from the United States played an important role for both countries. They are now societies with mature democracies and highly developed market economies. Their rapid economic development has made them two of the "four Asian dragons" (also called the "four little dragons" or the "Asian tigers").

3.2.2.1 South Korea

2015 Political Freedom Index (1 = best, 7 = worst): 2 (free).

2015 Economic Freedom Index (100 = best, 0 = worst): 72 (mostly free).

The entire Korea Peninsula (including both the North and South) was under Japanese occupation from 1910 to the end of World War II. After the war Korea was split into two: the North became a communist state while the South became an infant democracy. Park Chung-hee took power in 1961 through a coup and ruled until his assassination in 1979. Park's ruling strategy was a combination of political dictatorship with state-led market economy. Politically, he ruthlessly suppressed oppositions; economically, he was pro-development and ordered the big businesses such as Samsung to work not only for making money but also for lifting the country out of poverty (Huang & O'Neil-Massaro, 2001). Concretely, the state policy was to restrict imports and consumption, and mobilize the country to export and invest in industries and technologies. As a result, from the 1960s to the 1990s, South Korea's economy took off rapidly and eventually made it a leader in high-tech industries in the world. Along with economic development, South Korea's democratic development accelerated in the 1980s, and in 1987 it held its first free election for president. Now it is a mature democracy as shown by the Political Freedom Index (CIA, 2015; Freedom House, 2015; Heritage Foundation, 2015).

Traditionally, businesses in South Korean have heavily relied on the relation-based governance. The organization that best demonstrates the dominance of relation-based governance in South Korea is *chaebol* (재벌), which literally means a clan that owns wealth or property. The *chaebol* is a South Korean-style business conglomerate with the following characteristics: Typically, it is a holding (controlling, or parent) company that owns numerous enterprises that operate globally. The head of the holding/controlling company, which is usually the head of the family that founded the conglomerate, controls all operations. There are several dozen such *chaebols* in South Korea. It is commonly believed that there is widespread informal collusion among the *chaebols*. They maintain their close relationships through marriages and through industrial associations, such as the Federation of Korean Industry. In recent years, especially after the 1997 financial crisis, South Korea has made a great effort to adopt a more rule-based governance (CIA, 2015; Huang & O'Neil-Massaro, 2001).

3.2.2.2 Taiwan
2015 Political Freedom Index (1 = best, 7 = worst): 1.5 (free).

2015 Economic Freedom Index (100 = best, 0 = worst): 75 (mostly free).

In 1949, after a long civil war in China, the Chinese Communist Party defeated the ruling Nationalist Party (Kuomintang, or KMT), which fled to the island of Taiwan and continued its rule. This separation precipitated a race of political and economic development. On the mainland China, the Communist Party exercised a proletarian dictatorship and centrally planned economy; at the other side of the Taiwan Strait, the KMT tightly controlled the political power and allowed a market economy. In 1949, both sides had similar income per capital at about $50 per year; but by the late 1980s, Taiwan's income had reached $5275 (1988), about 19 times of China's ($280 in 1988) (Li, 1989)—obviously Taiwan has won the race. Since Taiwan and China had the same cultural tradition, the difference is not due to culture but due to the contrasting political and economic institutions. In 2000, Taiwan successfully made its first transition of power from the long-ruling KMT party to the opposition party, the Democratic Progressive Party, ushering Taiwan into a mature democracy.

Under the rule of the two generations of the Chiangs (Chiang Kai-shek ruled 1948–75 and Chiang Ching-kuo ruled Taiwan 1978–88) from the 1950s to the 1980s, Taiwan adopted an export-oriented economic policy, developed strong manufacturing industries, and achieved impressive economic growth. The current economy features high-tech, electronics, machinery and tools, and petrochemicals. Unlike South Korea, in which big conglomerates dominate the economy, Taiwan features small and medium sized firms that are adaptable, flexible, and resilient.

Traditionally, Taiwan was a relation-based society. Along with its rapid democratization, Taiwan is moving toward a more rule-based society. During the transition, clashes between the traditional relation-based way and the newly established public rules have been frequent (Park, Li, & Yeh, 2015).

3.2.3 Singapore and Hong Kong

Singapore and Hong Kong are often mentioned as a comparative pair in the political and economic analyses of competitiveness of countries, especially in Asia. They share many similarities: both are city-states, both were British colonies, and they complete fiercely for talents, investments, and international rankings. In the 2015 ranking of Economic Freedom Index, Hong Kong beat Singapore by 1 point to achieve the highest ranking in the world with Singapore a close second. Their economic achievement has made them two of the "four Asian dragons."

3.2.3.1 Singapore

2015 Political Freedom Index (1 = best, 7 = worst): 4 (partly free).

2015 Economic Freedom Index (100 = best, 0 = worst): 89 (free).

Historically, Singapore was founded as a British colony. In 1963, it became part of Malaysia, and was expelled by Malaysia 2 years later. Since its independence in 1965, under the leadership of Lee Kuan Yew (1923–2015), Singapore became a highly developed free market economy, as can be seen from the high rating in Economic Freedom Index. Politically, it is a parliamentary democracy. However, Lee kept a strong grip on power and destroyed any opposition leaders who challenged him by using the law. He was also effective in fighting official corruption, making Singaporean government one of the least corrupt in the world. His ruling style has earned him terms such as "paternalistic," "authoritarian," or "benevolent dictator" (Meadows, 1988; Spencer, 2015). The combination of nominal elections (in which Lee's ruling party always won) and restrictions on political rights prompted commentators to coin a phrase to describe Singapore as a "democracy without liberty."

The success of Singapore's economy can be attributed to its free market policy, the British common law system (which provides good protection of property rights) (La Porta, Lopez-de-Silanes, Shleifer, & Vishny, 1998), investor-friendly business environment, its favorable and strategic location as a major trading port, low government corruption, highly competent civil servant force, highly educated labor force, and a strong hardworking culture. Like South Korea and Taiwan, Singapore relies heavily on exports. Its strong industries include consumer electronics, information technology products, and medical and pharmaceutical products. It also has strong transportation, business, and financial services sectors.

Compared to other East Asia countries, Singapore is less relation-based due primarily to its long and strong heritage of British rule and the common law tradition.

3.2.3.2 Hong Kong

2015 Political Freedom Index (1 = best, 7 = worst): 4 (partly free).

2015 Economic Freedom Index (100 = best, 0 = worst): 90 (free).

Hong Kong, one of the most vibrant metropolitan areas in the world, was a fishing village less than 200 years ago. In 1841, following China's defeat in the Opium War, Hong Kong was given to Britain permanently. In 1871, New Territory (adjacent to Kowloon of Hong Kong) was leased to Britain for 100 years. Under the British rule and its laissez-faire, "positive noninterference" economic policy, Hong Kong's economy flourished and it has become a center of international finance and trade, with one of the highest income levels and lowest tax rates. The economic policy, political attitude, and social culture can be characterized as pro-business, money-making, efficiency, law-abiding, and low social welfare.

From the 1930s to the 1970s, a large stream of refugees flowed in from China, creating a shortage in social services and bringing in a bad habit of bribing officials. By the early 1970s, corruption by public officials, especially the police, ran rampant, which prompted the Governor of Hong Kong to decide to clean up corruption. In 1974, the Governor founded a powerful agency called the Independent Commission Against Corruption (ICAC), which would prove to be extremely effective in eradicating corruption. Within a few years, corruption was drastically reduced and the Hong Kong government has become one of the least corrupt governments in the world (Li, 2004; Transparency International, 2015).

Under the British rule, the governor of Hong Kong, the highest officer, was appointed by the British government, the local people had few opportunities to participate in the political process and policy-making. Nevertheless, even though there was no democratic political participation under the British rule, the rule of law based on the English common law was well established and impartially enforced, making Hong Kong one of the most law-abiding societies. The Hong Kong people under the British rule enjoyed fully protected political liberty and freedom of expression. Thus contrary to Singapore, Hong Kong is dubbed as having "liberty without democracy" (Ke, 2014).

In 1997, Hong Kong was returned to China and the Chinese Communist Party promised to keep Hong Kong's political and economic systems, which are different from China's, intact for 50 years—a policy called "one country, two systems." However, evidence shows that increasingly China is interfering with Hong Kong's systems, especially the political system. Ironically the Chinese Communist Party has kept Hong Kong's tradition of having "liberty without democracy." The 2015 political freedom survey by the Heritage Foundation confirmed this by giving Hong Kong a better score in civil liberty and a lower score in political rights (Heritage Foundation, 2015).

Due to the long, well-established British legal tradition and British rule, Hong Kong has been more rule-based than most other East Asia societies. At the same time, due to its close ties with China and the strong influence of the Chinese culture, Hong Kong people understand the relation-based way very well, and can seamless switch to the relation-based way when doing business in relation-based markets such as China.

3.2.4 China and Other (Former) Communist Countries in Southeast Asia

3.2.4.1 China

2015 Political Freedom Index (1 = best, 7 = worst): 6.5 (not free).

2015 Economic Freedom Index (100 = best, 0 = worst): 53 (mostly unfree).

In 1949, the Chinese Communist Party, led by Mao Zedong (1893–1976), won a two-decade long, on-and-off bloody civil war against the then ruling Nationalist Party (Kuomintang), and established a communist society called the "People's Republic of China." From 1949 until his death in 1976, Mao ruled China with absolute power with an ultra-leftist economic policy that drove the country's economy to the verge of total collapse. After Mao's death, Deng Xiaoping (1904–97) was the de facto leader of the Chinese Communist Party and China until his death in 1997. Deng was a pragmatic communist who seized the opportunity provided by Mao's death and the overwhelming desire of the whole country to end the ultra-leftist economic policy, and played an instrumental role in China's opening up and the start of economic reform in the late 1970s. The key characteristics of China's reform is that it allows peasants who work in collectively owned communes to take back their share of the commune land and keep the residual (surplus) after satisfying the commune's quota, and gives state-owned enterprises (SOEs) the freedom to lease the state-owned firm to its manager so that the manager can keep the residual profit after he/she fulfills the revenue or profit quota set in the leasing contract. Both of these measures in the commune and SOEs substantially improved productivity and output and are de facto privatization of the communes and the SOEs, which eventually became de jure privatization of the economy. Today, most of the Chinese economy has been privatized except the most lucrative industries that are monopolized by the state (usually in the name of "state security") such as the energy, banking, aviation, railroad, telecom, weapon, and tobacco industries. While the Communist Party loosens up the economy, it continues to firmly control its political system by maintaining its absolute power. To understand the political system in China, one must understand the characteristics of the Communist Party. The first communist party in power was founded in Russia by Vladimir Lenin (1870–1924). He led the Russian Communist Party to overtake Russia by force and established the Soviet Union (now Russia) in 1917. Lenin developed the organizational structure of the **communist party** as follows:

1. Selective membership. One must apply to join the party, have two party members to support his/her application, and take an oath to protect the party with his/her life.
2. The party is centrally controlled with a standing central committee (politburo), with propaganda and personnel departments.
3. Party rules are above public laws. The party will use any means to achieve its end.

As can be seen, these rules are similar to the rules of secret societies such as mafia organizations. To Lenin's credit, communist parties are also called "**Leninist parties**." They are very different than the political parties in a democracy, and are more like a mafia organization.

During the 20th century, as many as 30 countries were once ruled by a communist party. Now, there are only five countries that are still under the rule of a communist party, and four of them are in East Asia (except Cuba): China, Laos, North Korea, and Vietnam.

The Chinese Communist Party is founded by copying the ideology and organizational structure of the Russian Communist Party. The top decision-making body is the small group of politburo standing members, which currently has seven members. The top party chief is the general secretary of the party, who is also the president of the country. Politically, the party monopolizes power and has made it clear that it will never relinquish its monopoly. Economically, the party has a pro-business, pro-development policy. Under such a combination, China has had very fast economic growth—it averaged about 10% for decades until the 2008 financial crisis—and has become the world's largest manufacturing base and an export powerhouse. The way business is conducted in China is highly relation-based (Li, 2014).

3.2.4.2 Other (Former) Communist Countries in Southeast Asia

Vietnam

2015 Political Freedom Index (1 = best, 7 = worst): 6 (not free).

2015 Economic Freedom Index (100 = best, 0 = worst): 52 (mostly unfree).

Laos

2015 Political Freedom Index (1 = best, 7 = worst): 6.5 (not free).

2015 Economic Freedom Index (100 = best, 0 = worst): 51 (mostly unfree).

Cambodia

2015 Political Freedom Index (1 = best, 7=worst): 5.5 (not free).

2015 Economic Freedom Index (100 = best, 0 = worst): 58 (mostly unfree).

Vietnam, Laos, and Cambodia went through a similar path: The communist party overthrew the pro-Western government by violent civil wars and seized power, abolished the market system, and established central-planning that drove these countries into absolute poverty, which forced the communist parties in these countries to start economic reform just like China's. While Laos and Vietnam are still ruled by the communist party, Cambodia has democratized, as can be seen from its better scores in both the Political Freedom Index and Economic Freedom Index.

Myanmar

2015 Political Freedom Index (1 = best, 7 = worst): 6 (not free).[1]

2015 Economic Freedom Index (100 = best, 0 = worst): 47 (repressed).

While it is not quite in East Asia, Myanmar is very close to East Asia and shares many cultural and ethnic ties with East Asia. Most importantly, Myanmar is undergoing a rapid democratization process, which is opening many new opportunities for international business and foreign investment.

3.2.5 North Korea

2015 Political Freedom Index (1 = best, 7 = worst): 7 (worst of the worst). 2015 Economic Freedom Index (100 = best, 0 = worst): 1.3 (repressed).

North Korea, formally known as the Democratic People's Republic of Korea, is the last communist stronghold in the world that has not opened up and embarked on economic reforms. In spite of its democratic name, the state is neither "democratic" nor a "republic." The political system is an absolute communist dictatorship with a family dynasty flavor: the founder of this "Democratic People's Republic" was the "Great Leader" (the official title) Kim Il-sung (1912–94); after his death, his son, the "Dear Leader" Kim Jong-il (1941–2011), took over; and after his death, his son, the "Great Successor" (the "xxx Leader" title has yet to be decided) Kim Jong-un (1983–), assumed power. So the country is not really the "People's" as the formal name suggests; it is Kim's, at least de facto.

The Chinese people who visited North Korea all have the same comment: "it is just like China in the pre-reform 1970s" (Guo, 2014). Due to the ultra-leftist economic policy, North Korea has very low income per capita—estimated to be $1300 (CIA, 2015). Of course, the poorer the country is, the more opportunities there are for foreign investors to invest and develop. The country cannot be closed forever. Under the draconian dictatorship and a closed economy, the income gap between North Korea and its cousin in the south (and the rest of the world) will remain or even increase, which in turn will put pressure on the dictator to open the country up for economic changes.

If North Korea begins opening up, its path may likely follow that of China's. In view of its close relationship with China and its ethnical tie with South Korea, both economic powerhouses with rich economic development experience and resources, North Korea should achieve rapid economic development if it is opened up.

3.3 EAST VERSUS WEST: TWO CONTRASTING LEGAL TRADITIONS[2]

3.3.1 Blind-Folded Versus the Third Eye

East Asia, having a long totalitarian tradition and being relation-based, has a legal tradition culture that is the opposite of the Western tradition.

The Western legal tradition (or rule-based) is fairness and impartiality, typified in the statue of the Goddess of Justice, who is blindfolded and holding up a scale (to weigh the facts) (Fig. 3.3).

Figure 3.3 Western Goddess of Justice.

The judge presiding over a trial in a rule-based society acts more like a referee in sports, whose main objective is to make sure that the two adversaries—the plaintiff and defendant—are treated equally and fairly. Both have a fair chance to present their arguments.

In totalitarian societies, especially the ones in East Asia, the government assumes a paternalistic role teaching and disciplining its subjects. Contrary to the rule-based tradition that judges should be blindfolded, the totalitarian legal tradition emphasizes the mission of the judge to not only take a position in the disputed case but also claims to have the ability to pinpoint who is guilty. While an exact counterpart of the Goddess of Justice does not exist in the Asian culture, there is a legendary judge by the name of Bao Gong in Chinese folklore, who has the superpower to read people's mind and see past events so that he has never made a single mistake in ruling. In a sharp contrast to the blindfolded Goddess of Justice, the legend has it that Bao Gong has three eyes—the third eye in the middle of his forehead—to help him see through people! (Fig. 3.4).

Thus the main function of the legal system in totalitarian-ruled societies is to identify and punish people deemed bad by the regime, at any cost. The judge's role is to assist the state in carrying out its political agenda by legalizing state policies and volitions. In a court, especially a criminal

Figure 3.4 Chinese God of Justice, Baogong.

court, the judge takes an active, inquisitive role to interrogate the accused, making the judge almost like a prosecutor.

In the legal literature, these two traditions are called "**adversarial**" (Western) versus "**inquisitorial**" (Eastern). In contrast to the inquisitorial approach, the adversarial way lets the two opposing parties try their best to present their evidence and logical arguments, and the rigorous cross examination tends to result in more thoroughly uncovering the facts about the case and thus having a more fair trial. This is especially true in a juried trial, which is not used in totalitarian (mostly relation-based) countries. On the other hand, the inquisitorial approach may raise the chance of a forced confession and a higher conviction rate in trials.

3.3.2 How to Protect Oneself in Countries Without Fair Rule of Law

In totalitarian-ruled or relation-based countries, laws are made to primarily protect the powerful insiders and the government. So what can foreign investors do in such countries to protect themselves and their investment?

Before entering a foreign market, one must thoroughly review the legal system there. If the risks associated with the weak legal system outweighs the potential benefit of doing business there, do not go.

Figure 3.5 Ex ante monitoring.

Figure 3.6 Interim monitoring.

If the potential benefit outweighs the potential risks, and the prospective investor decides to go, then he/she should follow what I call the **three monitoring mechanisms**:

Ex ante monitoring: Before entering into a relationship with a prospective partner, check out his history. If anyone in his family was ever involved in a cheating scandal, it is likely that he will cheat as well. So stay away from him (Fig. 3.5).

Interim monitoring: The ability to follow up on the financial status and performance of one's partner. One must be able to ensure that one's partner is in good standing and is not about to disappear (Fig. 3.6).

Figure 3.7 Ex post monitoring.

Ex post monitoring: This is the most important—the ability to punish any breach of agreement by a partner. If the foreign investor's partner takes advantage of him, does the investor have an effective measure to deal with the situation, especially in the absence of fair and effective public rules (laws)? If not, do not enter into the partnership (Fig. 3.7).

3.4 THE ROLE OF THE STATE: A COMPARISON OF EAST ASIA AND THE UNITED STATES

The impressive performance in economic development in East Asia and the active role of the government in it has prompted a debate on the role of the state in economic development and the merit of neo-authoritarianism (Sautman, 1992), which essentially argues that an authoritarian state is conducive to economic development. More recently, the rapid economic ascendance of China and the economic recession in the United States triggered by the 2008 subprime mortgage crisis has rekindled the debate and strengthened the case for an authoritarian state to actively interfere with the economy to achieve fast growth.

The argument for neo-authoritarianism is that an authoritarian government such as China's does not have to appeal to voters who may favor redistribution through taxes over economic growth, thus it can make unpopular policies such as keeping social welfare expenditure low and subsidizing businesses to spur investment to achieve economic growth.

While anecdotal evidence, such as China's high economic growth, seems to support such a theory, it is clear that for mature democracies such as the United States, it is virtually impossible to revert to authoritarianism, new or old. In fact, as our analysis of the performance of state intervention during the 2008 crisis between the United States and China shows, the argument for the superiority of the Chinese government over the US government in effective interference in the economy is incorrect (Park, Li, & Zhang, 2015).

To combat the 2008 recession, both the Bush and Obama administrations intervened with great government spending to bring the economy out of the recession. The measures included giving tax refunds, injecting capital to banks, bailing out major auto makers, providing incentives for startups, etc. The short-term impact of these efforts is that it averted the total collapse of the US economy and restored people's confidence. The longer term effect of the interference has been that the market mechanism has been restored to normal functioning, large corporations turned around and paid back the bailout funds with interest, and the economy went through adjustment and recovery, and has entered the expansion mode with healthy growth in the job, consumption, and housing markets.

During the 2008 crisis, the Chinese government unleashed RMB 4 trillion ($666 billion) to stimulate the economy, which is the largest single stimulus of all countries. This, plus the multiplication effect, undoubtedly gave the Chinese economy a great push. The short-term goal of this effort was to ensure that the GDP growth reached 8%, or "bao-ba," as the Chinese policy succinctly puts it. And it indeed achieved this goal. The long-term effect of this effort is less cheerful: many government investment-induced projects became "rotten tail projects" and were never finished. Production capacities are over built in many industries. Local governments' debts are at least doubled; huge amounts of cash entered the real estate market, creating a housing bubble; the nonperforming loans of state banks and loan defaults of the informal lending houses rose sharply; and, last but not least, the stock market has been on a roller coaster ride due to the government's heavy interference.

What can attribute to these contrasting results of government interventions in the United States and China?

While a comprehensive answer to this question is beyond the scope of this book, we can take a look at how local governments in the United

States and China make economic decisions to get some clues. In the United States, local governments are governed by a group of elected council members, who are answerable to none of the upper level governments (state or federal) but the local voters. So the economic decisions of these council members will reflect what their constituents want, which, as we all know, may not necessarily be the most economically efficient goals. So an economic decision, such as the choice between preserving a wildlife reservation and using the land to build a shopping mall, must be a compromise between pro-development, pro-conservation and whatever other interest groups. While this process has the drawback of being slow and lack the focus of economic development, it can prevent the government from betting large sums of money on risky or wasteful projects, such as building a pyramid. In fact the state and federal governments have similar checks and balances that can safeguard their economic policies.

The Chinese model, on the other hand, is a total negation of the US model: the lower level governments are appointed and thus answerable to the higher level governments all the way to the central government, which controls enormous resources and has virtually absolute power over the economy. This has enabled the government, especially the central government, to drive the economy in any direction it sees fit, and to do it swiftly with all the resources of the country. Needless to say, it can be very efficient and effective, especially during an economic crisis, but such a system is not without considerable costs. For example, can the government make sure that the economic resources, such as the stimulus money, are spent efficiently and effectively on improving people's welfare in the long run? The answer is that it cannot, because the officials who decide on such issues are answerable to the upper level officials, not to the people in the region, and it is the local people themselves, not the upper level government, who know the best about what they want. Without the mechanism of following the people's preferences, the best the central government can do is to use GDP growth as the sole measure of local officials' performance, which, of course, is a great improvement over using the loyalty to Chairman Mao as the sole promotion criterion in the past.

Charged with increasing GDP at any costs, local officials began to build anything and everything that would enlarge GDP: manufacturing plants, shopping malls, apartment buildings, highways, and government offices that are so big that they dwarf the Capitol Hill in Washington. A lot of these newly built high-rise apartments and shopping malls remain empty, creating many ghost cities throughout China.

The conclusion of this comparison is clear: setting GDP as the only goal of development, which is the best an authoritarian government can do, can lead to distorting market signals and wasting resources, because no one—including the authoritarian government—knows what the goals of development should be except the constituencies themselves. Only through public debates and elections can officials learn and represent the diverse goals of development for a region or for the whole society for that matter. But such debates can only be possible and effective in a mature democracy, such as the United States's.

QUESTIONS

1. Plot the position of the following countries on Fig. 3.2: China, North Korea, Cambodia, and Japan.
2. Based on what we learned from this chapter, is there anything in East Asia's political and economic systems that the United States can learn to help improve its economic performance?
3. Pick an East Asian country of your choice, and study it using external sources (suggestion: a good source is the World Factbook at www.cia.gov) and identify the political and economic challenges it faces.

ENDNOTES

1. The value of the 2015 index does not reflect the recent political change as shown in the 2015 election.
2. Adopted from Li, S. (2009). *Managing international business in relation-based versus rule-based countries*. New York, NY: Business Expert Press.

REFERENCES

CIA. (2015). The World Factbook. www.cia.gov.
Freedom House. (2015). Freedom in the world survey: www.freedomhouse.org.
Guo, H. (2014). Interview by author, Macau.
Heritage Foundation. (2015). *Index of economic freedom*. Washington, DC: The Heritage Foundation. www.heritage.org.
Hill, C. (2005). *International business: Competing in the global marketplace* (5th ed.). New York, NY: McGraw-Hill.
Huang, Y., & O'Neil-Massaro, K. J. (2001). *Korea first bank (A) and (B)*. Boston, MA: Harvard Business School Case.
Huntington, S. P., & Nelson, J. M. (1976). *No easy choice: Political participation in developing countries*. Cambridge, MA: Harvard University Press.

Ke, W. Z. (2014, December 10). Singapore: Democracy without liberty; Hong Kong: liberty without democracy. *Facebook,* https://zh-hk.facebook.com/choiyuendavid/posts/786528751414656.

La Porta, R., Lopez-de-Silanes, F., Shleifer, A., & Vishny, R. (1998). Law and finance. *Journal of Political Economy, 106*(6), 1113–1155.

Li, S. (1987). The road to freedom: Can communist societies evolve into democracy? *World Affairs, 150*(3), 183–189.

Li, S. (1989). What China can learn from Taiwan. *ORBIS: A Journal of World Affairs, Summer 33*(3), 327–340.

Li, S. (1999). Relation-based versus rule-based governance: An explanation of the East Asian miracle and Asian crisis. *Paper presented at the American Economic Association annual meeting in New York,* January. Listed on the Social Science Research Network (<http://papers.ssrn.com/paper.taf?abstract_id=200208>), 2000. Reprinted in *Review of International Economics,* 2003, *11*(4), 651–673, *American Economic Association Annual Meeting in New York.* New York.

Li, S. (2004). Can China learn from Hong Kong's experience in fighting corruption? *Global Economic Review, 33*(1), 1–9.

Li, S. (2014). The inevitable and difficult transition from relation-based to rule-based governance in China. *Corporate Governance: An International Review, 21*(1), 145–172.

Li, S. (2015). International business operations—An online course.

Meadows, D. (1988, May 5). Singapore leads the good life under a benevolent dictator. *Sustainability Institute* http://www.donellameadows.org/archives/singapore-leads-the-good-life-under-a-benevolent-dictator/.

Park, S. H., Li, S., & Yeh, K. (2015, April 8). Governance paradox in East Asia: Too many rules in fast-changing societies. *Forbes.com.* http://www.forbes.com/sites/ceibs/2015/04/08/governance-paradox-in-east-asia-too-many-rules-in-fast-changing-societies/.

Park, S. H., Li, S., & Zhang, R. (2015, August 27). Government stimulus: Pyramids, national parks, and ghost cities. *Forbes.com.* http://www.forbes.com/sites/ceibs/2015/08/27/government-stimulus-pyramids-national-parks-and-ghost-cities/.

Przeworski, A., Alvarez, M., Cheibub, J., & Limongi, F. (2000). *Democracy and development: Political institutions and well-being in the world, 1950–1990.* Cambridge: Cambridge University Press.

Sautman, B. (1992). Sirens of the strongman: Neo-authoritarianism in recent Chinese political theory. *The China Quarterly, 129,* 72–102.

Spencer, R. (2015, March 23). Lee Kuan Yew: A model for the new authoritarians or a one-off genius? *The Telegraph.* http://www.telegraph.co.uk/news/worldnews/asia/singapore/11489273/Lee-Kuan-Yew-a-model-for-the-New-Authoritarians-or-a-one-off-genius.html.

Transparency International. (2015). Corruption perception index: http://www.transparency.org.

Wang, Z. (2014, January 6). Neo-authoritarian reform needed in transition. *Global Times.* http://www.globaltimes.cn/content/837919.shtml.

Yuasa, S. (2008, November 2). They're young, educated, scared, poor. *The Virginian-Pilot & The Ledger-Star.*

CHAPTER 4

The Role of Culture in Economic Development: Does Culture Give East Asia an Edge Over America in Economic Competition?

4.1 WHAT IS CULTURE?

4.1.1 Case: What Is Missing in Inner-City Schools in America?

It is well known that public high schools in the inner cities in America have a poor quality and produce low-performing students, and Mathew F. Maury High School, an inner-city school in downtown Norfolk, an old city in Southern Virginia with a lower income level and higher concentration of minorities than its neighbors, seems to fit this image squarely. More than 60% of Maury students are nonwhite and many are from poor neighborhoods. Its academic performance is below the state average: 27% of Maury students failed the 2007 Virginia Assessment Algebra I test, as opposed to a 6% fail rate statewide. However, a visit to the school may surprise you in a positive way: the school has a good infrastructure—an indoor swimming pool, a nice library and an up-to-date computer lab; teachers are dedicated with advanced degrees from esteemed universities, such as Duke University and University of Virginia. But why does a school with a good infrastructure and high quality, dedicated teachers fail to be a top school? It is the desire to learn, the motivation to succeed academically that is missing among most students, many of whom are from broken families with one or both parents absent, or with parents who simply do not care about education. For example, it is not uncommon for Maury students to hang out late at night: a few years ago its football team captain was gunned down on the street around 1 am after returning from a party.

For the small number of students from families that do value education, they excel at Maury. And Maury teachers thrive from their achievements. For example, the physics teacher would use his own funds to

East Asian Business in the New World.

award a $100 scholarship to everyone who gets the top possible Advanced Placement test score in his class. Every year Maury will send a few students to some of the best universities: Harvard, Princeton, Yale, or MIT.

What sets the failing and the successful students apart in Maury, aside from their different intellectual abilities, is not the infrastructure or the teachers, but a **culture** that propels students to either value their education or forgo it.[1]

4.1.2 Culture Defined

What exactly is culture? There are many different definitions of culture, but most of them agree on the essential points. The Merriam–Webster dictionary defines culture as "the integrated pattern of human knowledge, belief, and behavior that depends upon the capacity for learning and transmitting knowledge to succeeding generations." The American Heritage New Dictionary of Cultural Literacy defines culture as "the sum of attitudes, customs, and beliefs that distinguishes one group of people from another. Culture is transmitted, through language, material objects, rituals, institutions, and art, from one generation to the next." Hofstede, Hofstede, and Minkov use the analogy of computing to describe culture: "the collective programming of the mind that distinguishes the members of one group or category of people from another" (Hofstede, Hofstede, & Minkov, 2010). These definitions and definitions by others (eg, Hill, 2005) have the following characteristics more or less in common: (1) the idea of culture is broad and includes knowledge, beliefs, customs and attitudes; (2) culture shapes people's behavior and the way of living in a given group of human beings, such as a society; (3) different groups or societies may have different cultures; and (4) culture is passed on from generation to generation.

4.1.3 Religious and Ethical Systems and Economic Performance

In countries that have religions, which include most of the countries in the world except the atheist countries such as communist countries in which religions are banned, religions act as perhaps the most important indoctrination force to teach people values and norms. Here we will review some religious and ethical systems that have played significant roles in economic performance in general and in East Asia in particular.

German sociologist Max Weber is a pioneer in examining the role of religion in economic performance and wrote a seminal book *The Protestant Ethics and the Spirit of Capitalism* (Weber, 1958 (1904–1905)), in which he compared the two major denominations of Christianity, Catholics and Protestants, in terms of their impact on economic performance, and argued that the **Protestant work ethics** are more conducive to economic performance. In Weber's view, Protestants differ from Catholics in organizational structure and work ethics. First, compared to Catholics, the organization of Protestants is highly decentralized. Each church is more autonomous and each Protestant is equal in front of God. This decentralized operation is congruent with the free market principle. Second, Protestants emphasize work for the glory of God and live a frugal life. Hard working, in a fair and competitive free market, will result in creating wealth, and being frugal means that one cannot indulge oneself with consuming all the wealth. The result is that the hard-working Protestants invest their wealth back into creating more wealth. This work ethic, according to Weber, has greatly contributed to the creation of modern capitalism.

While Christianity has had relatively few adherents in East Asia, East Asia does have an ethical system with a 2000-year tradition that holds similar values as the Protestant work ethics: Confucianism, which is an ethical and philosophical system (sometimes also described as a religion) developed from the teachings of the Chinese philosopher Confucius (551–479 BCE).

Confucianism has been designated by Chinese emperors as the official belief in China for thousands of years. Because of this, governments and scholars added all the virtuous values and norms into it, making it a collection of oriental virtues. The core values of Confucianism that are relevant to economic performance include: respect for authority, reciprocity (returning favors), filial piety, frugality, humanistic value (universal love and the ultimate concern for humanity), and respect for education and knowledge. Most of them are consistent with Max Weber's "Protestant work ethics." With that being said, we must emphasize that the most important and unique core value of Confucianism is reciprocity, which eventually grew into one of the most important concept in business in East Asia: *guanxi* (relationship or connections).

Historically, the cultures and countries strongly influenced by Confucianism include mainland China, Taiwan, Hong Kong, Macau, Korea, Japan, and Vietnam, as well as various territories settled predominantly by Chinese people, such as Singapore. Some scholars argue that the rapid economic growth in East Asia in the past 50 years or so can be partially explained by the cultural dominance of Confucianism in the region (Hofstede & Bond, 1988; Zhang & Zhu, 2012).

4.1.4 Hofstede's Cultural Dimensions

That culture is important in affecting economic performance is not difficult to understand and has been widely accepted. What is difficult is how to quantify culture. Without quantifying it into measurable variables, we cannot systematically study it and gage its effects on economic performance. There have been numerous efforts by scholars trying to quantify culture. One of the most successful endeavors was made by Geert Hofstede, who developed six dimensions to delineate culture (Hofstede, 2015b). Below we briefly describe them (Table 4.1).

Power Distance. Power distance "is the extent to which the less powerful members of organizations and institutions (like the family) accept and expect that power is distributed unequally." This dimension measures inequality in a culture. A society that has a large power distance tends to have a high level of inequality. One indication of larger power distance in a workplace is that the relationship between the supervisor and the subordinate is more formal (eg, the subordinate addresses the supervisor by surname with title rather than by first name). The power distance score for the United States is 40, whereas for East Asia it is 66, which means that compared to their counterparts in the United States, people in East Asian societies emphasize obedience more and have greater respect for authority. Managers are more powerful and employees are expected to be told and follow orders without asking too many questions. This culture trait tends to be conducive to the productivity of low-skilled workers, such as assembly line workers or garment workers.

Individualism. Individualism as a cultural trait is the opposite of collectivism. It measures "the degree to which individuals are integrated into groups" (Hofstede, 2015a). Individualism gives individuals greater importance as opposed to groups or society as a whole. It emphasizes individuality and being unique and different, rather than conformity, consensus, and commonality. As can be seen from Table 4.1, East Asian societies and the United States are on the two extremes in this measure. The low individualism in East Asia can be attributed to the long history of absolute monarchy and the more recent authoritarian/totalitarian rule in these countries. Economically, individualism encourages creativity so it is conducive to the development of entrepreneurship and innovation. It is also positively associated with social mobility. Conversely, collectivism encourages teamwork and conformity so it is conducive to improving the efficiencies of unskilled work and assembly-line works. Collectivism's emphases on family background and family ties may negatively affect social mobility.

Table 4.1 Hofstede's cultural dimensions, East Asian countries and the United States

Country/region	Power distance	Individualism	Masculinity	Uncertainty avoidance	Long-term orientation	Indulgence
China	80	20	66	30	87	24
Hong Kong	68	25	57	29	61	17
Japan	54	46	95	92	88	42
Korea (South)	60	18	39	85	100	29
Singapore	74	20	48	8	72	46
Taiwan	58	17	45	69	93	49
East Asia (average)	66	24	58	52	84	35
United States	40	91	62	46	26	68

Source: Hofstede, G. (2015b). *Dimensions of national cultures.* http://geert-hofstede.com/countries.html.

Masculinity. Masculinity, as opposed to femininity, "refers to the distribution of emotional roles between the genders" (Hofstede, 2015a). According to Hofstede, women's values include being modest and caring, whereas men's values tend to be assertive and competitive. Socially, a more masculine society has greater gender inequality. Economically, masculine culture emphasizes material success. East Asia and the United States are similar in their degree of masculinity. However, Japan has a very high degree of masculinity, which supports the commonly held view that Japan has a larger gap in gender equality.

Uncertainty avoidance. Uncertainty avoidance "deals with a society's tolerance for uncertainty and ambiguity" (Hofstede, 2015a). Cultures with low uncertainty avoidance nurture risk-taking attitudes and behavior, which are vital for entrepreneurship and innovation. On the other hand, people with a culture of avoiding uncertainty like to obey rules and orders and thus tend to be good followers and unskilled workers, which may contribute to the high productivity in the early stages of economic development. The level of uncertainty avoidance of East Asia is similar to that of the United States and both are in the middle.

Long-term orientation. "Long-term oriented societies foster pragmatic virtues oriented towards future rewards, in particular saving, persistence, and adapting to changing circumstances" (Hofstede, 2015a). This is a trait that is highly valued in East Asia.

Indulgence. Indulgence, as opposed to restraint, "stands for a society that allows relatively free gratification of basic and natural human drives related to enjoying life and having fun," whereas "restraint stands for a society that suppresses gratification of needs and regulates it by means of strict social norms." This measure overlaps with long-term orientation and thus we will not further discuss it.

Investing money or time first and enjoying the fruits of the investment later is called delayed gratification in economics. For example, how people park their cars can be used to gage such behavior: Reverse backing into a parking space takes more time, but makes it easier, quicker, and safer to leave later. In a study of productivity using parking behavior, the author found a high correlation between them (Li, 2015) (Figs. 4.1 and 4.2).

4.1.5 Names and Address: Differences Between the East and West

Western names such as English and American names are given name first and family name last; whereas Eastern names such as Chinese or Korean

Figure 4.1 A Parking garage in Norfolk, Virginia, USA, 2013.

Figure 4.2 A Parking lot in Kaohsiung, Taiwan, 2013.

names are the opposite. This can provide further evidence that the Western culture emphasizes the individual and the Eastern culture views the family as more important. In practice, for Western names, the given names have clearer patterns, and are more common and easier to remember than last names, such as John, David, or Alice; for the Eastern names, the opposite is true: family names are more common and easier to remember, such as Lee (Li), Park, Wang (Wong), Zhang (Chang), or Liu.

Addresses have a different format between the East and West. In the West an address begins with the individual first, the smallest unit (house) to largest (country); in the East it is the opposite: country, province, city,.., individual.

The English calendar format is dd/mm/yy; the Eastern calendar is yy/mm/dd.

All these reflect that cultural differences can be summarized as being in the West, individual first—without the individual, there will be no collective or aggregate. In the East, the aggregate comes first, whereas individuals are merely elements of the aggregate.

4.2 CULTURE AND ECONOMIC PERFORMANCE

4.2.1 Why and How Culture Matters for Economic Performance

Culture is shaped by the political and economic forces in a society, and it shapes the political and economic systems in the society as well (Li, Park, & Li, 2004). A more pro-business and hard-working culture will help a country's economy to grow faster, and conversely, a culture that looks down on business money making activities and overemphasizes spiritual achievement may experience slower economic development (Li, Park, & Selover, 2015). More specifically, economists argue that certain cultural traits would help a person become a more productive worker. These traits include hard working, emphasizing independence, self-reliance, thrift, and education, for example. The mechanisms by which culture affects economic performance include the following: people who are long-term oriented tend to invest their time and money in education, which in turn makes them more knowledgeable and skillful, and therefore can create more output and value. People who are frugal do not indulge themselves with their earnings and thus reinvest them back into production; people who are hard working are more productive; people who respect authority are efficient in jobs requiring attention to detail and following orders closely (Li et al., 2015).

Li, Park, and Selover conducted a study that linked culture to economic performance (Li et al., 2015). They regressed labor productivity on a number of cultural traits across more than 40 emerging countries (eg, countries with a capita income below $10,000) and identified three groups of cultural factors that significantly affect labor productivity in these countries.

The first group is economic-related culture, including people's perception about their own financial situation, their attitudes toward income inequality and taxes. They found that people who are not satisfied with their financial situation tend to plan for the longer term and are willing to take greater risks, and this attitude in turn helps to improve productivity. They also found countries with high productivity gains have a social attitude that tolerates inequality more and dislikes taxes.

The second group is the attitude toward authority and freedom. They found that the following three cultural factors are conducive to labor productivity gains: a culture that accepts and expects great power distance (eg, less powerful people are willing to accept the fact that power is not distributed equally); people who perceive that they don't have much freedom tend to be more productive; and a social attitude that prefers government to assure social safety and stability rather than a deregulated society in which people are responsible for their own actions. In sum, the culture of the high productivity-gain countries tends to be more authoritarian and less free.

The third group of factors is all about family value. The family—the most basic element in a society and the primary organization in which a person is brought up and is socialized—plays the most important role in forming the culture of a person. It is the most important vehicle through which culture is passed from generation to generation. When the family is broken, it will adversely affect the children's learning of the established culture of a society. The authors examined three family value related attitudes: the view on the happy family, the view on single mother, and marital status. High productivity gains countries tend to frown on nontraditional family arrangements, and hold a view that "a child needs a home with both a father and a mother to grow up happily" (World Value Survey). These cultures also disapprove of single motherhood as a conscious lifestyle choice. Statistically, high productivity countries have lower divorce/separation rates. In general, the higher productivity-growth countries tend to have stronger traditional family values and more intact families.

Combining the three groups of factors, Li et al. created a single "Cultural Index" that captures the most important elements of a culture that is conducive to encouraging people to work hard and be productive. As can be seen from the chart below, there is a strong correlation between the Cultural Index and productivity gains: countries high in the Cultural Index are also high in productivity gain (Fig. 4.3).

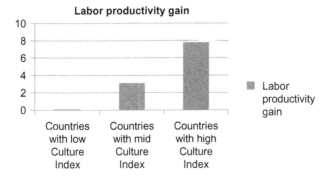

Figure 4.3 *Li, S., Park, S. H., & Selover, D. (2015). Cultural dividend: A hidden source of economic growth in emerging countries: Old Dominion University.*

It should be pointed out that countries that have a strong productivity-enhancing culture and have achieved high economic growth rates all have implemented economic reforms. Without a market-oriented economic reform, productivity-enhancing culture alone cannot achieve high economic growth. In other words, economic reform, or economic institutional change, is a prerequisite for a country to capture the cultural dividend. Both have to interact to bring prosperity to a country.

An interesting and important finding in the Li, Park, and Selover study is that while both economic reform and culture can positively affect productivity gains, the latter has a longer-lasting effect on improving productivity than that of economic reform. More specifically, the positive effect of economic reform on productivity gains will disappear when income rises to a relatively low level, ranging from $5000 to around $10,000; whereas the positive effect of culture on productivity gains will not taper off until income reaches a much higher level, from approximately $15,000 to $60,000 income per capita.

4.2.2 More Evidence of Culture's Effect on Economic Performance

4.2.2.1 The Triple Package Argument

In their book, *The Triple Package: How Three Unlikely Traits Explain the Rise and Fall of Cultural Groups in America*, Jed Rubenfeld and Amy Chua studied the cultural ethnical groups in America that significantly outperformed the rest of the population, and attempted to identify what cultural factors they all possess that contributed to their success (Rubenfeld & Chua, 2014). They identified eight such cultural groups: Chinese, Cuban exiles, Indians, Iranians, Jewish, Lebanese-Americans, Mormons, and Nigerians, and found that they all possess three distinctive traits: a **superiority complex**, **insecurity**, and **impulse control**.

According to the authors, superiority complex is "a deeply internalized belief in your group's specialness, exceptionality, or superiority." Insecurity is "a species of discontent—an anxious uncertainty about your worth or place in society, a feeling or worry that you or what you've done or what you have is in some fundamental way not good enough." And impulse control is "the ability to resist temptation, especially the temptation to give up in the face of hardship or quit instead of persevering at a difficult task," which is similar to the economists' notion of delayed gratification.

The positive effect of these cultural traits on economic performance is intuitive and not difficult to understand. What is more insightful in their study is that the authors pointed out that while the triple package was the mainstream culture in America many years ago, the contemporary mainstream American culture is an antithesis of the triple package: instead of the feeling of superiority, the American culture teaches us that everyone is equal and no one is special; the opposite of insecurity, the American popular culture is "feel good about yourself" and be content. As for impulse control, Americans today are known for instant gratification. What is even more intriguing and ironic is that while the American mainstream culture emphasizes equality, feeling good, and an enjoy-it-while-you-can attitude, the American political and economic system still rewards the opposite of that, namely, hard-working, competitive, and save and invest. This incongruent combination creates a rare opportunity for fresh immigrants who still possess the triple package to outperform the majority. However, even the authors warned about the possible side effect of the triple package if taken too far:

> The Triple Package has a dark underside too. Each of its elements carries distinctive pathologies; when taken to an extreme, they can have truly toxic effects. Should people strive for the Triple Package? Should America? Ultimately, the authors conclude that the Triple Package is a ladder that should be climbed and then kicked away, drawing on its power but breaking free from its constraints (Rubenfeld & Chua, 2015).

4.2.2.2 The Role of Culture in China's Rapid Economic Growth[2]

While it is widely recognized that the economic reform has played a key role in China's fast economic growth in the past three decades, there is less known about the role of culture in it.

The hard-working, pro-business culture in contemporary China is a result of the simultaneous existence of several important cultural factors that are molded by the unique historical events that define China today.

Historically, Confucianism contributed to economic prosperity in the majority of the Tang (618–907) and Song Dynasty (960–1279). From 1949 to 1976, Mao ruled China with ultra-leftist anti-market policies that brought China into absolute poverty. Tens of millions of people died of starvation under Mao. Mao's draconian rule made the Chinese people frugal, obedient, resilient, and tough. In 1976 when he finally died, the Chinese economy was on the verge of total collapse. The horror and poverty under Mao has left an indelible imprint in the minds of all Chinese. Mao's death ushered in a new era and his successor Deng Xiaoping seized the opportunity to open up China and initiate economic reform.

Deng's slogan was "getting rich is glorious" (Li, 2002), and all Chinese felt liberated and took his call of making money fully to heart.

In summary, China has created the most pro-economic growth culture for political, economic, and historical reasons. Traditionally the Confucian culture, of frugality, hard working, and respect for the family is conducive to economic efficiency and productivity. Politically, the authoritarian political system has shaped a population that respects authorities; traits that contribute to efficiency for low skilled work such as manufacturing assemblies. Economically, decades of poverty under Mao's rule made people extremely motivated to work hard to make money. The weak rule of law and lack of a legal tradition nurtured a relation-based culture that encourages people to circumvent the laws and get things done using private relations. All these cultural traits contributed to China's high economic growth. Paradoxically, without Mao's cruel rule, the Chinese would not work this hard today; without his death, the Chinese would not be able to work this hard today either.

4.3 CHANGING THE CULTURE TO BE MORE PRODUCTIVE

4.3.1 Cultural Change Is Hard, But Can Be Done

Our discussion on the role of culture in economic growth suggests that countries should adopt a more productive culture in order to improve their economic performance. However, unlike the political and economic systems that can be changed by policies, government orders, or elections literally overnight, culture is difficult to change. The fundamental difficulty is that there is no effective way to actively apply a force external to a person to reengineer his/her mind to make him/her think certain ways. Old habits and traditions dead hard, and inertia can be strong. So in general, cultural changes take a long time, sometimes several generations.

Nevertheless, with deliberate social efforts by a variety of social forces, culture can be changed relatively quickly. For example, through the efforts of the health service sector, the education sector, government policies, news media, and community campaigns, the social attitude toward smoking has been drastically changed in many parts of the world.

Today the world is still slowly climbing out of one of the biggest recessions in contemporary history and all countries are seeking policy tools to revitalize their economies. Our study on culture may help this effort by looking into the role of culture in economic growth, and finding that there are certain cultural factors that are more conducive to productivity growth. The implication of our study is that social institutions, including governments, firms, schools, and families, can actively help nurture such productivity growth friendly cultures. It is our belief that this effort is much needed and will have an impact on the global recovery, especially on the emerging countries which have garnered much hope from the world to be the engine of growth in the coming decades.

Based on our above analysis on how culture can positively affect productivity, we believe that there are some measures that governments can do to promote productive culture.

4.3.2 Some Policy Considerations for Emerging Countries[3]

Government policies often have either intended or unintended effects on culture, which in turn affect productivity gains. Here are some things a government can do (or avoid doing) to encourage a more productivity enhancing culture.

First, we found that the following economic related attitudes are associated with higher productivity growth: unsatisfactory feeling toward one's financial situation, an attitude against taxes, a belief that differences in income are an incentive for people to work hard, and the willingness to take risks. Several policy implications can be drawn from these. For example, high taxes and high social welfare that aim to reduce income inequality do not help to nurture a productivity growth culture. Governments should institute economic policies that encourage risk-taking, entrepreneurial behavior, such as making it easier to start a business (simplifying the process and instituting automatic approval of business registration). An extension of the above discussion is that governments should not raise the wage level of regions with low labor productivity, because doing so does not address the source of the low productivity; on the contrary, it may exacerbate the problem by nurturing an entitlement culture that hinders productivity growth.

Second, our finding regarding the attitude toward authority and freedom and its relationship with productivity gain shows that there is a positive association between a more authoritarian cultural environment and productivity gains in the emerging countries (with income level less than $10,000).

For the low income, less developed, emerging countries, the state should strengthen their capacity to formulate and implement policies that can nurture a productivity gain friendly culture. The educational policy should allow the school to have more authority over students' learning and discipline. Especially for the least developed nations, implementing policies that can help establish an obedient and disciplined labor force may help increase productivity growth. These policies work best if combined with economic reform that aims at instituting the free market and the rule of law.

Third, we found that family is important in nurturing a productivity growth culture. There is a strong association between high productivity gains and low divorce rates, a strong disapproval of single mother as a life-style choice, and a view that a happy family must have both father and mother present.

While we do not intend to engage in the moral debate about the traditional family values versus alternative lifestyles, our study indicates that government policies in the less developed, emerging countries that either directly or indirectly encourage traditional family values will be conducive to productivity growth. Governments should not institute policies that directly or indirectly encourage teenage childbirth (which tends to end up with the child living with a single mother), births out of wedlock, or facilitate or even encourage the disintegration of the family.

4.3.3 America: A Need for a Cultural Revolution

As the authors of *The Triple Package* pointed out, "America itself was once a Triple Package culture. It's been losing that edge for a long time now" (Rubenfeld & Chua, 2015). What can America do to revitalize such a culture? Addressing this question is particularly difficult and the role of the government is especially limited due to the fundamental belief that Americans hold dear that individuals are free to choose their way of life and government should not impose its view on the people. With this being said, we should not dodge this important issue. There is a dearth of research on how America should go about revitalizing its productive culture. While more studies are urgently needed, one clue we can draw based on the relationship between the hard institutions (political, legal, and economic regulations and policies) and the soft institutions (culture) is that culture is also shaped by the hard institutions (North, 1990). This means that the American government should initiate changes in the political and economic policies that may incentivize people to adopt a more productive culture.

A powerful force for cultural changes in America toward a more productive culture is global competition, especially the competition from East Asia. To be competitive, Americans may need to be more hard-working, longer-term oriented, more respectful to authorities, value education more, and restore and preserve the traditional family values. These indeed are contrary to the contemporary cultural trend in America and many of these changes will be painful. But in order to reverse the losing of ground in the competition with East Asia, these changes are necessary. We call for more studies on the issue of how to effectively help America adopt a more productive culture, especially on the role of the government in such an effort.

QUESTIONS

1. Briefly describe the most important values you have learned in your life.
2. Based on your experience and observation, what attitudes or believes in the American popular culture hinder Americans' productivity the most?
3. The hard-working culture in American society is losing ground. Suggest some measure(s) that the United States could take to help restore such culture.

ENDNOTES

1. Source: Interviews and school visits by author (2005–2012); University of Michigan: "Inner-City Schooling." http://sitemaker.umich.edu/mitchellyellin.356/student_achievement Accessed 19.09.12; City-Data.com, "Maury High School in Norfolk, Virginia (VA)." http://www.city-data.com/school/maury-high-school-va.html Accessed September 1909.12; The Virginia-Pilot, "Captain of Maury football team slain in Park Place shooting," (2009, January 5). http://hamptonroads.com/2009/01/captain-maury-football-team-slain-park-place-shooting.
2. Adopted from Li, S., & Park, S. H. (2013). The hard working culture. *The BRIC Magazine*, 3. http://www.bricsmagazine.com/en/articles/the-hard-working-culture.
3. Adopted from Li, S., & Park, S. H. (2013). The hard working culture. *The BRIC Magazine*, 3. http://www.bricsmagazine.com/en/articles/the-hard-working-culture.

REFERENCES

Hill, C. (2005). *International business: Competing in the global marketplace* (5th ed.). New York, NY: McGraw-Hill.

Hofstede, G. (2015a). *Dimensions of national culture.* http://www.geerthofstede.nl/dimensions-of-national-cultures.

Hofstede, G. (2015b). *Dimensions of national cultures.* http://geert-hofstede.com/countries.html.

Hofstede, G., & Bond, M. (1988). The confucius connection: From cultural roots to economic growth. *Organizational Dynamics, 16*(4), 5–21.

Hofstede, G., Hofstede, G. J., & Minkov, M. (2010). *Cultures and organizations: Software of the mind: Intercultural cooperation and its importance for survival* (3rd ed). New York, NY: McGraw Hill.

Li, S. (2002). The coexistence of booming and looting in China. *China Brief*, *2*(21), 3–6.

Li, S. (2015). Assessment of and outlook on China's corruption: Stagnation in the authoritarian trap? *A chapter for the project "China in 2030" at Cambridge University.*

Li, S., & Park, S. H. (2013). The hard working culture. *The BRIC Magazine*, *3*. <http://www.bricsmagazine.com/en/articles/the-hard-working-culture>.

Li, S., Park, S. H., & Li, S. (2004). The great leap forward: The transition from relation-based governance to rule-based governance. *Organizational Dynamics*, *33*(1), 63–78.

Li, S., Park, S. H., & Selover, D. (2015). Cultural dividend: A hidden source of economic growth in emerging countries: Old Dominion University.

North, D. (1990). *Institutions, institutional change, and economic performance.* Cambridge: Cambridge University Press.

Rubenfeld, J., & Chua, A. (2014). *The triple package: How three unlikely traits explain the rise and fall of cultural groups in America.* New York, NY: Penguin Press.

Rubenfeld, J., & Chua, A. (2015). *About the book.* http://www.thetriplepackage.com/.

Weber, M. (1958 (1904–1905)). *The protestant ethics and the spirit of capitalism.* New York, NY: Charles Scribner's Sons.

Zhang, C., & Zhu, X. (2012). Confucianism and market economy. In G. P. Prastacos, F. Wang, & K. E. Soderquist (Eds.), *Leadership through the classics* (pp. 255–271). Berlin Heidelberg: Springer.

CHAPTER 5

Why Some East Asia Countries Thrive Despite Corruption*

5.1 EFFECT OF CORRUPTION ON ECONOMIC GROWTH

Corruption in international business is a major challenge for both multinational corporations and governments, including the multinationals's home-country government and the government of the countries these companies invest in. After reviewing the characteristics of the relation-based markets, the reader may have the impression that corruption may be more prevalent in relation-based societies, which, as will be shown later in this chapter, is correct. In this chapter, we will discuss how corruption is carried out in societies with different governance environments and how it affects the economy, and why East Asia thrives despite corruption (Fig. 5.1)

5.1.1 Corruption Is Bad for Society as a Whole, as Well as for Corrupt Officials

Corruption by government officials, which refers to the sales of government goods or services for the corrupt official's private gains, is epidemic worldwide. It ranges from multibillion-dollar government projects illegally awarded to private businesspeople who bribe the officials in charge, to petty corruption in which a policeman extorts cash from a hapless tourist who does not know what laws he has broken.

Scholars of political economy have long argued that corruption is bad for a society because the citizens and firms are the ones that have to pay for the corruption, and those payments will be displaced from productive use by the citizens and firms. Furthermore, corrupt officials, for fear of being caught, usually hide the ill-gotten wealth in secret places, which is not always the optimal way to employ capital. A third reason that corruption is bad for the economy is that it distorts the allocation of resources in a society. The corrupt officials have a strong incentive to use their power to encourage the type of businesses

---

* Adopted from Li, S. (2009). *Managing international business in relation-based versus rule-based countries*. New York, NY: Business Expert Press.

East Asian Business in the New World.

© 2016 Elsevier Ltd.
All rights reserved. 71

Figure 5.1 "Approved!"

that are easy for them to extort, such as complicated projects that require many approvals, so that at each approval the official in charge can ask for bribes. An example of these projects is real estate development in many countries. Another kind of resource-distortion project is the expensive, one of a kind, custom-designed project that cannot be easily benchmarked so that the corrupt official and the briber can collude to jack up the total cost and split the illegal gains. Projects of this sort include nuclear power plants and mega construction projects such as airports and highways. Corruption-induced distortion has plagued many underdeveloped countries. For instance, traveling in poverty-ridden African countries, one would see underfunded and rundown elementary schools but expensive highways that could be used for landing airplanes. A possible reason for this disparity is the cost of building new schools can be relatively easy to calculate on a per-student basis and thus has little room for squeezing out bribery to pay officials, whereas the construction of an expensive highway is a more lucrative project for seeping funds.

In sum, corruption can be said to be universally bad. It is even bad for the corrupt officials—because they face the prospect of being locked up in prison or even being executed in certain countries, such as China. It is a vicious circle: more corruption makes an economy poorer; a poorer economy makes the per capita income lower and thus the corrupt official's paycheck smaller, which prompts the corrupt official to extort more bribes, increasing his chance of being caught.[1] Logically, we can argue that cleaning up corruption is beneficial for the *corrupt* officials because as the society

Figure 5.2 Map of corruption level in the world (the darker a country, the more corrupt). *Transparency International. (2015). Corruption perception index. http://www. transparency.org.*

has more resources freed from corruption to invest in the economy, the per capita income will rise and so will the official's income. The higher income of the officials reduces the drive for extorting bribes, which reduces their chance of being caught. The success stories of Hong Kong and Singapore in fighting corruption are cases in point (Li, 2004).

5.1.2 How Bad Is Corruption Worldwide?

In order to assess how bad corruption is in different countries, we need some qualitative data. It is difficult to get reliable corruption data, since neither the corrupt official nor the businessman who pays bribes to officials is willing to tell a surveyor about their illegal activities. Most corruption data are indirect estimates. The most used measurement of corruption across countries is the Corruption Perception Index (CPI) developed by Transparency International (TI), an international nongovernmental organization headquartered in Berlin (Transparency International, 2015). TI conducts an annual survey of business executives, financial journalists, and country experts about their perception of corruption for each country and builds its CPI database accordingly. The CPI ranges from 0 (totally corrupt) to 10 (free of corruption) (Fig. 5.2).

Countries in a dark color have more corruption and countries in a light color have less corruption. As can be seen, more countries are in a dark than in a light color. Corruption is a serious problem worldwide.

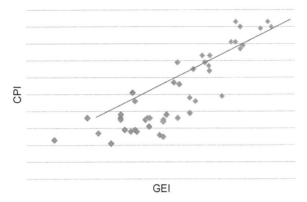

Figure 5.3 Governance Environment Index (GEI) and Corruption Perception Index (CPI). *Note*: X = GEI (high = rule-based), and Y = CPI (low = corrupt). *Author and Transparency International.*

5.1.3 Corruption and the Governance Environment

A closer look at the data would indicate that the more corrupt countries tend to be less rule-based. If we overlay the Governance Environment Index (GEI) and the corruption score, we can see that **the more rule-based a country is, the cleaner (less corrupt) it tends to be** (Fig. 5.3).

The average corruption score for the more rule-based countries (ie, GEI is positive) is 6.9, whereas the corruption score for the less rule-based countries (GEI is negative) is 3.4. The nonrule-based countries, namely, the relation-based countries and the family-based countries, tend to have higher levels of corruption.

5.1.4 Corruption and Economic Efficiency

A further examination would show that most of the less corrupt countries are affluent while the more corrupt countries are poor. Thus the political economists are right that corruption is bad for a country's economy, as shown by Fig. 5.4: The higher the corruption level, the lower the income level in a country (Fig. 5.4).

So far we have only examined the relationship between corruption and income level. However, if we plot annual economic growth rate against corruption level, the trend is much less clear. In terms of economic **growth**, there are some countries that have had quite impressive

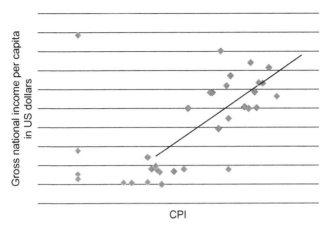

Figure 5.4 Corruption level and income level across countries. *Note:* Y = gross national income per capita in US dollars; X = Corruption Perception Index, 0 = most corrupt and 10 = most clean. *Transparency International and World Bank.*

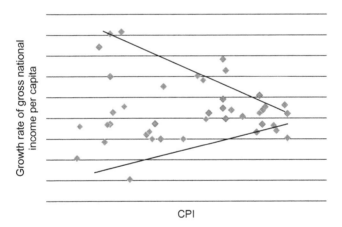

Figure 5.5 Corruption level and economic growth. *Note:* Y = growth rate of gross national income per capita in US dollars; X = Corruption Perception Index, 0 = most corrupt and 10 = most clean. *Transparency International and World Bank.*

economic growth despite high corruption, such as China. Upon further examination, we can see that while economic growth rates of the less corrupt countries (mostly rich) fall in a narrower band, the economic growth rates of the more corrupt countries are spread widely, from negative to highly positive (see Fig. 5.5). In other words, it seems that while many corrupt countries have suffered slow or negative economic growth, some have enjoyed very rapid economic growth. How do we explain this?

5.2 WHY DO SOME ECONOMIES GROW FAST DESPITE CORRUPTION?

Political economists have long conjectured that corruption may help economic efficiencies in some ways (Lui, 1985). For example, in a communist economy, the government exerts absolute control over virtually all production and consumption activities and thus takes away any incentives for the bureaucrats to take any efficiency-enhancing initiatives or engage in any productive activities. Under such a circumstance, business activities are extremely slow and getting permission to do business is difficult. To incentivize the bureaucrats to loosen up their control and make doing business possible, bribery may be necessary. Actually this is what happens in most reforming economies in which the government is powerful and monopolizes most of the country's resources. Bribing the officials who can make business possible is what one might call "greasing the wheels." Thus some political economists argue that some corruption is necessary to liberalize a rigid government-controlled economy. Scholars use the term "efficiency-enhancing" to describe such corruption (Li & Wu, 2010).

What social conditions will make corruption less predatory (or more efficiency-enhancing)? Our study shows that in relation-based societies, corruption tends to be more efficiency-enhancing (Li & Wu, 2010). The main reason is that compared to other nonrule-based societies, such as the family-based ones, the relation-based societies tend to have a higher level of trust.

5.2.1 The Role of Trust in Corruption

It sounds paradoxical that corruption, an illegal activity in most societies, would need trust, which is associated with honesty and integrity, to be carried out. This is precisely because it is illegal, so trust between the briber and the corrupt official is crucial. When a corrupt official is contemplating taking a bribe, he must evaluate his risk—the risk of being caught and the subsequent punishment he may receive if being caught. Furthermore, there is also a risk of being cheated in a bribery-corruption transaction. While small-time corruption can be simultaneously transacted, such as a policeman extorting payment from a driver who was stopped for a traffic violation, large-scale corruption involving huge amounts of bribes and multiyear projects usually cannot be completed on a spot. The bribe payment and the delivery of the promised goods, such as a license, approval, or government projects, tend to be separated in time and space.

In such cases, there is always the age-old question in trade: Who should do it first? Should the corrupt official deliver the desired government goods or service first, or should the briber pay first?

If the corrupt official and the briber trust each other highly, then the temporal and spatial separation of payment and delivery is not a problem. Otherwise, when there is little trust between the two parties, a bribery-corruption transaction will be difficult because each party is afraid of being cheated by the other. This fear is further exacerbated by the fact that neither party can resort to the legal system for protection, since paying and taking bribes is illegal in all countries. For the corrupt official, there is an added risk of being blackmailed by the briber.

Once again, this is why trust plays an important role in corruption, which sounds paradoxical because in most cultures trust is associated with integrity and honesty, whereas corruption means conspiring in secrecy and is criminal. But following our analysis, readers will see that the relationship between trust and corruption is not black and white.

Trust is the confidence or faith one places on another person or other people. What are the implications of having or not having a high level of trust in a bribery-corruption relationship? We can do some logical deduction to help us better understand this issue.

Suppose there are two societies: A and B. In Society A, there is a high level of trust (note that we don't have to distinguish generalized or particularized trust), whereas in Society B, trust is almost nonexistent. In Society A, corrupt officials feel safe to take bribes from almost anyone, as the chance of being turned in by the briber is extremely low, due to the high level of trust. Bribers are confident to pay in advance and, likewise, corrupt officials can deliver the requested government goods and services first. The separation of payment and delivery in time and space does not pose a problem. Thus the corrupt official can sell his service (such as a government contract) to the highest bidding briber, who does not have to be a relative or close friend of the corrupt official, but must be a highly efficient businessperson, which enables him to pay a high bribe and still make a profit (provided that all the bidders more or less maintain similar qualities for their products or services). Under such an environment, bribery-corruption becomes a competitive market and the most efficient briber gets the economic opportunities controlled by the government, making corruption "efficiency-enhancing."

In Society B, there is little trust among people. Corrupt officials do not dare to take bribes from people they don't know well. In other words, they must keep such illegal deals within a very small circle of confidants—their family members and very few close friends. However, their cronies may not be in the right industry to take advantage of the opportunities the officials can provide, and the cronies' firms may be inefficient with low productivity. Thus in general, corruption does not lead to efficiency-enhancing in such societies.

Furthermore, in society B, if the government controls vast resources and the politicians are powerful, they must use their power and resources to extort rent (payment) from the society (citizens and businesses). Since the officials are afraid of engaging in bribery-delivery relationships as illustrated in the case of Society A, then they will extort payment from the society by force, such as announcing new taxes or imposing fees on businesses. What is worse is that the corrupt official does not have to deliver any government goods or services in such top-down extortions. As a result, corruption becomes **predatory**. It is an absolute loss for the society.

The next question is, among the societies with high levels of corruption (mostly not rule-based), which ones tend to have a higher level of trust? Chapter 2, Western Rules Versus Eastern Relations: A Fundamental Framework to Understand East Asia, has answered this question: The relation-based societies have a higher level of extended particularized trust than the family-based societies. These societies are more like Society A in our example above, and corruption in these societies tends to be more "efficiency-enhancing," whereas the family-based societies closely approximate Society B, with little trust beyond the family, and corruption in those societies is more "predatory." In the next section, we use cases of corruption in China and the Philippines to illustrate these two types of corruption (Li & Wu, 2007).

5.2.2 Corruption in China and the Philippines

China and the Philippines are developing countries with similar income levels, and both have experienced high levels of corruption. But the similarity seems to end there; what differs between the two is that China has a much higher level of trust and a higher level of economic growth rate, as can be seen from Table 5.1.

Corruption in China. As we know, China is a typical relation-based society, in which *guanxi*-based networks have been extensively developed and widely spread. These informal social networks were first established during the era of Mao Zedong's rule (1949–76) and were booming and dominant in China during the later years of Mao's rule, during which the economy

Table 5.1 Corruption, trust, and economic development in China and the Philippines

Country	GDP annual growth rate (%) (1990–2000)	GNI per capita (2001)	Corruption perception index (10 = best; 1 = worst) (2000)	Trust (1999–2004)
Philippines	3.3	1050	2.8	8.6
China	10.3	890	3.1	54.5

Transparency International. (2015). *Corruption perception index*. http://www.transparency.org; World Bank. (2015). World development indicators. Washington, DC: World Bank (World Bank, 2015); and World Value Survey. (2005). World Value Survey: World Value Survey Association (World Value Survey, 2005).

was on the verge of total collapse and consumer goods were in extreme shortage. In order to obtain daily necessities, jobs, or permission to move from one place to another, people resorted to a gray market for consumer goods and government goods and services that were distributed through these informal social networks based on exchanges of favors. After Mao died in 1976, the Chinese government led by Deng called for a market economy and encouraged people to make money. At the same time, when the economy took off at a rapid pace, the formal legal system was underdeveloped: laws were and still are made by one party—the Chinese Communist Party—in which judges are political appointees and corruption is rampant. As a result, people and firms in China rely on relation-based governance to protect their business interests.

Those informal social networks are based on extended particularized trust. A common practice in China is informal networking. For instance, in social gatherings or parties, some businessperson may mention that he is trying to get a project approved by a particular government department, but he does not know anyone there and will ask around if someone in the gathering knows officials in that department. Then someone in the party may volunteer (and will get compensated if he does help), "I don't know anyone there directly, but my sister-in-law's father has a former student who works there," and then this person would introduce this official to the businessman who was looking for help. Once the official and the businessman are introduced, they can quickly begin to negotiate a deal, which usually involves the businessman paying the official and the latter delivering the needed service to the former.

In a society that lacks trust, such a deal may be viewed as too risky. But in China, a deal in which an official is paid for a special service is quite common and the risk is quite low because although the two do not know each other well, they are introduced by people who know both of them well (a third party—see chapter: Western Rules Versus Eastern Relations: A Fundamental Framework to Understand East Asia) and can hold them accountable should they cheat. In other words, the strong particularized trust within each circle, and the easy connection of one circle with another make such a bribery-corruption relationship easy to establish and operate.

In *Losing the New China*, an insightful book about corruption in China, Ethan Gutmann vividly documents how multinational companies use bribes to get around China's corrupt market. These multinational corporations would set aside big "slush funds" and hire consultants to run these funds. The consultant would use the fund secretly to bribe government officials according to the agenda set by the corporations. A multinational firm's senior executive described one such operation this way: "The terms of the deal was…a ten million dollar discretionary fund. Hands off, no questions asked. Don't ask [the consultant] where the money goes…We know exactly what he was up to, and exactly how successful he would be" (Gutmann, 2004).

In China, such business-to-official transactions are so frequent that there is a need to provide discrete, secure places for them to make such deals. Some smart restaurant owners saw this opportunity and offered just the right environment for them. In Beijing, an expensive Cantonese seafood restaurant with several locations was known for such a service. The following is a description by a reliable source who wishes to remain anonymous: "I [the briber] invite my client [corrupt official] to a well-known Cantonese restaurant with several branches in Beijing. The meal costs an astronomical 20000 yuan [US$2,400] for two. On the way out, the restaurant passes a gift to my client and the client is told he or she can exchange the gift for cash if he or she does not like it. The gift is then exchanged by my client for about 10000 yuan. I have not discussed any such exchanges with my client. But just in case people get the wrong impression, the restaurant has covered my car's license plate in the restaurant's parking lot." As one can imagine, this kind of bribery-corruption deal is only possible when the trust between the parties is high.

Even the Chinese government realizes that corruption has reached a point that is difficult to control. A study that followed 47 corruption cases in 2007 calculated that on average these corrupt officials took 35 million yuan (US$4 million) in bribes. The Chinese Supreme Court and the Supreme Prosecutorial Commission explicitly promulgated

10 corruption activities that are illegal. Of the 10 types of bribery-corruption behavior, the one that is most relevant to our discussion here is "an official gives a favor to someone, and receives payment after the official leaves his post." Another feature of Chinese corruption is globalization: the corrupt official delivers the favor inside China and receives payment overseas in the form of luxury homes, Swiss bank accounts, gambling trips, or scholarships for the official's children to attend schools abroad. Clearly, the separation of time and space in the transaction needs a high level of trust to make such bribery-corruption deals possible.

Corruption in the Philippines. As can be seen from Table 5.1, the trust level in the Philippines is extremely low, which is an indication of a family-based environment (see chapter: Western Rules Versus Eastern Relations: A Fundamental Framework to Understand East Asia). Unlike corruption in China, corruption in the Philippines has been characterized by a pattern in which the head of state would control the entry of an industry or simply monopolize it, impose a tax or surcharge on all the firms in or products of the industry, or extract a fee on firms for entering the industry. After that, the head of state would then appoint one of his cronies to be in charge of the industry and steal all the collections from the state coffers. To the private sector payers, these taxes, surcharges, or fees were nothing more than robbery, a deadweight loss in the economic sense. The collecting officials simply imposed the fees on the payers without facilitating or helping any business activities. Furthermore, the victim of the corruption, the payers, would have no evidence to implicate corrupt officials (the collector of these charges) because the latter was simply carrying out a state order.

Several cases of major industries in the Philippines demonstrate this kind of corruption pattern (Wedeman, 1997). In the coconut sector during the 1970s (accounting for roughly 25% of the Philippines' export income), the former president Ferdinand Marcos imposed a tax on all sales of coconuts and copra. The agency in charge of collecting this tax was headed by his close friend Manuel Conjuangco. Conjuangco used the extorted money to buy banks, which in turn funded his acquisition of many coconut oil pressing mills. Then he put all the tax money into a fund and used the fund to subsidize the mills he and Marcos controlled.

A similar corruption pattern occurred in the cigarette industry as well. In 1975, Marcos imposed a 100% import duty on cigarette filters, but gave a special 90% import duty reduction to the Philippine Tobacco Filters Corporation, a company owned by one of his cronies, Herminio Disini.

Disini in turn supplied the filter at below-market prices to Fortune Tobacco, a major cigarette maker owned by another Marcos ally, Lucio Tan. Together they drove the competition out of the market and monopolized the cigarette industry.

The corruption in the sugar industry resembled a similar pattern. In 1974, Marcos ordered that all sugar exports be monopolized by the Philippine Exchange Company, which was controlled by his school mate Robert Benidicto. With the privilege given by Marcos, Benidicto manipulated sugar prices to profit at the expense of sugar farmers and producers in the country.

In all these corruption cases, there was little cooperation between the briber (the payer of the surcharges, entry fees, and other types of extortions) and the corrupt official. The bribers were forced to pay, and the official did not enhance the efficiency of their business. It is estimated that through these extortions, Marcos and his associates amassed wealth valued at between US$3 billion to US$6 billion!

5.2.3 More Countries Follow the Same Pattern

To further verify our argument, we also conducted a statistical test using pooled data in two time periods (1994–99 and 2000–05) from 53 countries. We examined how corruption level and trust level affect economic growth rate in a country, while controlling other important factors that may also affect economic growth. These controlled factors include income per capita, schooling, the political system, and time period. We paid special attention to the interaction of corruption level and trust level in a country.

The results support our view: the negative effect of corruption on economic growth is mitigated by a higher level of trust in a country. For example, if in a country the trust level is 0 (which means that 0% of people trust others), then the effect of corruption on economic growth would be −0.17%; however, as the level of trust increases, it will mitigate the negative effect of corruption on economic growth. On average, every 10% increase in trust would reduce the negative effect of corruption on economic growth rate by 0.03% (Li & Wu, 2010).

What can readers take away from this chapter? First, we are not saying that corruption is good. As we mentioned at the opening of the chapter, corruption has a negative effect on economic growth in all countries. However, this negative effect may be reduced when corruption interacts with a high level of extended particularized trust. Second, since the briber and the corrupt official both benefit from the deal, the briber has little

Figure 5.6 Three figurines depicting bribery-corruption relationship.

incentive to turn in the corrupt official, making corruption difficult to detect. In general, we conclude that **the high level of extended particularized trust in societies with predominantly "efficiency-enhancing" corruption implies that cleaning up corruption is very difficult.** A strong and thick social network makes it very hard for "whistle-blowing." Our analysis suggests that the prospect for eradicating corruption in highly relation-based countries, such as China, is not good.

QUESTIONS

1. Justify "cleaning up corruption is beneficial to corrupt officials."
2. Based on Fig. 5.6, (1) tell a story of corruption based on the figurines, and (2) describe the relationship among the figurines.

ENDNOTE

1. Of course, in a rampantly corrupt society, corrupt officials use their power to protect themselves, so their chance of being caught and prosecuted tends to be low.

REFERENCES

Gutmann, E. (2004). *Losing the New China: A story of American commerce, desire and betrayal.* San Francisco, CA: Encounter Books.
Li, S. (2004). Can China learn from Hong Kong's experience in fighting corruption? *Global Economic Review, 33*(1), 1–9.

Li, S. (2009). *Managing international business in relation-based versus rule-based countries.* New York, NY: Business Expert Press.

Li, S., & Wu, J. (2007, April). Why China thrives despite corruption. *Far Eastern Economic Review,, 170*(3), 24–28.

Li, S., & Wu, J. (2010). Why some countries thrive despite corruption: The role of trust in the corruption-efficiency relationship. *Review of International Political Economy, 17*(1), 129–154.

Lui, F. (1985). An equilibrium queuing model of bribery. *Journal of Political Economy, 93*(4), 760–781.

Transparency International. (2015). *Corruption perception index.* http://www.transparency.org.

Wedeman, A. (1997). Looters, rent-scrapers, and dividend-collectors: Corruption and growth in Zaire, South Korea, and the Philippines. *Journal of Developing Areas, 31*(4), 457–478.

World Bank. (2015). *World development indicators.* Washington, DC: World Bank.

World Value Survey (2005). World Value Survey: World Value Survey Association.

CHAPTER 6

Information and Investment in East Asia: What We Need to Know When Investing in Relation-Based Societies*

When I teach about information and investment across countries, I ask my students the following question: "suppose you got some money and decided to invest it in the stock market by buying some stock, how do you go about getting the information about what stocks to buy?" When I asked this question to students in the United States, the most frequent replies are "search online," or "read the companies' annual reports." When the same question is asked of students in China, the most common answer is "talk to someone who has inside information," or "follow someone who is in the know." In a class in Taiwan, a student said, "Follow A-Chen!" Seeing that I was totally lost, he explained that A-Chen was the nickname for Wu Shu-chen, wife of the former president of Taiwan, Chen Shui-bian, who was convicted of corruption. His wife is known for her "ability" to always pick the winning stocks. When I pressed my Asian students further with the question, "What about studying the annual report?" they would always dismiss it by saying, "Most companies cook the numbers. So who would trust their annual reports?"

Why do Americans tend to rely on public information such as annual reports and East Asians value private information to make investment decisions? In this chapter we will discuss this issue and will show that the choice of information is determined by the governance environment.

6.1 INFORMATION IN RELATION-BASED SOCIETIES

As we have shown earlier, relation-based governance primarily relies on private information to monitor social exchanges because public information,

---

* Adopted from Li, S. (2009). *Managing international business in relation-based versus rule-based countries.* New York, NY: Business Expert Press.

such as government information releases or company accounting records, is not reliable or trustworthy. Both the public sector and the private sector in relation-based societies manipulate their information.

6.2 INFORMATION MANAGEMENT BY A RELATION-BASED GOVERNMENT

An example of information management by a relation-based government is the Chinese government's long history of manipulating public information, going back to Mao Zedong's era. Mao Zedong ruled China from 1949 to 1976 with a radical communist ideology and totalitarian control over the society. Mao ignored the legal rules he set up and believed that the end justified the means. It was reported that when US President Richard Nixon visited him in 1972, Mao told Nixon, "I don't obey any laws!"[1] Even Nixon, who did not have much respect for the law either, was shocked. Mao manipulated public information for his benefit. Perhaps the largest information manipulation was the concealment of the great famine from 1959 to 1962, during which tens of millions died of starvation. Even today, the Chinese Communist Party refuses to tell the world how many died in the famine. Estimates run from 27 million to over 40 million (Yang, 2008).

Another example of information management in relation-based societies is the government's alteration of photos to manipulate public opinions (well before Photoshop became available). During the Soviet era, Joseph Stalin, the communist party head, doctored photos based on the relationship he had with other leaders in the photo. When someone lost his favor, this person would be removed from the picture. Like Stalin, Mao manipulated who should be retained or wiped out from photos taken with other comrades depending on who was in favor with Mao at any given time. Even today, the Chinese Communist Party still practices this technique (Zhou, 2009).

Local officials in China routinely manipulate economic statistics to serve their agendas: If an official wants to get promoted, he makes the numbers such as the economic growth rate larger; if he wants to get aid, he shrinks the numbers. This practice is jokingly referred to in China as "officials make numbers, numbers make officials."

Not only does the government suppress or invent news, it also schedules major, newsworthy projects and chooses when to release the major positive news. Major government-sponsored projects, such as nuclear weapon tests and space programs (eg, launching a satellite), must be timed to gain the highest impact or to distract the public from major negative news. For instance, in Sep. 2008, a major scandal was exposed in which leading dairy companies in China sold melamine-tainted milk that made tens of thousands of babies sick and caused several deaths. The Chinese government then announced that it would move a space shuttle launch to earlier than originally scheduled. Critics suspected that the government used the shuttle launch and the space walk to steer the world's attention away from the tainted milk scandal (Chi, 2008).

Restricting the free flow of information is another dimension of information management by relation-based government. In China, the internet is under tight control by the government, which filters all information on the net using what is known as the "great firewall." Youtube, Facebook, and many other websites deemed "subversive" are blocked by the Chinese government. Chinese citizens who spread information that the government does not like face arrest and imprisonment.

As a result of public information management by the government, people in China have not had much faith in official news or statistics. Public information in general is less trustworthy in relation-based societies, and people living in these societies are always seeking reliable information from informal channels, such as rumors and hearsay.

6.3 INFORMATION MANAGEMENT BY FIRMS

In an environment where the government manipulates public information, there is very little reason why firms should not do the same to their advantage, so they mimic what the government does and manipulate their operating information. According to our interviews with accountants in China, it is common for firms to manipulate their earnings reports.

Private firms tend to lower earnings to avoid taxes. Studies show that tax evasion by firms in China is widespread. Large losses tend to trigger auditing by the tax authorities, so the firms that manipulate earnings in order to avoid taxes only show a small loss.

Managers of state-owned firms report more earnings to get promoted or to simply keep their jobs. In their study of executive compensation and firm performance in China, economists Kato and Long found that "Chinese executives [of state-owned firms] are penalized for making negative profits" (Kato & Long, 2006). But they also found that the executives are not further rewarded for profits that are much greater than zero. Their study confirms the existence of a very strong incentive for Chinese state firm executives to

engage in earnings management to bring the profit rate into positive territory. But there is also no further incentive to push profits higher.

These two tendencies suggest that firms in China tend to manipulate
their profit rate close to zero. To verify this, my colleagues and I did a
simple statistical analysis: We created a distribution of all manufacturing
firms in China by their profit level as measured by return on assets (ROA)
(Li, Selover, & Stein, 2011), as shown in Fig. 6.1.

In Fig. 6.1, the tallest curve is the ROA distribution of Chinese firms,
the second tallest curve is the ROA distribution of US firms, whereas the
most flat curve is a hypothetical normal distribution curve in the absence
of earnings management.

Compared to the ROA distribution of US firms, Chinese firms show
a much greater spike around zero on the positive side, which is a strong
indication that Chinese firms adjust their ROA to a slightly positive value.

While the purpose of earnings management in China may be tax evasion or promotion seeking, a serious unintended consequence results.
Outsiders cannot rely on a firm's financial report to accurately evaluate the
firm, which means that outsiders may not be willing to invest in the firm.
This deterrent explains why relation-based firms tend to rely on internal
and informal financing.

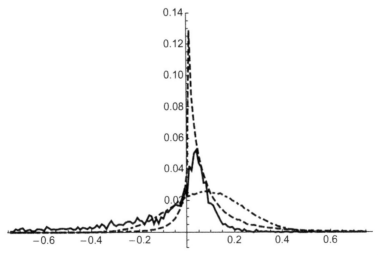

Figure 6.1 Distribution of return on assets in China, the United States, and normal distribution. *Note*: China: long dotted line; The United States: solid line; Normal distribution: short dotted line. *Li, S. (2009). Managing international business in relation-based
versus rule-based countries. New York, NY: Business Expert Press.*

6.4 RELATION-BASED WAYS OF FINANCING

According to research, the Chinese business community in Thailand relies primarily on informal means to raise capital for their business expansion (Ueda, 2000). The most common way to raise capital is the *chae*, which is a rotating credit society in which all members contribute and each member takes his turn to borrow a sum contributed by all members. The key to the functioning of this credit society is careful screening and admitting members who have a good reputation and are trustworthy. Another way to finance their business is to engage in discounting postdated checks, which means to cash a check with a future date with a discount. The risk of receiving a bad check is reduced by the community's ability to verify and monitor the borrower's business and credit. A third way to raise capital is an equity joint venture in which the fund provider will invest in the fund seeker's project. All the above financing methods require efficient and accurate monitoring mechanisms that can verify the prospective fund seeker's credit worthiness (*ex ante* monitoring), his ability to perform his duty (interim monitoring), and where his assets are in case he fails to deliver (*ex post* monitoring). If the parties involved are outsiders, such as banks, then this kind of monitoring mechanism would be almost impossible to use, or the cost of doing so would be too high to make business sense.

In such an environment, formal credit risk management does not work efficiently and banks often incur high losses from bad loans. For example, in China, nearly 50% of bank loans to small borrowers cannot be collected, whereas loans arranged privately using the above monitoring mechanism seldom go bad (Bradsher, 2004). As a result, banks charge a very high transaction fee and interest to compensate for the risk associated with the difficulty of evaluating credit in a relation-based market. As commented by a researcher who studied Vietnam's real estate market, getting loans from banks "was the most expensive option" to finance a project (Kim, 2008).

6.5 WHY FOREIGN INVESTMENT FLOWS TO COUNTRIES WITH POOR LEGAL SYSTEMS

In relation-based economies that lack publicly reliable information and effective and efficient public ordering to protect investment, how do foreign investors enter those markets and protect their investment?

The inflows of foreign investment across countries have some interesting patterns, which, as one would expect, are influenced by the governance environment, namely, how investments are protected in a country.

Researchers have studied this issue extensively and have accumulated a great deal of knowledge about how a country's legal system affects the inflow of foreign investment. In general, they have found that a poor legal system deters foreign investment. This finding is hardly surprising: intuition would tell us that if the legal system does not offer effective and efficient protection of property rights, investors will be reluctant to invest.

However, this argument fails to explain why countries with a poor legal system attract sizable foreign investment. Take the case of China, its legal system is controlled by a single party—the Chinese Communist Party—and judges are political appointees that tend to be corrupt. Despite this, China has been attracting huge amounts of foreign investment.

Of course, one may argue that the huge market in China provides great opportunities for production and consumption. While this is certainly a major factor in attracting foreign investment to China, it does not address the issue of how investment is protected in countries like China, where the rule of law is weak. In order to better understand this question, we need to distinguish two types of foreign investment: direct and indirect investment.

6.6 DIRECT INVESTMENT AND INDIRECT (PORTFOLIO) INVESTMENT

Capital investment, including both foreign investment and domestic investment, can be classified into two types: direct and indirect. Direct investment refers to an arrangement in which the investor *invests and controls* (*manages*) the project or entity in which he or she invests. This is usually the case when the investor invests a large share of the total investment and thus controls the investment. The investor can access all the information about the investment, manage it, and make all the decisions about it. An example of direct investment would be someone investing to build and operate a restaurant or a garment factory.

Indirect investment refers to the type of investment in which the investor cannot directly control or manage the investment. Usually the investment accounts for a small percentage of the total investment, so that the investor cannot directly exercise his control right or management right. In this case, the investor becomes a passive investor; he does not have firsthand, unlimited access to information relative to the investment such as the accounting books or board meeting minutes. He has access to information about the state of the operation he has investment in through annual reports and shareholders meetings. An example of indirect investment would be buying a few shares of stocks of a large company such as AT&T. In general, indirect investments include securities offered in the public market, such as stocks or bonds of publicly listed companies. This kind of investment is commonly referred to as "portfolio investment." We will use "indirect investment" and "portfolio investment" interchangeably in this book.

When we break down the total foreign investment that flows into China, we find an unbalanced distribution. Most investment is direct investment, and portfolio investment accounts for a small proportion. For example, in the 3-year period from 2004 to 2006, China received a net of $181 billion foreign direct investment (FDI) and a net of −$53 billion foreign portfolio investment (FPI). In the same period, the United States received net of −$71 billion FDI and $1.9 trillion FPI. (Interestingly, most of the FPI in the United States is sent by the Chinese government and other Chinese investors. Obviously China has faith in the public financial market of the United States.) The popular view that China is the largest recipient of foreign investment is not correct. It is only correct in terms of FDI. In terms of total foreign investment, the United States is still by far the largest.

6.7 TYPES OF INVESTMENT AND MODES OF GOVERNANCE

The two types of investment require different governance mechanisms for protection (Li, 2005). In portfolio investments, since the investors do not have direct access to operational and managerial information or direct control over the managers, they must rely on *publicly* available information, such as annual reports or company press releases, to aid their investment decisions. For the portfolio investors, the timeliness and accuracy of the public information is vital. If disputes arise between the investors and the management of the investment, they usually resort to public rules, through the courts, to resolve them. The court must rely on publicly verifiable information to make a ruling.

In sum, *portfolio investment requires a rule-based governance environment for effective and efficient protection.* Two anecdotes about information distortion and stock price manipulation in China may illustrate this point. In the late 1990s, there was a listed company called Tiange Technology whose products included freshwater snapping turtle, a delicacy in China. In order to manipulate its stock price, management would issue statements such as "due to a flood, our turtles were washed away" to drive the price down;

if it wanted to boost the price, it would issue something like "the flood receded and our turtles swam back" (Zhang, 2002). Li Jiange, a former vice chare of China's Security and Exchange Commission, revealed that "there is a close correlation between the restrooms of listed companies and the unusual fluctuation of their stock prices." This is because government officials would invite themselves to the board meetings of these companies, and after they learned the inside information from the meeting, they would rush to the restroom and then the stock price would suddenly change violently (Ling, 2016, January 1).

When I taught this topic in my international business class, I always asked my students, "What information would you rely on and where would you get it when you evaluate whether to buy a listed company's stock?" Most American students would start with "studying the prospective company's annual report and quarterly filings." My students in Asia, on the other hand, would suggest ways such as "talk with someone with inside information" or "follow someone who is in the know."

As for direct investment, there is no separation between investors and management. The investors are the insiders who are also directly involved in managing the investment and share the information about the investment *privately* among themselves, which substantially reduces the information gap between the investors and the management that exists in portfolio investment. The direct control by owners in direct investment makes it easier for the owners to protect their assets *privately* than that to protect portfolio investments. In other words, the need for an effective and efficient legal system to protect the investment is not as high for direct investment as for indirect investment.

Now let us consider the type of investment and mode of governance together. Based on the above analysis, we may conjecture that in rule-based societies, foreign investment tends to be in the form of portfolio investment, whereas in the relation-based societies, foreign investment should be in the form of direct investment. Is this pattern supported by evidence? We need to examine the relationship between the mode of governance and the type of investment using data.

If we compare the combination of FDI and FPI in three of the least rule-based countries—China, Azerbaijan, and Pakistan—with three of the most rule-based countries—the United States, Australia, and the Netherlands—we get the following numbers: During the 3-year period from 2004 to 2006, the relation-based group attracted $63 billion FDI per annum, while losing $16 billion in FPI yearly, whereas the rule-based group incurred a loss of $64 billion in FDI, while gaining $701 billion in FPI annually. This pattern suggests that when investors invest in relation-based countries, they prefer direct investment. In order to further confirm this, I plotted FDI over total foreign investment against the Governance Environment Index (GEI), which was introduced in Chapter 2, Western Rules Versus Eastern Relations: A Fundamental Framework to Understand East Asia. The pattern is quite clear: The less a country is rule-based, the higher the proportion of the total foreign investment that is direct investment. When foreign investors invest in countries with poor legal systems and unreliable public financial information, they tend to choose direct investment over indirect investment.[2]

Fig. 6.2 shows that the less a country is rule-based, the greater the proportion of foreign investment is direct investment.

This finding helps us to better understand why China attracted so much FDI and relatively little portfolio investment. Foreign investors

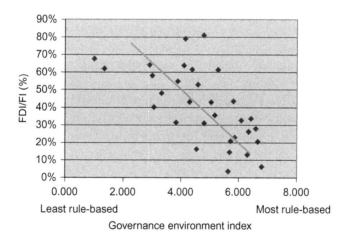

Figure 6.2 Governance environment and foreign investment. *Note:* The horizontal axis is the score of GEI, which has been adjusted to a scale of 0 (least rule-based) to 8 (most rule-based). The vertical axis is the proportion of foreign direct investment in the total foreign investment in a country: FDI/FI= (foreign direct investment)/(total foreign investment). Each dot in the chart represents a country. *Li, S. (2005). Why a poor governance environment does not deter foreign direct investment: The case of China and its implications for investment protection. Business Horizons, 48, 297–302.*

choose direct investment in China *because of*, rather than *despite*, the absence of the rule-based governance environment. When public ordering is not effective and efficient, direct investment gives them more control and thus better protection through private relationships. This finding also explains why in some of the least rule-based countries, such as Rwanda, Kyrgyzstan, or Armenia, some 99% of foreign investments were in direct investment, whereas the percentage was substantially lower in rule-based countries, such as the United States (23%) or Finland (6%) (IMF, 2003).

6.8 IMPLICATIONS OF INVESTMENT TYPE AND GOVERNANCE MODE

The above discussion on investment type and governance mode has several implications. First, investors must study a country's governance environment before deciding whether to invest there and what mode of investment is optimal for the protection of the investment. Second, due to the low quality of public financial information, the risk of investing in the public financial market, such as the stock market, is higher. Following the same logic, due to the fact that firm's accounting information is less reliable (as reflected in the high level of earnings management in Chinese firms), outside investors are reluctant to invest in relation-based firms. These facts suggest that the capital market is limited mostly to relational investment, and the cost of capital in the public capital market is higher in a relation-based economy.

The complexity of property rights differs from industry to industry. In general, the property right structure is relatively simple in manufacturing industries, such as the shoe and the garment industries, where the quality and quantity of the products are easy to verify and thus workers and manufacturers can be paid on a regular basis. Logically, the protection of property rights and investments in those industries is relatively straightforward. On the other hand, in the financial industry, the property rights structure can be very complex, such as in initial public offering of stocks, options, and other complex financial deals. For those products and services, the property rights protection is complicated and requires strong legal protection, which is better in rule-based societies. Thus, in general, for investors who are evaluating different industries in which to invest in a relation-based market, if everything else is equal, the investors should favor industries that have simpler property rights structures.

QUESTIONS

1. Elaborate why high-quality public information is vital for the stock market of a county.
2. What are the reasons of why the quality of public information is low in relation-based societies?
3. Is investing in a relation-based market more dangerous than investing in a rule-based market?

ENDNOTES

1. Mao was using a Chinese proverb "an old monk with a leaky umbrella" meaning a lawless person. See Sydney Morning Herald. (1973, April 29). Mao: The lone monk with leaky umbrella, *The Sydney Morning Herald.* https://news.google.com/newspapers?nid=1301&dat=19730429&id=cJ8pAAAAIBAJ&sjid=HeUDAAAAIBAJ&pg=6613,401208&hl=en.
2. Another major factor affecting the type of foreign investment inflow is the government's regulation on the capital market. In some countries, the stock market is not completely open to foreign investors. In our analysis, we have controlled for such effect.

REFERENCES

Bradsher, R. (2004). Informal lenders in China pose risks to banking system. *New York Times.*
Chi, Y. (2008). *Chinese Communist Party promotes space walk, Netizens: can't save the party.* Epochtimes.com.
IMF. (2003). International Monetary Fund. *International Financial Statistics.*

Kato, T., & Long, C. (2006). Executive compensation, firm performance, and corporate governance in China: Evidence from firms listed in the Shanghai and Shenzhen Stock exchanges. *Economic Development and Cultural Change, 54*(4), 945–974.

Kim, A. M. (2008). *Learning to be capitalists.* Oxford: Oxford University Press.

Li, S. (2005). Why a poor governance environment does not deter foreign direct investment: The case of China and its implications for investment protection. *Business Horizons, 48,* 297–302.

Li, S. (2009). *Managing international business in relation-based versus rule-based countries.* New York, NY: Business Expert Press.

Li, S., Selover, D., & Stein, M. (2011). "Keep Silence, Make Money": The institutional pattern of earnings manipulation in China. *Journal of Asian Economics, 22,* 369–382.

Ling, A. (2016, January 1). Retired high-level officials reveal shocking information 退休高官披露資訊令人震驚!, Open 《开放》. http://www.open.com.hk/content. php?id=2662#.Vo8SSFmKKh0.

Sydney Morning Herald. (1973, April 29). Mao: The lone monk with leaky umbrella. *The Sydney Morning Herald.* https://news.google.com/newspapers?nid=1301&dat=1973042 9&id=cJ8pAAAAIBAJ&sjid=HeUDAAAAIBAJ&pg=6613,401208&hl=en.

Ueda, Y. (2000). The entrepreneurs of Khorat. In R. McVey (Ed.), *Money and power in provincial Thailand* (pp. 154–194). Honolulu, HI: Hawaii University Press.

Yang, J. (2008). *Tombstone: Documenting China's great famine in the 1960s.* Hong Kong: Cosmos Books (Tian-di).

Zhang, W. (2002). What is behind the disputes over the ownership of Tiange Technology? *China Economic Times.*

Zhou, S. (2009). *Chinese Communist Party doctors photo, erasing "Republic of China".* Epochtimes.com.

CHAPTER 7

The Currency Exchange Market in East Asia

The currency exchange market plays a vital role in influencing the domestic economic policies and development as well as in international trade and investment. In this chapter we will provide the background on the foreign exchange market and international monetary system, and explain the rationale behind the currency valuation and exchange policies of East Asian countries.

7.1 THE FOREIGN EXCHANGE MARKET

The foreign exchange market is the global market for exchanging currencies of different countries. It is decentralized in a sense that no one single authority, such as an international agency or government, controls it. The major players in the market are governments (usually through their central banks) and commercial banks. Firms such as manufacturers, exporters and importers, and individuals such as international travelers also participate in the market. There are a few key concepts we need to understand the market. **Foreign exchange** is the action of converting one currency into another. The rate that is agreed upon by the two parties in the exchange is called **exchange rate**, which may fluctuate widely, creating the **foreign exchange risk**. As will be seen in the case of Japan Airlines (JAL) below, the risk can be high.

There are two types of exchange rates that are commonly used in the foreign exchange market. The **spot** exchange rate is the exchange rate used on a direct exchange between two currencies "on the spot," with the shortest time frame such as on a particular day. For example, a traveler exchanges some Japanese yen using US dollars upon arriving at the Tokyo airport. The **forward** exchange rate is a rate agreed by two parties to exchange currencies for a future date, such as 6 months or 1 year from now. A main purpose of using the forward exchange rate is to manage the foreign exchange risk, as shown in the case below.

East Asian Business in the New World.

The main functions of the market are to (1) facilitate currency conversion, (2) provide instruments to manage foreign exchange risk (such as forward exchange), and (3) allow investors to speculate in the market for profit.

7.2 CASE 1: JAPAN AIRLINES

In 1985, JAL ordered aircrafts from Boeing. JAP earns its income mostly in Japanese yen but needed to pay Boeing in US dollars for the purchase, and the payment would not be due until 1994. So JAL entered a 10-year forward exchange rate contract to buy US$3.6 billion with Japanese yen (¥). The exchange rate in 1985 was $1= ¥240. The common forecast was that the yen was going to rise against the dollar, and the prevailing forward exchange rate based on the forecast was $1= ¥185, which seemed to be a pretty good deal for JAL, as it was substantially higher than the spot rate of $1= ¥240. But in reality the yen appreciated much faster. By 1992, the rate was $1= 120, and by 1994 it was $1= ¥99! If JAL could have used the spot rate in 1994 to pay Boeing at the delivery, it would have paid much less than the amount using the $1= ¥185 forward exchange rate. However, JAL was bound by the contract and thus could not take the advantage of the strong yen in 1994. As a result, JAL paid an estimated $1.5 billion more over the spot rate in 1994.[1]

As shown in the above case, the market fluctuates widely and is difficult to predict because many factors affect it. In sum, the nature of the market is that it is huge, highly volatile, and never sleeps—when the Tokyo market closes, the London Market opens, and then New York market takes over—and many factors affect the exchange rates of currencies. Below we review some economic theories on the determination of exchange rate.

Purchasing power parity (PPP). PPP argues that the exchange rate between two currencies should reflect the purchasing power of these currencies, especially in the long run. For example, if maintaining a middle class life style for a family of four in the United States and Japan, based on a basket of goods (food, clothes, transportation, housing, etc.) requires $80,000 and 10 million yen, respectively, then the exchange rate between the two should be $80,000/¥10,000,000, or $1= ¥125. If the actual exchange rate deviates from the PPP-based exchange rate, then it will be adjusted toward towards the PPP-based exchange rate in the long run.

Interest rates and exchange rates. Irving Fisher proposed a formulate depicting the relationship between real and nominal interests and inflation (the **Fisher Effect**):

$$i = r + I,$$

where i is the nominal interest rate, r is the real interest rate, and I is the inflation rate. What Fisher is trying to show is that the real interest rate (r)—the cost of borrowing—should be independent of monetary policies that affect inflation and thus the nominate interest rate. In other words, r is relatively stable, and the change in the nominal rate (i) reflects mostly the change in inflation rate (I).

Projecting the Fisher Effect into the international market, it becomes the **International Fisher Effect**, which states that the difference in the nominal interest rates between two countries reflects the market expectation on the trend in the spot exchange rates of the two countries. Numerically, the exchange rate between the two currencies will change the same amount as the gap between the nominal interest rates in the opposite direction. This is because the currency with the higher nominal interest rate is expected to have higher inflation and thus it will depreciate against the other currency. For example, if the spot exchange rate between currencies A and B is 1/1.5, currency A's nominal interest per year is 5%, and currency B yearly nominal interest rate is 7%, then the exchange rate 1 year later will be 1/(1.5 × (1 + 0.02)), or 1/1.53.

A logical extrapolation of the International Fisher Effect is that if two countries, X and Y, have the same inflation rate, but the government of X decides to raise its nominal interest rate, then capital will flow from country Y to X to seek higher real return (namely, firms and people will convert the currency of Y into the currency of X).

7.3 EXCHANGE-RATE REGIMES IN THE WORLD

Every country has a policy on how its currency is exchanged in the foreign exchange market (ie, its relationship to other currencies), and how its exchange rate is managed and determined. Such a policy is called the **exchange–rate regime**, which is set by the authority of the national government or the central bank. Broadly speaking, the way the exchange rate is determined ranges from completely freely floating to completely fixed, with many gradations in between. We will briefly review some major types below.

Float. This is to let the market determine a currency's exchange rate, which is the most common regime today. All the major currencies in the world—the US dollar, euro, yen, and British pound all have a floating rate. However, the governments behind these currencies often intervene by buying or selling their currencies to stabilize their exchange rate. Such intervention in the floating regime is called **managed float** or **dirty float**.

Pegged. Some countries peg their currency's exchange rate to a major currency, usually without the consent of the government of the major currency. For example, Hong Kong and China peg their currencies to the US dollar.

Fixed. If a group of countries mutually agree to fix their exchange rates to each other, a fixed exchange-rate regime exists. Historically, after World War II, 44 countries, led by the United States agreed to fix the exchange rates among them. The regime worked for a while and eventually collapsed in 1973.

"Beggar thy neighbor" refers to an economic policy that tries to enhance a country's economic performance by taking advantage of trading partners. For example, a country can devaluate its currency to make its exports cheaper to other countries, at the expense of other countries' exports that will be more expensive to sell to the devaluating country (Fig. 7.1).

Figure 7.1 What happens if one can keep selling without buying.

7.4 THE EXCHANGE-RATE REGIMES OF EAST ASIA

A common feature related to the exchange-rate regime and foreign exchange policy among East Asian countries is that they tend to maintain a trade surplus, have a high foreign reserve in US dollars, and keep their currencies' exchange value low in order to support their export sector.

When making their foreign exchange policies, East Asian governments must address two questions. First, should they fix their currency's exchange rate with a major currency? Second, if so, which major currency should they pick?

Addressing these questions are not easy, as each policy option has its cost and benefit. For example, maintaining a fixed exchange rate has the benefit of certainty, which is conducive to long-term planning, but it also requires the government to defend its fixed rate, which may be very costly and even impossible, and may force the country to coordinate with its partner countries at the expense of its domestic economic policy.

In reality, most East Asian countries and regions choose to have a regime that is neither fixed nor completely floating, while keeping a strong hand over its exchange rate. In terms of which major currency to peg, most (except Japan) use the US dollar as their benchmark to manage their exchange rate. Such a policy is called the "East Asia dollar standard" (Volz, 2011), which has the following benefits. First, it promotes export growth, especially to the United States, which is the largest importer of their goods. Second, it helps them to achieve macroeconomic stability. Third, it facilitates regional economic integration. Following such a strategy, East Asian countries have enjoyed a fast growth in exports, which in turn has boosted their manufacturing sector, achieved trade surpluses, and accumulated large foreign reserves (in US dollars).

However, there are also costs associated with such a strategy. First, pegging one's currency to the US dollar makes the economy vulnerable to the swings of the dollar's value. Second, in the same logic, the country may become a hostage of US domestic policies. For instance, in Dec. 2015, the US Federal Reserve decided to raise their interest rate to keep inflation in check in the US economy, which has recovered better than the rest of the world. Such a decision is primarily based on the domestic economic situation in the United States. However, due to the US dollar's status as the world's foreign reserve currency and as a pegged currency for many countries, such a decision may adversely affect the economic recovery and expansion of these countries (Wei, 2015, December 15). Third, a fundamental problem with the "East Asia dollar standard" is what economists termed as the "conflicted virtue." By artificially suppressing the value of their currency, they increase their exports. The trade surplus resulted from the increased exports then makes them hold a large amount of the dollar. Their trade surplus and dollar reserve pushes their currency exchange rate higher, which in turn dissipates the value of their dollar assets. Furthermore, the higher exchange rate will hurt their export growth (Volz, 2011).

Recently in 2015, China began to slowly and gradually move away from dollar standard. Of course, such a move is risky and may hurt China's export growth and trigger capital flight in the short run, because if people expect the Chinese yuan to delink from the dollar and to further depreciate, they may convert the yuan into dollars and move them outside of China. But such a measure is necessary if China wants to make the yuan a freely traded currency.

In Nov. 2015, the International Monetary Fund decided to include the yuan into the basket of the world's leading currencies for the IMF's Special Drawing Rights, which is used as the standard for maintaining financial reserves of its 199 member countries (The Wall Street Journal, 2015, December 1). While achieving such a status does not have immediate impact on the yuan, which only accounts for less than 3% of world trade and has virtually no significance as a foreign-exchange reserve, the inclusion signifies China's progress toward the liberalization of its currency control and future economic reform. A major reason that hinders the yuan from becoming a major foreign-exchange reserve currency is China's mercantilist trade practice, namely, the government actively supports exports and discourages imports, creating a huge trade surplus in foreign currencies, especially in the US dollar. In order to become a foreign-exchange reserve, the Chinese government must allow other countries to hold the yuan, which can only be possible if China imports more and incurs a trade deficit, like the United States.

7.5 CASE 2: WHY QUANTITATIVE EASING HAS DIFFERENT RESULTS IN THE UNITED STATES AND CHINA?

To boost economic growth during the 2008 financial crisis, the US Federal Reserve started a quantitative easing (QE) policy, which increases the broad money supply and aims to encourage private bank lending by buying mortgage-backed and Treasury securities. From late 2008, when the QE started, to 2014, when it was halted, the Fed accumulated $4.5 trillion in assets in its EQ program. The effort is widely credited for accelerating recover and boosting economic growth. The main concern of QE is that increasing the money supply in a large scale will induce inflation. However, that has not happened. One of the main reasons is that many countries absorbed the newly increased dollars as reserve.

But one country is not very happy about US QE, China, which is understandable. China was the largest holder of the US dollar—over $1 trillion in 2008. If the US dollar depreciated as a result of the US QE, China would see its dollar reserve evaporate in value to the Chinese yuan and there was little China could do to stop the US QE.

"If you can't beat them, join them." So China decided to do its own QE by releasing a large quantity of the Chinese yuan. Around 2008, the Chinese government unleashed RMB 4 trillion ($666 billion) to stimulate the economy, the largest stimulus in Chinese history, hoping to achieve similar results as that of the United States—boosting economic growth while keeping inflation at bay. Unfortunately, it did not work like that. One of the main reasons is that the Chinese yuan is not a reserve currency for other countries and thus no countries bought it as a reserve, plus the yuan is controlled by the Chinese government and there is no free market for it. So the Chinese government needed to find outlets to absorb all these newly available yuans. The government encouraged people to buy real estate and other big-ticket items and luxury goods. During the 2008 crisis, real estate prices in major cities in China grew rapidly, causing complaints from ordinary people who could not afford to buy apartments. For example, the average price of housing to income ratio is 54:1 in Beijing, as compared to 7:1 for the United States.

QUESTIONS

1. Based on Case 1, what is the purpose for JAL to enter into the foreign exchange contract?
2. Initial condition in year t: the exchange rate between the yen and the dollar is: $1= ¥100$; the interest rate of the yen, $i(¥) = 6\%$; the interest rate of the dollar is $i(\$) = 2\%$. What is the exchange rate between the yen and the dollar exactly 1 year later in year $t + 1$?
3. If the US Federal Reserve raises the interest rate of the dollar, how does the rise impact the Chinese yuan and the China's capital market, and China's export sector?
4. Based on Case 2, what are the factors that may have attributed to the different results of QE efforts between the United States and China?

ENDNOTE

1. Compiled based on Hill, C. (2003). *International business: Competing in the global marketplace* (4th ed.). New York, NY: McGraw-Hill.

REFERENCES

Hill, C. (2003). *International business: Competing in the global marketplace* (4th ed.). New York, NY: McGraw-Hill.

The Wall Street Journal. (2015, December 1). The yuan and Chinese reform. *The Wall Street Journal.*

Volz, U. (2011). On the choice of exchange rate regimes for East Asian countries. In V. K. Yin-Wong Cheung & G. Ma (Eds.), *The evolving role of Asia in global finance (Frontiers of economics and globalization)* (Vol. 9, pp. 123–156). Bingley: Emerald Group Publishing Limited.

Wei, L. (2015, December 15). China's problem with the dollar. *The Wall Street Journal, C3.*

CHAPTER 8

Business Strategies in East Asia

8.1 INTERNATIONAL BUSINESS STRATEGY

8.1.1 What Is Strategy?

Strategic management is the effort by the top management of a firm on behalf of the owners to formulate the firm's major goals and implement these goals. The goals are based on the firm's resources and the competitive environment.

Firms may have different goals. But the most common and perhaps the ultimate goal of operating a business is to make and increase **profit**, which can be defined as the difference between the cost and revenue.

How do firms increase profit? Generally, there are two ways to increase profit: increasing the selling price of the product or service the firm is producing and selling, or decreasing the cost of producing the product or service.

Based on this logic, business scholars such as Michael Porter have identified two types of competitive advantages: **lower cost** or **differentiation** relative to its rivals (Porter, 1980). Firms that are good at cost control and efficiency may profit from producing and selling products that have lower costs than its rivals. Alternatively, firms that excel at innovation, advanced technologies, or superb customer services may earn higher profit by differentiating its product from the competition by offering products that have unique features with high quality. Extending these two types into the international arena, firms may profit globally by either competing on cost or differentiation (localization).

8.1.2 Profiting From Global Expansion

Firms can increase their performance by going global in the following ways:

Achieving location economies. Location economies can be achieved by locating different activities in the value creation to either maximize profit or minimize cost. For example, a computer maker may locate its design in the Silicon Valley, California to access designing talents, its CPU production in Taiwan which is a leading player in the sector, its

East Asian Business in the New World.

LED production in Japan, its parts and accessories production in South Eastern Asia where there is a semiskilled work force, and carry out the final assembly in China to tap into the vast inexpensive labor supply. In doing so, the firm can make the product competitive in cost and quality. Without doing so, the firm risks being left behind by its rivals that do so.

Realizing Cost Economies. Cost economies can be realized by improving efficiency through quickly advancing through the experience curve. The experience curve effect exists in the production of goods or services such that when the volume of production increases cumulatively, the unit cost of production (including direct and indirect costs associated with the production) decreases.

Leveraging Core Competencies. Introduced by Prahalad and Hamel, the concept of core competency is the unique set of skills and resources possessed by the firm that enable it to distinguish itself in the marketplace (Prahalad & Hamel, 1990). In order to achieve core competencies, a firm must be able to create high value and benefit to the customer in a wide variety of markets and, most importantly, such an ability must be difficult to imitate by competitors.

If a firm has developed a set of core competencies in its home market, which has been saturated, the firm may go to foreign markets to further profit from its core competencies. For example, Procter & Gamble, the giant consumer product maker, has strong core competencies in marketing and turning its product into a dominant brand. Since this unique and powerful set of core competencies has already been developed in the home market, P&G can relatively easily take it to foreign markets and profit from it by developing and marketing its products to dominate the new foreign markets.

Leveraging Subsidiary Skills. Companies go abroad to learn from their foreign operations (branches, subsidiaries, or joint venture operations). While it is true, especially for companies from highly developed countries, that home country companies going abroad often bring new technology and business knowledge to the host countries, especially developing countries, it is also true and important that home country companies can and should learn from the host country operations, such as new technologies, new production methods, new corporate culture, etc. For example, KFC's Japanese operation developed a 12-piece "mini-barrel" (as opposed to the 21-piece set offered in the United States), and small store layouts with a flexible kitchen design. KFC Japan even experimented with chicken nuggets in 1981.

8.1.3 Key Factors to Consider for Firms Going Global

When bringing its product or its production to foreign markets, what are the major challenges a company must consider? In other words, what are the major factors that will determine the success of its product in foreign markets? What are the major factors that will determine the success of its locating its production activities in foreign markets?

8.1.4 Pressure for Cost Reduction and Local Responsiveness

Firms doing business globally face two major challenges: the pressure to reduce cost and the pressure to make their products or services fit the each foreign market (Hill, 2005).

Pressure for cost reduction. The pressure for cost reduction arises from the following factors. First, it is due to the type of the product. If the product is mass produced with a highly standardized process with few unique features, such as steel, fine chemicals, or certain standardized tools or machinery, the cost reduction pressure tends to be high. If the users of the product/service can easily switch from one supplier to another without high cost, such as the users of personal computer, then customer loyalty is low and the product/service faces cost reduction pressure.

Second, it is a function of the type of the industry supply/demand condition. If the industry persistently has high idle capacity, in other words, if the supply is always higher than demand, then the cost reduction pressure will be high. The 2015 oil industry resembled such a condition, in which the global capacity of oil production greatly outpaced the demand, giving the oil producers a tremendous pressure to reduce cost and driving the high-cost producers (such as the Canadian oil-sand producers) out of the market.

Third, an industry with some suppliers located in countries with below average production cost tends to face a great pressure of cost reduction, provided that suppliers compete globally. For example, the combination of huge supply of low cost labor and the high productivity of the Chinese workers has made China a low-cost manufacturing base for garments.

Fourth, there are industries that have greater international competition, such as household appliance manufacturing, and therefore face greater cost reduction pressure.

For firms that face the above pressures, in order to reduce cost, they must go global to optimally locate each link of the value creation chain to minimize cost.

Pressure to localize product/service. Although some products can be globally standardized, many need to be localized to fit the market. Obviously, localizing a product incurs extra cost. The pressure to localize is influenced by the following factors.

First, for many products, consumer taste and preference vary substantially from country to country. For instance, if we go in a convenience store in the United States looking for a snack, we will see chips, all sorts of chips; if it is in Japan, we will see many types of seafood-based snacks with spices.

Second, differences in government regulations and infrastructure across countries dictate the need to localize. For example, electricity supply varies across countries; some countries require headlights to be on during daytime for cars. In some countries people drive cars on the left-hand side of the road. Some host country governments require that a multinational enterprise selling its product in the host country must use parts provided by the country.

Third, distribution channels differ across countries. Some countries ban advertising of certain products, such as alcoholic beverages or cigarettes. Some countries ban direct selling.

If the foreign market for a product is highly localized, then the firm marketing such a product must localize its offer to enter the market.

In some industries, the firm may face both pressures, or may face little of each (Fig. 8.1). Graphically, the combination of the two pressures is as follows:

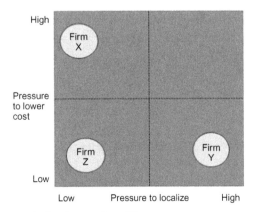

Figure 8.1 Pressures facing international firms.

8.1.5 Four Strategic Choices

As can be seen from the above graph, there are four positions: LL (low cost pressure-low localization pressure), HL, LH, and HH. For example, each of the three companies on the graph faces a different combination of the two pressures. Corresponding to the four positions, **there are four strategies for multinational firms** (Hill, 2005) (Fig. 8.2):

Traditional Strategy (LL). This strategic position assumes that the firm in the global market faces little pressure to reduce costs or localize. Ideally, firms taking this strategy can offer products or services that host countries do not have and must depend on. Firms taking a Traditional Strategy tend to be in dominant or even monopolistic positions worldwide. An example of such a strategy is Microsoft's Window operating system, which has had a near monopoly so it faces little pressure to lower cost (or price), and needs minimal localization, for example, the display language, since its source code does not change across country.

Global Standardization Strategy (HL). This strategic choice is usually taken by firms that face great pressure to lower cost. In order to achieve cost reduction, they must realize location economies to the fullest extent by strategically locating each activity of the whole production process in the best location in the world to minimize cost or maximize efficiency. Implementing such a strategy requires **centralization of decision-making**, namely, the headquarters must exercise the authority to coordinate all the firm's branches and subsidiaries throughout the world so that together they can achieve low cost. In other words, its subsidiary in a foreign country or one of its plants cannot have the autonomy to decide

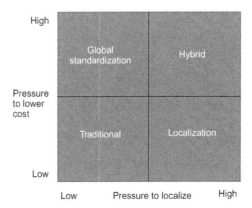

Figure 8.2 Basic strategic positioning.

what or how it wants to make or sell. A good example of firms taking a Global Standardization Strategy is Apple's global allocation of its production of the iPhone. Many countries are allocated parts of its production ranging from the United States, countries in Europe, and Asian countries, depending on the resources, capabilities, and cost. The most technology-intense, core processes are done in the United States; the processes requiring specialized technologies are allocated to Europe, Japan, South Korea, and Taiwan, and the final assembly is in China (Financeonline.com, 2015).

Localization Strategy (LH). Opposite to the Global Strategy, this strategy focuses on making its products or services fit the host country market. If organizational requirement of the Global Strategy is high centralization, then **the organization requirement of the Localization Strategy is decentralization** in the sense that operation decisions, such as product development and marketing, must be delegated to the management in the host country, not at the headquarters. For example, for a multinational firm taking processed snack foods to sell globally, it must rely on its local marketing team in each market to develop and market the products that fit the local taste and preference.

Hybrid Strategy (HH). The strategy intends to achieve both low cost and localization, a very ambitious and difficult objective. Of course, companies that can achieve this are superior to most of their peers. Sometimes the nature of the industry or the intensity of the global competition demands firms to adopt such a strategy. While realizing both strategic imperatives can put the firm in the highly advantageous position, it is difficult to do because to lower cost, the firm must centralize decision-making to allocate its facilities and functions globally; at the same time to localize, it must decentralize decision-making so that local teams can develop products that best fit the local market. How can a firm be centralized and decentralized simultaneously? The answer, as scholars have suggested, is to have **flexibility and networking**. The headquarters work closely with local teams, and staff members work across division or location to tap into different talent from problem solution and collaborate beyond one's own unit to achieve the strategic goal.

An important note: Students usually have difficult to classify which strategic position a firm belongs, as it appears to belong to several positions. This is quite normal, because **these four strategic positions are relative**. The label of these strategic choices is **heuristic**. It is primarily an **industry-based view** of strategy, meaning that the industry structure and product characteristics determine a firm's strategic position.

8.2 STRATEGIES IN EAST ASIAN COUNTRIES

8.2.1 Low Cost Production

Since the end of World War II, East Asia has been the low-cost manufacturing base, which has helped its economic development and also benefited consumers worldwide and especially consumers in the mature economies by providing inexpensive consumer goods. The key factor for the success of the low-cost manufacturing base is low labor cost coupled with high productivity, which is the result of the hard-working culture (see chapter: The Role of Culture in Economic Development: Does Culture Give East Asia an Edge Over America in Economic Competition?). In the 1950s and 1960s, Japan was the low-cost–high-efficiency manufacturing base; from the 1970s to 1980s when its labor cost became high along with the rising living standard as a result of high economic growth, South Korea and Taiwan took over from Japan as the low-cost–high-efficiency manufacturing bases; in the 1980s, when labor in these two countries became expensive, the base shifted to China, which has become the largest manufacturing base of the world.

Now China's manufacturing sector is repeating what happened to those of Japan, South Korea, and Taiwan: with the rapid economic growth and the rising of living standards, labor cost has risen so high that it has begun to threaten China's dominant position as the world's low-cost manufacturing base (Chu, 2015, December 3).

As can be seen from Fig. 8.3, the labor cost in China increased drastically from 2000 to 2015, surpassing Taiwan, which has a much higher income per capita ($22,500) than China ($7400) (World Bank Group, 2015).

Now many low-cost manufacturers that have been operating in China have begun to shift their operations to other Asian countries that have lower labor costs with relatively high productivity, such as Malaysia and Vietnam, whose labor costs are 75% and 33% of China's, respectively (Chu, 2015, December 3).

A major challenge to the low-cost production strategy in East Asia is the low fertility rate in the major East Asia countries that has steadily reduced the labor force there. As can be seen from Table 8.1, the fertility rates of the major East Asian countries and regions are far below the replacement level (the number of children per woman required to sustain the current population). (Recently China changed its birth control policy from one child per couple to two children per couple. However, due to

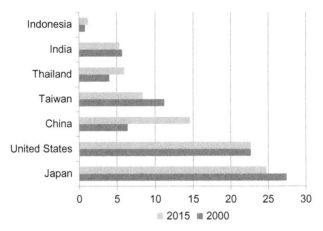

Figure 8.3 Changes in manufacturing labor costs in US dollar per hour adjusted for productivity, 2000–15, assuming US cost remains constant from 2000 to 2015. *Chu, K., & Davis, B. (2015, November 24). A nation of 1.4 billion faces a labor shortage. The Wall Street Journal, 2.*

Table 8.1 Fertility and net migration in East Asia and the United States, 2013

Countries/regions	Total fertility rate (children/ woman)	Net migration (millions)	Net migration rate (%)	Population (millions)
China	1.7	−1.80	−0.13	1357
Hong Kong	1.1	0.15	2.14	7
Japan	1.4	0.35	0.28	127
South Korea	1.2	0.30	0.60	50
Taiwan	1.0	0.02	0.09	23
United States	1.9	5.00	1.58	316
Replacement level fertility	2.1			

Source: Wikipedia. (2015). *Demographics in Taiwan.* Wikipedia.com (Wikipedia, 2015); World Bank. (2015). *World development indicators.* Washington, DC: World Bank (World Bank, 2015).

the high cost of raising children, most people in China do not want to have more children, and such a policy change will have a limited effect on raising the fertility rate (Burkitt, 2015, December 16).) In addition, net migration is too small to compensate for the low fertility in order to replenish the labor force in these countries, with the exception of Hong Kong. In comparison, the United States is in a much better shape in its demographic trend: it has a fertility rate that is close to the replacement level and a relatively high net migration rate.

8.2.2 Localization

The importance of localization in East Asia cannot be overemphasized. Due to their unique cultural and consumer tastes, government policies, and infrastructures (Associate Press, 2015, December 11), multinational corporations that want to market their products in East Asia must carefully evaluate the need to localize and determine the optimal level of localization. Examples of localization can be easily seen in the snack food market, in which consumer tastes differ widely across regions. Walking into a 7-Eleven store in Taipei to survey the snack foods shelf, one would find items that are not seen in a 7-Eleven in the United States. According to BuzzFeed, the top five Asian snacks are the Chinese hawthorn fruit chips, dried squid, cuttlefish chips, lychee jelly, and Asian rice crackers (Chen, 2013, November 4), whereas the top selling snacks in the United States are mostly made of wheat, corn, and potato (Culliney, 2012, September 27).

The rise of nationalism and consumer rights in East Asia, especially in newly emerging countries such as China, has put more pressure on the multinational corporations to localize (Park, Zhao, & Li, 2015, October 13). This effort includes catering products and services to local market and consumption characteristics, relying on local talent, and developing business and political networks. For example, Electrolux, one of the largest appliance manufacturers headquartered in Stockholm, Sweden, claimed to be "Making Foreign Brand Local"; P&G proposed to "Being A Chinese Citizen"; KFC has provided a local style breakfast in Asia; and L'Oreal has created cosmetics friendly to the skin of East Asians.

While these measures can be effective, there are pitfalls in them that multinational corporations must be aware of and thus avoid. For example, if the localization effort is seen as a purely economic decision to maximize profit, then it may be viewed suspiciously and meet resistance from local stakeholders (local communities, consumer rights groups, and nationalists). A common error the multinational corporations tend to commit is to underestimate the local stakeholders' expectations. Such expectations have been for a long time marginalized in the multinational corporations' business considerations. As a result, many multinational corporations in China that relied on growth supported by fast and deep localization have fallen into growth traps.

Another common error is fast localization without carefully mapping out the steps and being prepared for the challenge. When an multinational corporation's localization is rapidly implemented, it often faces shortage of local talents and overreliance on its local partners for supplying and marketing, which are vulnerable to fraud and weak quality control. For example, to fight fraud and counterfeiting in the local market, multinational corporations often hire local detectives to catch the offenders and close the counterfeiting factories. An in-depth report by Associated Press revealed that these detectives often are counterfeiters themselves and create fake arrests and closures to claim rewards (Associate Press, 2015, December 11).

Fast localization may also result in hiring unqualified local workers and underpaying them. This can cause not only quality issues, but also a backlash from the local stakeholders who protest against the "multinational corporation's exploitation," which may escalate into a public crisis for the multinational corporation. Such a crisis has happened to many multinational corporations in East Asia, including Dell, Honda, and Carrefour (the French based department store chain) (Park et al., 2015, October 13).

8.3 THE NEW HYBRID STRATEGY: MASS CUSTOMIZATION

With the rapid advancement in technologies, new solutions are emerging to overcome the challenges to the low-cost production strategy in East Asia posed by the rapid shrinkage of the labor force and the rise in labor cost.

8.3.1 Automation: The Answer to the Rising Labor Cost and Shortage

Facing up to the coming shortage of workers, East Asian countries are investing heavily in substitute workers: robots. For example, the Chinese Communist Party Chief Xi Jinping in 2014 urged the country to start "an industrial robot revolution" (Chu & Davis, 2015, November 24; Knight, 2015, December 7). As can be seen from Fig. 8.4, three of the top five markets for industrial robot sales are in East Asia. While the "revolution" is not an overnight paradigm shift, policy makers and businesses are optimistic about the prospect of using automation to solve, or at least to mitigate, the rapidly aging labor force that is shrinking worldwide. They see a wide range of applications for automation including housekeeping work, 3-D printing, assembly line work, caring for the elderly, and construction work, for example Hagerty (2015, November 24).

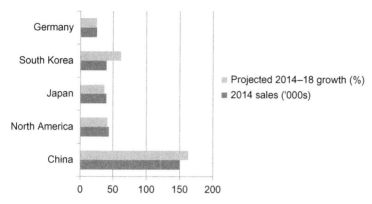

Figure 8.4 Top five markets for industrial robot sales (Future: automation. Hagerty, 2015, November 24). *Hagerty, J. R. (2015, November 24). The robots are coming, but don't worry yet. The Wall Street Journal, 1.*

8.3.2 Mass Customization: The New Hybrid Strategy

Mass customization is a marketing and production strategy that has been enabled by the information technology revolution that began in the 1990s (Rogers, 1993). It is a marriage of two polarized approaches in marketing. Customized production and marketing is to treat each customer individually and custom-tailor the product and service to fit his/her needs, whereas mass production and marketing is to produce a product in a large quantity and market it to a large customer base. The cost and benefit of the two approaches are opposite to each other: while customization fits the unique needs of each individual, it is costly to do; and although mass production and marketing has a low cost, it cannot fit the varying needs of all customers. It had been a dream for marketers to be able to provide customized products and services at the mass production cost, and this dream has been fulfilled by the advancement in computing and communication technologies.

In general, mass customization is possible due to the following two capabilities:

1. Powerful computing and data management capability enables marketers to collect, store, and analyze large amounts of data on customers' attitude and behavior.

2. Telecommunication and internet technology enable marketers to interact with customers in real time.

Based on these two capabilities, marketers can rely on computers to systematically identify and predict customers' needs, and execute orders to produce a product or service to meet the needs and therefore there is a high likelihood that a customer will buy it.

An example of adopting such a strategy is Levi, the leading garment maker in the world. Facing the rising labor cost and worker shortage in China, Levi has gradually shifted its emphasis from low-cost mass production to mass customization. According to a *Wall Street Journal* article, Levi is "moving toward agility. Liz O'Neill, Levi's senior vice president of product development, told the newspaper that 'The real money is having the right product in front of the customer at the right time'" (Chu & Davis, 2015, November 24).

8.4 STRATEGIC CONSIDERATIONS

Several issues stand out in East Asia that require strategic considerations for multinational corporations doing business there.

The first is the importance of **geopolitical issues** in East Asia, which can be best illustrated from the disputes and conflicts on the South China Sea and the artificial islands built there by the Chinese government. Along with the rapid economic rise of China, China has begun to exert its territorial claim in the Pacific region and is trying to assume the leadership role in Asia. Such efforts have been received with concern by the neighboring countries in East Asia. The clashes between countries in the region may adversely affect multinational corporations doing business in East Asia. For example, there has been a dispute between China and Taiwan, which have been separated since 1949, with the former regarding the latter as a renegade province and the latter wanting to maintain its independence. In Dec. 2015 the US government announced that it would sell $1.83 billion worth of weapons to Taiwan, and China lodged a strong protest and announced that it will boycott the American companies that sell arms to Taiwan, which are primarily Raytheon and Lockheed Martin (Wong, 2015, December 17).

Closely related to the first issue is another important issue: the **rise of nationalism** in the region, especially in China. Along with economic development and prosperity, Asians are increasingly feeling proud of their identities and heritages and exerting such feelings more explicitly in the international arena (Lehmann, 2013, January 4). International political economist Jean-Pierre Lehmann warns that "[T]he specter of rising nationalism in the area now threatens to undo the gains that global interdependence has brought to the region…While China, Japan and

South Korea may have embraced economic globalization, they have emphatically not embraced one another...If the fuse goes off on the Northeast Asia powder keg, the consequences will be immediate, global and dramatic" (Lehmann, 2013, January 4).

Marketing studies show that due to cultural and historical factors, such as the Japanese invasion of China during the World War II, consumers in Asia are sensitive to the country of origin in brand perception and acceptance. For example, studies show that Chinese consumers show hostility to Japanese brands (Fong, Lee, & Du, 2014).

At a more fundamental level, the rise of nationalism poses a particular challenge to Western firms since in the West there is the view that basic human rights, such as individual freedom, override national sovereignty, whereas East Asian traditions may place the nation-state above individual freedoms. Translating this into business issues, a dispute between a Western firm and East Asian consumers or a competition between a Western firm and the domestic firm can be easily labeled as an "East versus West" issue, such as shown in the case of Starbuck's coffee shop being forced to move out of the Forbidden City in Beijing (New York Times, 2007, July 15).

QUESTIONS

1. Plot the position of the following firms on Fig. 8.2: Proctor & Gamble, Dell, Coca-Cola, Dow Chemicals, US Steel, McDonald's, Wal-Mart.
2. Are the following global standardization industries or localization industries: bulk chemicals, pharmaceuticals, branded food products, moviemaking, PCs, airline travel?
3. What do you see as the main organizational problems likely to be associated with the implementation of a transnational strategy?
4. Case Study and Discussion: Kentucky Fried Chicken (Japan) Ltd.
   Read "Kentucky Fried Chicken (Japan) Ltd." by Christopher A. Bartlett, 1986 (revised Dec. 1992), Harvard Business School Case. Suggested video for the case: The Colonel Comes to Japan, PBS business series, 1981. Review and answer the following questions:
   a. What should Dick Mayer do about Loy Weston?
   b. What does it take to succeed in the fast food franchising business?
   c. What is the major challenge in *international* operation of fast food business?
   d. Evaluate Dick Mayer's "stage theory."

e. What recommendation would you make to Dick Mayer on the issues he raises at the end of the case?

5. Conduct research online and compare the cost of manufacturing in China and the United States. How can the United States improve its competitiveness in attracting manufacturers?

REFERENCES

Associate Press. (2015, December 11). Fraud rampant in fight against Chinese fakes. *Taipei Times.*

Burkitt, L. (2015, December 16). Chinese families reluctant to let go of one-child model. *The Wall Street Journal.*

Chen, T. (2013, November 4). 15 iconic Asian snacks you need to try. *BuzzFeed.com.*

Chu, K. (2015, December 3). China loses edge on labor costs. *The Wall Street Journal, 2*

Chu, K., & Davis, B. (2015, November 24). A nation of 1.4 billion faces a labor shortage. *The Wall Street Journal, 2.*

Culliney, K. (2012, September 27). Top 10 US snack brands: A consumer choice. *bakeryandsnacks.com.*

Financeonline.com. (2015). How iPhone is made: The global assembly line. *Financesonline.com.* http://financesonline.com/hello-world-the-economics-of-iphone/.

Fong, C., Lee, C., & Du, Y. (2014). Consumer animosity, country of origin, and foreign entry-mode choice: A cross-country investigation. *Journal of International Marketing, 22*(1) Retrieved from http://search.proquest.com/docview/1507458539?accountid=1507412967.

Hagerty, J. R. (2015, November 24). The robots are coming, but don't worry yet. *The Wall Street Journal, 1.*

Hill, C. (2005). *International business: Competing in the global marketplace* (5th ed.). New York, NY: McGraw-Hill.

Knight, W. (2015, December 7). China wants robots to replace millions of low-paid workers. *MIT Technology Review.* http://mashable.com/2015/12/07/china-workers-robots/#wLmU2xKrUZqa.

Lehmann, J.-P. (2013, January 4). Nationalism rises in Northeast Asia, *YaleGlobal.* http://yaleglobal.yale.edu/content/nationalism-rises-northeast-asia.

New York Times. (2007, July 15). Starbucks closes coffeehouse in Beijing's Forbidden City. *The New York Times.*

Park, S. H., Zhao, M., & Li, S. (2015, October 13). From silent majority to strategic challengers: China's new stakeholders for MNCs. *The Financial Times.*

Porter, M. (1980). *Competitive strategy.* New York, NY: Free Press.

Prahalad, C. K., & Hamel, G. (1990, May–June). The core competence of the corporation. *Harvard Business Review, 68,* 79–91.

Rogers, M. (1993). *The one-to-one future: Building relationship one customer a time.* New York, NY: Doubleday.

Wikipedia. (2015). *Demographics in Taiwan.* Wikipedia.com.

Wong, C. H. (2015, December 17). China has few options in protesting U.S. arms sales to Taiwan. *The Wall Street Journal.*

World Bank, (2015). *World development indicators.* Washington, DC: World Bank.

World Bank Group. (2015). *Doing Business 2016.* www.worldbank.org.

CHAPTER 9

Market Structures in East Asia: Why Selling to Some Countries Are So Difficult?*

9.1 CUSTOMER SERVICE QUALITY IN DIFFERENT SOCIETIES

For global business travelers, perhaps the first difference they observe is in service quality. In some countries the service experience is pleasant: the people who serve customers—flight attendants, waiters/waitresses, convenient store clerks—are fast, reliable, and care; and in some other countries, the people whose job is serving the customers do not serve well, and there are societies in which the service people are the king (Arlen, 2008, October 24)!.

9.1.1 Service Quality in Communist Societies

In societies without competitive markets, such as the communist societies, there tend to be a shortage of consumer goods, which creates a seller's market. Sales peoples became powerful as they control the goods in shortage. As a result, they do not have to please the customer, as depicted in the cartoon (Fig. 9.1).

9.1.2 Service Quality in Capitalist Society (Market Economies)

The United States. The American culture emphasizes equality. Servers and the serviced are equal. It has been a market economy for 400 years since the Europeans settled here and is now a mature market economy. This long history of capitalism may have made the service culture in the United States tired and dull.

---

* Adopted from Li, S. 2009. *Managing international business in relation-based versus rule-based countries.* New York, NY: Business Expert Press.

Figure 9.1 *"Can you please show me that?" Author (based on memory of a cartoon seen in China in the 1980s).*

East Asia. Compared to the United States, the East Asian culture is more hierarchical in which the power distance is greater, and the service culture treats the customer literally as king. The relationship between the server and the served is like between servant and his/her master. In addition, capitalism is relatively young in East Asia, especially in China, making the service culture vibrant and overzealous in pushing "customer is king" to the extreme (see Video: Customer service in a convenience store in Taiwan, (Li, 2011a) and Video: Train conductor in Japan 1-2, (Li, 2011b)).

9.2 SALIENT FEATURES OF RELATION-BASED MARKET STRUCTURE

In general, the market structure in a relation-based society is different from that of a rule-based society. In this section, we will discuss some of the main features of the market structure in relation-based societies and contrast them with those in rule-based societies.

9.2.1 Government and Business

The role of the government in a relation-based society can be summarized as very powerful. As we discussed in the introduction, the fundamental reason why people and businesses try to avoid formal rules and rely on private relationships to conduct business and protect their interest is that the formal rules tend to be opaque and unfair, and the state cannot enforce them impartially. This situation results from the unbalanced power of the state, especially when the executive branch overshadows or controls legislative and judiciary functions. The state controls most lucrative industries, usually in the name of protecting domestic industries or "national security." For instance, the Chinese government explicitly stated that it must maintain "absolute control" over the following seven industries: defense, electricity production and distribution, petrochemical, telecommunication, coal, civil aviation, transportation, and shipping. (Xinhuashe (New China News Agency), 2006). Under such a policy, the Chinese government created some extremely large companies that are in monopolistic positions with rich resources and lucrative markets given by the state, and make huge profits (Nanfangwang, 2006; Zhang, 2011, July 12). According to the 2014 Fortune Global 500 list, all the top ranked firms from China are state-owned, such as Sinopec, China Natural Petroleum, State Grid Corp, and Industrial and Commercial Bank of China (Fortune, 2015).

Meanwhile, relation-based governments usually give privileges to certain private business people who have close relationships with the government. For example, in Thailand, lucrative industries are tightly controlled by the government and demand "an especially close relationship with 'the centers of power'" to enter (Hewison & Thongyou, 2000). These industries include natural resource extraction, building and engineering contracting, and alcohol distribution and retailing. In general, opportunities are open only to the business people who are well connected with government officials. As analysts have observed, there is a key axis of powerful military officials and financiers that dominates the urban political economy in Thailand, and "spectacular success in the growing urban economy was reserved for the small number of business groups that clustered around this axis" (Phongpaichit & Baker, 2000).

In China, the government has stated that it would allow certain private investors to enter some of the state controlled industries. The investment must be under state planning and must be qualified as being offered by "high quality private firms" (Xinhuashe, 2005). The online comments about this policy suggest that it will give well-connected investors the opportunity to enter these lucrative industries. One commentator said, "This policy is nothing more than creating a few oligarchs who control China's economy. It is to legitimize transferring the lifeline of our national economy to the children of high-ranking officials." Another said, "[Allowing] non-state capital [to enter] the controlled industry? Who has that kind of money to play such a game? Who can win (against the state)? Only the children of the policy makers can play. Only they can win" (Xinhuashe, 2005).

A seasoned and very successful entrepreneur in China, Feng Lun, made the following observation about the role of ordinary private businesses under the watchful eyes of the state:

> *Private businesses in China must realize that they have been and will always be appendices of the state-owned businesses. Thus, the best survival strategies are the following: you can stay far away from the industries in which state-owned firms dominate, being satisfied with your own small plot, contributing actively to philanthropy, and building roads and bridges in your community. Alternatively, you can partner with the state capital to create a mixed ownership. Leveraging on your professional and managerial ability, you must first preserve the state capital and deliver a good return for it, and then you may gain legitimacy and enjoy a relatively safe environment...Facing the state-owned businesses, private businesses must cooperate, not compete; supplement, not replace; follow, not surpass (Wu, 2008).*

In addition to the tight control over many industries by the state, another common feature of market entry barriers in a relation–based society is that while an industry may be formally open to private or foreign investment, the informal barriers, created by the powerful regulatory officials and the exclusive network of incumbents, can be insurmountable. A spokesperson for a national business association in China, Huang Mengfu, complained,

> *Publicly, some industries appear to be open, but when you try to enter, you will find many hurdles that are so high that it is impossible for you to enter. We call this a 'glass door' that is locked. You can look through it, but you can't get in. If you try, you will hit a wall (Wu, 2008).*

A Vietnamese entrepreneur described a similar situation in his country: "It's government policy not to discriminate between the state and private sectors, but in reality the officials who implement the policies often don't treat us equally" (Hiebert, 1996).

9.2.2 The Tendency to Have More Formal Rules in Relation-Based Societies

Readers who have traveled to relation–based countries, especially to the ones undergoing rapid changes, may observe that compared to rule–based countries, these relation–based countries that are not supposed to closely follow formal public rules actually have *more* formal rules than rule–based countries. Take the case of China, for instance. The formal rules of setting up a limited liability company, the most common form of business organization, are many and complicated. At the turn of the century (late 1990s and early 2000s), I had an experience of setting up a company from scratch and acquiring an existing firm in China. One of the major steps in setting up a new firm was to register it with the local business administration bureau, which first required that a prospective new firm submit a feasibility study (which could be simply rejected by the bureau as "not feasible," a decision we first received), that the owners have valid local resident cards (eg, Beijing residents may not register a firm in Shanghai), that the company had leased or bought a physical location, and that it deposit the minimally required registered capital in the bank, ranging from 100,000 yuan ($12,000 in 1999) to 30 million yuan ($3.6 million in 1999), depending on the nature of the business and its type of ownership structure. Furthermore, the required cash deposit for the startup must be verified by the government, which typically charged 0.3% of the total investment as the cost of "performing" the verification. The naming of a startup was stringently controlled by the state. The format is "location" + "adjective" + "nature of business," for example, "Shenzhen City Prosperous Fishing Gear." The words "China," "national," "international," or anything that implied a national or international scale were owned by the government; any firms that want to use them must get special permission from the state. (Of course, for someone who has a strong relationship with the authorities and offers them an appealing deal, such words can be part of the company name.) In the case of one company acquiring the other, the regulation is that the acquiring company's registered capital (not the total assets) must be greater than that of the acquired company. If not, even if the acquiring company has enough cash on hand, it cannot buy the other company.

In Vietnam, for example, the state regulation for urban land development involves 22 permits and approvals (Kim, 2008). Not surprisingly, a feasibility study is required, and it has to be reviewed and approved by two separate agencies. Ultimately, all land development projects must go all the way up to the Vietnamese Prime Minister's Office to get approval! (Imagine if all land development applications had to be approved by the White House in the United States....) In Indonesia, even in the post-Suharto (who was very corrupt) era, after substantial changes, the approval procedure for foreign firms to enter "remains lengthy and tedious" (Risk Management, 2009).

How do we explain the tendency of relation-based governments to set up more formal rules? The reason for this abundance of rules is that the government in a relation-based country is generally more powerful and controls more public and economic resources than its counterparts in rule-based countries. We should keep in mind that the key feature of relation-based societies is not that they lack public rules; it is that the public rules are not fairly made and are not consistently applied. People with close relationships to officials can easily circumvent the rules. In this sense, these stifling rules are evidence of a relation-based system. Researchers commenting about Thailand's complicated business regulation system said this: "The tangle of licensing controls and miscellaneous red tape…provided opportunities for the generals to favor their friends" (Phongpaichit & Baker, 2000). If someone does not have a good connection or refuses to go through private relationships, then doing business in such societies is very difficult. For example, an American developer in Vietnam—who did not use private connections or pay bribes—spent 5 years to get project approval, 1 year to get a construction permit, and 2 years to get the land use certificates! (Kim, 2008).

9.2.3 High Market Entry Barrier

In an economy that relies on private relationships to conduct and protect business activities, business people invest heavily in establishing good relationships with the people who can help them in their business. These people include government officials and established business people. Investment in relationships is "sunk capital" in a sense that once invested, the investor cannot redeem his investment because he cannot resell his established relationship to others.

Private relationships are exclusive, just like a marital or dating relationship, and thus the people who are in a relationship carefully guard it from existing or potential competitors. Any newcomers that try to budge their way into an existing relationship are not welcome.

Thus, the market structure of a relation-based economy tends to have high entry barriers. In Jun., 2009, I was helping a UK-based telecom group with their market entry strategy in China. I asked the group's marketing executive what their major difficulty in doing business in China was. The executive replied: the lack of relationships with the established players in the market. Below is a typical case of what usually happens to his marketing effort.

> Since I don't know anyone in the major telecom companies in China, I would make cold calls to pitch our services. Well, it is not completely a cold call; I would do my homework on the person I would call and be well prepared. When I call the

prospective client, in order to get through to his secretary, I would say that I have an appointment with him. When I get to the target person, he usually asks where I found his name, how I learned about his background, and who introduced me to him. He would first be impressed by my knowledge of him. But once he learned that I was not introduced by anyone, he would say, "come back when you get a proper introduction" and hang up.[1]

In relation-based economies, major industries tend to be dominated by a few insiders. Those insiders are the business people or firms who either are designated players by the government or have close relationships with the government so that they can get special permissions to enter the market. Once they become insiders, they, along with their benefactor—the government regulatory agency—will try to make the entry barrier high so as to protect their (sunk) investment.

In Indonesia, although many sectors appeared to be completely open to foreign investors, few investors would be confident enough to go in solo because the informal barriers were high and complicated. The properly informed foreign investors always went in with a powerful local player, even though such an option was costly due to "fees" or outright corruption. As one researcher noted, experienced foreign investors "knew the value of having a savvy and influential domestic counterpart with good connections who could navigate the still unreformed bureaucracy." The process was so complicated and difficult that it required the Indonesian president's children to help the foreign firms to "sail through this maze" (Borsuk, 1998).

9.2.4 High Market Exit Barrier

While the reason for high market entry barriers in a relation-based society is easy to understand, why markets in relation-based society have high exit barriers is not so obvious. To understand this, let us examine the entry and exit mechanism of a mafia group—an extremely relation-based organization. To be admitted into a secretive society such as the mafia, the prospective member needs a proper introduction from senior members, and he usually needs to complete a difficult, often dangerous, task asked by the organization to show his commitment and loyalty. An example might be obtaining (often through illegal means) valuable artifacts or information, or even killing someone. After a period of informal probation, if he has fulfilled his tasks, he will be admitted. At that point, the organization has invested substantial effort and resources in this new member. If a member wants to quit the organization, not only will all the sunk investment in him be lost, but more importantly, he will take many assets with him, such as the secrets of the organization and the connections or networks the organization has given him. In other words, he knows too much to let him go. To deter such damaging behavior, the mafia organization must exterminate quitters, as shown in numerous cases of organized crime.

It is difficult to obtain cases that reveal in detail the cost and difficulty involved in players quitting business relationships, since such relationships are secretive. Nevertheless, we can indirectly assess the difficulty by examining some high-profile cases of exiting a powerful relation-based business network. The late Indonesian president Suharto was a powerful ruler who had forged an extensive and corrupt government-business alliance. When he was forced to step down in 1998 due to the popular uprising, many business people who were closely associated with him or his family suffered great losses in their business ventures (Borsuk, 1998). Many of these people invested into these ventures not because the business had cutting-edge technology or superior products or services; they did it simply because Suharto's power would guarantee an above-market average return no matter what the business did. Similarly, when the powerful businessman turned prime minister of Thailand, Thaksin, fled the country, many of his business associates suffered big losses (Brown, 2008). Needless to say, the value of their investment into such a relationship was rapidly becoming worthless. And worse yet, some of them may be prosecuted by the new regime on bribery and corruption charges related to the former rulers. We can reasonably conjecture that the business partners of Suharto and Thaksin would do whatever they could to prevent the two from leaving, if they were able.

9.2.5 Business Groups in Relation-Based Markets

Based on our analysis so far, it is no surprise that most successful business people in a relation-based society have cozy relationships with the government. Once a business person has developed a good relationship with the government, it is easy for him to get the entry permission for his chosen industry. In fact, since the relational investment to cultivate a cordial relationship with the government is sunk, he should use the established relationship as much as possible. Thus, instead of entering one industry, the relationship holder may as well enter as many industries as he can. Because most industries are restricted by the government and competition is limited, whoever has the privilege to enter is likely to make money, even though they may not have expertise or experience in the industry.

This logic may partially explain why in relation-based economies there are some huge business groups whose businesses span widely into many unrelated areas. For instance, in Thailand, once well-connected business-men became successful in a core business, they would use "their privi-leged access to capital and patronage to extend sideways into related fields. Each had come to dominate a conglomerate of multiple companies" (Phongpaichit & Baker, 2000). By the late 20th century, some 20 families dominated the urban economy of Thailand. Since they had already estab-lished close relationships with the official regulators, they entered many sectors that needed special blessings by the government, and they earned high profits in these restricted businesses (Phongpaichit & Baker, 2000). In Indonesia, big conglomerates owned by some prominent families such as the Suharto family were so dominant that the Indonesian people made the expression "it's all in the family" a political joke. The largest conglomerate in Indonesia is the Salim Group, which, through some 600 subsidiaries, extends its businesses into "food manufacturing, agribusiness, distribution and retail, telecommunications, automobile, building materials, real estate, hotels and resorts, banking and financial services, infrastructure, chemical manufacturing, and international trade sectors" (Bloomberg, 2015; Habir, 1999). In Japan, South Korea, and Hong Kong, the economies are still dominated by big conglomerates (family-owned business groups in Hong Kong, the *keiretsu* in Japan, and the *chaebol* in Korea) that are the legacies of the old or passing relation-based system.

9.2.6 Other Features of Relation-Based Markets

Compared to markets in the rule-based environment, relation-based mar-kets have the following characteristics: the distribution channel tends to be more exclusive, namely, the market is more difficult for outsiders to enter; marketing information tends to be privately held by the insiders, and dis-putes tend to be resolved privately (Li, 2009; Li, Karande, & Zhou, 2005).

9.3 TRADE FLOWS BETWEEN RULE-BASED AND RELATION-BASED COUNTRIES

If the market entry barrier is higher in relation-based countries, does it affect the trade flowing in and out of them? In this section, we exam-ine how the governance environment affects international trade flows, namely the import (buying) and export (selling) of goods across countries. Essentially, we want to answer the following question:

9.3.1 Which Are Easier to Trade With, Rule-Based or Relation-Based Countries?

Based on our definition, rule-based countries (ie, representative democracies) are the ones in which public rules (laws and regulations) are fairly made with input from different constituencies and are transparent and universally enforced effectively and efficiently by an impartial state. Thus in the most ideal situation, in rule-based countries, trade rules and regulations tend to be open and equally applied to everyone. Anyone who is interested in conducting international trade can access and study the rules and trade, even if this person is from a relation-based society. Of course, this is the ideal situation; in reality, there are still hidden trade barriers even in rule-based countries. But, it is fair to say that in comparison with relation-based countries, the rules of entering rule-based markets are more transparent and thus easier to follow. In relation-based markets, the formal rules are more likely to be just ink on paper, and one must not only know the hidden barriers and the informal rule of the game but also have strong connections with the insiders who control the market entry. Here the concept of "a glass door" is quite appropriate to describe the high entry barrier to relation-based market. The "magic word" to open the glass door would be one's private connections with the authorities that control the market gate.

Therefore, *everything being equal, it is easier for a relation-based firm to enter a rule-based market to trade than a rule-based firm to enter a relation-based market.* The reasons are as follows. First, it is difficult for outsiders to have access to the private information about the hidden norms of trade. For them, even getting all the required permits and licenses can be an insurmountable task. Second, due to the weak rule of law in relation-based societies, actually conducting trade is difficult and risky. Compared with domestic trade, international trade requires stronger property rights protection and contract enforcement because of the greater geographic and time separation of delivery and payment. In many relation-based countries, these protections are very weak or even nonexistent. For example, we interviewed a Hong Kong businessman who sold luxury watches to China. He told us that due to the lack of protection for the credit market, he could not ship goods to his distributors in China on credit; he must demand cash payment for his shipment, since the temptation of disappearing with the watches was too high and the legal enforcement was difficult. On the other hand, obviously, it was not very safe to carry a large bag of cash while traveling long distances in China. So he capped his goods delivery at a cash value of about 500,000 Yuan (US$60,000). (It still sounds very dangerous to carry that much money in cash.) This practice limited the scale of his business.

9.3.2 Trade Flows Between Rule-Based and Relation-Based Countries

There are four types of possible trade relations between rule-based and relation-based countries, as depicted in Fig. 9.2: (1) a rule-based country sells (exports) to another rule-based country; (2) a rule-based country exports to a relation-based country; (3) a rule-based country sells to a relation-based country; and (4) a relation-based country exports to another relation-based country.

Let us review each type in turn. The first type, trade between two rule-based countries, is easy in terms of getting through the regulation and market entry. As we discussed earlier, there are some commonalities among all rule-based societies in terms of their political and economic institutions, such as the existence of checks and balances. Furthermore, in order for most people and firms to follow the formal rules and regulations, they must be relatively easy to follow, be transparent, and be fair. For example, in the United States, import and export do not require any special license or permit (except the restricted items to certain nondemocratic countries that can be used for military purposes). In sum, for an exporter who is familiar with his home country's import and export regulations, learning to navigate in another rule-based market should be relatively easy compared to the task of entering a relation-based market.

In the second case, it is much more difficult for an exporter in a rule-based country to sell to a relation-based country. In a relation-based environment, the formal trade rules tend to be very restrictive. For example, in China the right to import and export is strictly controlled by the state. According to export and import laws, it is totally up to the discretion of

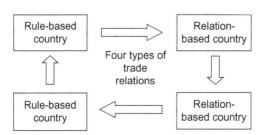

Figure 9.2 Trade patterns between rule-based and relation-based countries.

the state to restrict and require a license on any export or import item. The process of applying for an import or export license is complicated, and qualifications are not automatic. A visit to the official Website of China's trade regulation agency would reveal a substantial number of products that require a license to import. The official Website maintains a long list of firms that were punished for violating import or export regulations. The punishment varies from suspending the license for 6 months to revoking the license indefinitely (Ministry of Foreign Trade and Economic Cooperation, 2009). Similar situations exist in Vietnam, where the state tightly controls international trade, and it is very difficult for ordinary private firms to get a license (Hiebert, 1996). In sum, if the foreign seller does not have good relationship with the officials in charge or the powerful players in the industry, it would be very difficult to get in.

In the third case, however, when a firm in a relation-based country exports to a rule-based country, it is more or less on the equal footing with any other firm, including the domestic firms, as far as the regulation and market access are concerned. There is also no additional difficulty imposed specifically on a relation-based firm from outside.

In the last case, in which a firm from a relation-based country sells to another relation-based country, getting through the regulation and gaining market access may not necessarily be easy simply because both are relation-based. While rule-based countries share many similarities in their political and economic institutions, each relation-based country is unique in terms of who has the power to control the private network and how the key players set up the often hidden norms to regulate the insiders. A firm that is very well connected in one relation-based environment may not be able to transfer its connections to a new relation-based country. Thus, the trade between two relation-based countries may not necessarily be easy; it is certainly not as easy as trade between two rule-based countries.

The above argument has been confirmed by data. We conducted a statistical analysis to verify the trade pattern in Fig. 9.2 (Li & Samsell, 2009). We used 44 countries for which we had the GEI score as the study sample, and for each country we obtained a list of countries it exported to (up to 43 countries) and the volume of the export in US dollars. So in total we have over 1800 pairs of trading flows among the 44 countries, representing about 90% of world trade. We found the following patterns: first, rule-based countries trade more than relation-based countries. In other words, countries in which laws and regulations are more transparent and fair tend to conduct more international trade. Second, in general, countries with large differences in their governance environments (such as between a highly rule-based country and a highly relation-based country) have low trade flows between them. Third, trade flows between two relation-based countries are also low. Fourth, compared to the trade volume of rule-based countries selling to relation-based countries, the volume of relation-based countries selling to rule-based countries is relatively larger. In sum, all countries like to trade with rule-based countries, while the volume of trade that involves a nonrule-based country tends to be lower.

9.3.3 Policy and Strategic Implications

The policy implication for relation-based countries is that if the government wants to promote trade, it should realize that political and economic reforms that will make the governance environment more rule based will actually help trade, including both imports and exports.

Exporting firms, especially the ones from rule-based countries, should study not only the prospective partner in a target country but also the governance environment of that country. Understanding the governance environment will help the exporter access the difficulty and risk of entering the country.

9.4 COUNTERFEIT GOODS IN EAST ASIA

The production and selling of counterfeit goods in East Asia is a major issue not only in East Asia but in the world. Alibaba, the largest e-commerce firm in Asia which is listed in the United States, has been and still is marred by counterfeiting and its inability to clean it up (CNN, 2014). One type of counterfeiting is called "**yuandan**" (原单) product. Yuandan means original order. An example of a yuandan product is a well-known brand owner places an order to a factory in East Asia to produce its product. The factory secretly produces more than the order and puts the extra in the market through channels that are known for allowing the sale of counterfeits, such as taobao.com owned by Alibaba. So yuandan products are identical to the genuine products except they are sold illegally without the knowledge of the name brand owner. In other words, they are genuine fakes (yahoo.com, 2016).

According to a survey by the US Homeland Security, about 90% of counterfeit imports it seized are from East Asia, especially from China (Homeland Security, 2015).

As can be seen from Table 9.1, among the top 10 countries exporting counterfeits seized by the US government, seven are from Asia, and six are

Table 9.1 Top 10 countries exporting counterfeits seized by United States, 2014

	Value based on manufacturer suggested retail price (MSRP) (US$)	%	Population	MSRP (US$) per capita
China	772,629,008	63.0%	1,364,270,000	0.57
Hong Kong	310,437,365	25.3%	7,241,700	42.87
Canada	12,460,242	1.0%	35,540,419	0.35
India	5,540,652	0.5%	1,295,291,543	0.00
UAE	3,791,268	0.3%	9,086,139	0.42
Taiwan	3,081,838	0.3%	23,434,000	0.13
Singapore	2,538,079	0.2%	5,469,700	0.46
Korea	2,514,596	0.2%	50,423,955	0.05
Vietnam	2,422,050	0.2%	90,730,000	0.03
Kenya	2,292,982	0.2%	44,863,583	0.05
All others	108,639,461	8.9%	4,334,648,961	0.03
Total	1,226,347,540	100.0%	7,261,000,000	0.17

Source: Countryeconomy.com. (2016). *Taiwan population, 2014.* http://countryeconomy.com/ (Countryeconomy.com, 2016); Homeland Security. (2015). *Intellectual property rights seizure statistics, Fiscal Year 2014.* https://www.cbp.gov/sites/default/files/documents/2014%20IPR%20Stats.pdf; World Bank. (2015). World development indicators. Washington, DC: World Bank. (World Bank, 2015).

from East Asia. China exported the most counterfeits seized both in total value and on per capita basis except for Hong Kong, which exports counterfeits produced in China. Hong Kong and Singapore have high counterfeit value seized per capita because they are major trading ports and export large volume of goods originating from other countries such as China. Compared to its large population and economy, the value of counterfeits seized from India is small.

QUESTIONS

1. What are the possible explanations for East Asia's higher quality customer service?
2. Why do relation-based markets have high exit barrier?
3. What are the implications to the trade volume of the relation-based countries if they become more rule-based?
4. Why is counterfeiting rampant in China?

ENDNOTE

1. Telephone interview conducted by author with A. Watkin in Shanghai from Norfolk, VA (2009).

REFERENCES

Arlen, C. (2008, October 24). The 5 service dimensions all customers care about. *Service Performance.* http://www.serviceperformance.com/the-5-service-dimensions-all-customers-care-about/.

Bloomberg. (2015). Company overview of Salim group. *Bloomberg.* http://www.bloomberg.com/research/stocks/private/snapshot.asp?privcapId=9682271.

Borsuk, R. (1998). The Suharto regime blew many chances to amass wealth. *Wall Street Journal.*

Brown, P.J. (2008). US twist to Thaksin court case. *Asian Times.* http://www.atimes.com/atimes/Southeast_Asia/JH02Ae01.html.

CNN, (2014). Alibaba has a major counterfeit problem, www.money.cnn.com, Sep. 11, 2014.

Countryeconomy.com. (2016). *Taiwan population, 2014.* http://countryeconomy.com/.

Fortune. (2015). Fortune global 500. *Fortune.* http://fortune.com/global500/.

Habir, A. D. (1999). Conglomerates: All in the family?. In D. K. Emmerson (Ed.), *Indonesia beyond Suharto: Polity economy society transition* (pp. 168–204). Armonk, NY: M. E. Sharpe.

Hewison, K., & Thongyou, M. (2000). Developing provincial capitalism: A profile of the economic and political roles of a new generation in Khon Kaen, Thailand. In R. McVey (Ed.), *Money and power in provincial Thailand* (pp. 195–220). Honolulu, HI: Hawaii University Press.

Hiebert, M. (1996). *Chasing the tigers: A portrait of the new Vietnam.* New York, NY: Kodansha International.

Homeland Security. (2015). *Intellectual property rights seizure statistics, Fiscal Year 2014.* https://www.cbp.gov/sites/default/files/documents/2014%20IPR%20Stats.pdf.

Kim, A. M. (2008). *Learning to be capitalists.* Oxford: Oxford University Press.

Li, S. (2009). *Managing international business in relation-based versus rule-based countries.* New York, NY: Business Expert Press.

Li, S. (2011a). *Customer service in a convenience store in Taiwan.* https://www.youtube.com/watch?v=1axy9s93eD4.

Li, S. (2011b). *Train conductor in Japan 1 and 2.* https://www.youtube.com/watch?v=o MQ4KgkX_kc.

Li, S., Karande, K., & Zhou, D. (2005). The effect of governance environment on market exchange: The case of the diamond industry in the U.S. and China: Old Dominion University.

Li, S., & Samsell, D. (2009). Why some countries trade more than others: The effect of the governance environment on trade flows. *Corporate Governance: An International Review,* *17*(1), 47–61.

Ministry of Foreign Trade and Economic Cooperation. (2009). *Official Website of Ministry of Foreign Trade and Economic Cooperation.* http://www.cofortune.com.cn/moftec_cn/index.html.

Nanfangwang. (2006). *Five monopolistic industries account for 80% of new profits, encroaching other industries.* news.xinhuanet.com.

Phongpaichit, P., & Baker, C. (2000). Chao Sua, Chao Pho, Chao Thi: Lords of Thailand's Transition. In R. McVey (Ed.), *Money and power in provincial Thailand* (pp. 30–52). Honolulu, HI: University of Hawaii Press.

Risk Management, (2009, April). International profile: Indonesia. *Risk Management, 56,* 32–33.

World Bank, (2015). *World development indicators.* Washington, DC: World Bank.

Wu, X. (2008). *China: The era of grabbing wealth: Business history, 1993–2008.* Taipei: Yuanliu.

Xinhuashe (New China News Agency). (2005). *The Chinese state allows private capital entering controlled industries.* www.politeian.org.

Xinhuashe (New China News Agency). (2006). *Our government will maintain absolute control over seven major industries.* www.cenn.cn.

yahoo.com. (2016). What is yuandan? Is it the same as yuanchang? 請問原單的意思?跟原廠一樣嗎?, yahoo.com. https://tw.answers.yahoo.com/question/index?qid=20111113000010KK01266.

Zhang, M. (2011, July 12). The high monopolistic profits of state-owned enterprises hinder the economic transition. *Thesis by Well-Versed Economists.* http://202.119.108.161:93/modules/showContent.aspx?title=&Word=&DocGUID=b19ad0f54f344eba8e8f96c943a53c41.

CHAPTER 10

Human Resource Management in East Asia: Should You Speak Out During Company Meetings?*

10.1 MAFIA BOSS OR CEO?

In the heyday of the economic opening up in China in the 1980s and 1990s, the name Yu Zuomin was a household word. Mr. Yu was the head of the famous village enterprise called Daqiuzhuang, a village of some 4000 people that had operated a booming conglomerate of steel, piping, printing, electronics, and related upstream and downstream businesses since the start of the economic reform in 1978. By 1990, Daqiuzhuang had achieved a per capita income of $3400, 10 times greater than China's average. Its success had earned it titles such as "the richest village in China" and "China's first village."

A main factor of the success of Yu and his Daqiuzhuang was that Yu was an expert in cultivating cordial private relationships with key government officials, who in turn gave him inside information on government policies and granted many tax favors to Daqiuzhuang, giving it a huge advantage in the marketplace. Without Yu's ability to obtain these tips and concessions from the government, Daqiuzhuang would not have been as successful. So when Yu was asked about the ownership of the more than 1 billion yuan assets (about US$130 million in the 1990s) of the village, which on paper was owned collectively by the whole village, Yu answered, "You can say that it is mine" (Hudong, 2008).

Internally, Yu's management style was equally impressive. He commanded absolute authority. "We must follow him with no questions asked," villagers said when they were interviewed. His famous slogan in hiring senior managers was, "You may have your own ideas, as long as they are the same as mine. If not, you know who has to go." He appointed his family members and relatives as his lieutenants. But he also used people

---

* Adopted from Li, S. (2009a). *Managing international business in relation-based versus rule-based countries.* New York, NY: Business Expert Press.

who were not related to him. In fact the manager who played the second most important role in Daquizhuang's development was Mr. Liu, a nonfamily member recruited by Yu against some opposition in the village. The way Yu controlled his managers and employees was through requiring everyone to be unconditionally loyal to him and him only.

The downfall of Daqiuzhuang appeared accidental and yet fateful: It all started with the death of a general manager of one of the subsidiaries. Like Yu, the deceased general manager used to run his subsidiary as a dukedom, and he was the only one who controlled all the vital information. So his sudden death virtually paralyzed the subsidiary. No one knew where the real accounting books were or who had loaned to or borrowed from the subsidiary. All of this information went to the grave with the deceased manager.

Yu was upset and began to persecute the associates of the deceased manager. He illegally arrested them and tortured them. One of them was beaten to death by Yu's associates. When the government heard this, it sent police to the village to investigate. Yu asked the suspected associates to go into hiding, ordered all the villagers to barricade the village and waged a war against the police. Yu was subsequently arrested by the government in 1993 and given a 20-year sentence. He died in 1999. Ten years later, many villages in Daqiuzhuang still view him as a great leader who brought them out of poverty, not a criminal (Hudong, 2008).

Is Yu a mafia boss or a business CEO?

10.2 THE RELATION-BASED ORGANIZATION STRUCTURE AND MANAGEMENT STYLE

10.2.1 Organizational Structure

In a multicountry study of management style, the author Shimoni observed that the Swedish manager he studied seems to delegate more, whereas Thai managers centralize their power (Shimoni, 2008). The author did not use the rule- versus relation-based framework to explain the results, but based on the theory of rule-based and relation-based governance, we now know that Sweden is a rule-based society and Thailand is relation-based (Li, 2009a). In our leadership and management survey, we found that American managers delegate more than their counterparts in China (Li, 2009b), and we also know that the former is more rule-based than the latter.

Relation-based firms tend to have the following characteristics in organizational structure: they tend to be highly centralized; the head of the firm tends to exert absolute power; and the boss is less likely to delegate authority to his or her managers. The reason is that the head manages his or her firm by using his private connections to deal with external relationships, such as with customers and suppliers in the market or the government. These relationships are secretive (to prevent from his competitors intercepting them) and personal, and the information he relies on to make decisions tends to be private and unquantifiable (such as who is playing golf with whom). Thus, it is difficult to delegate those tasks to subordinates (Li, Park, & Li, 2004).

10.2.2 Private Relations are Hard to Transfer

This pattern was obvious in our field research in China. In a rule-based environment, CEOs use a secretary to answer telephone calls and make appointments. In China, many CEOs we interviewed did not use such a systematic way to handle communications and appointments. Some of them answered phone calls and made appointments themselves. Another interesting observation in China was that some executives would have several telephone sets on their desk, and the executive would be busy answering them. A similar pattern was seen among Vietnamese executives (Hiebert, 1996). Each of those phones was dedicated to a special relationship.

At first we were puzzled by this: Labor cost is much lower in China; so if a CEO in the United States can afford to hire one secretary, then a Chinese CEO of equal status should be able to hire five. Why do they handle these calls themselves? The answer is that a private relationship is not transferable. The boss cannot use subordinates to handle his important relationships. First, doing so may offend the other party. (Why doesn't your boss call me personally?). Second, there may be sensitive information between them, and the relationship is too subtle for the subordinate to handle. For example, sometimes we did reach a subordinate of the big boss, but the subordinate would not know how to reply to our calls since he or she did not know what the relationship between us and the boss was.

This fact brings up another point about handling relationships in a relation-based environment. During my research in China, I often contacted a CEO friend of mine and asked him to have lunch so that I could exchange management ideas with him. Usually he would say yes to the lunch but would not commit to a firm date. If I pushed for a date, he would say, "We will see" without a definite date. And without any warning, he would call me at 11:00 am and say, "Shaomin, let's have lunch at 12. I will send a car to pick you up."

This is typical relation-based relationship management. My CEO friend needs to leave his calendar open for more important relationships, such as with government officials, who dictate when to meet the CEO. Having lunch with me, a professor friend, is fun, but should not jeopardize his opportunity to meet his official friends because they are vital to his business. In the early 1990s, when the chairman of J. P. Morgan went to meet the party chief of the City of Tianjin in China with a confirmed appointment made in advance, the party chief was not there to receive him! The party chief's aide just told the chairman matter-of-factly, "By the way, the party chief is not available today."[1] One can only guess that the party chief must have had a more important relationship to take care of. Like the way my CEO friend treated me, appointments tend to be more fluid in a relation-based society.

10.2.3 Titles Don't Tell All

Deng Xiaoping, the late paramount leader of China, had no official title in the Chinese government or in the Communist Party, but the chairman of the central government, the state premier, and all the politburo members reported to him. When a researcher asked a business leader in Vietnam about his role in one of the companies he was associated with, he replied that he was "an unofficial vice-director" (Kim, 2008). It is interesting that his role is informal and yet so precise.

In a relation-based firm, the formal title may not accurately reflect the importance or power of an employee. For example, as shown in Fig. 10.1, in a relation-based firm, the CEO's secretary may have greater influence on the CEO than his lieutenants, because he or she may know

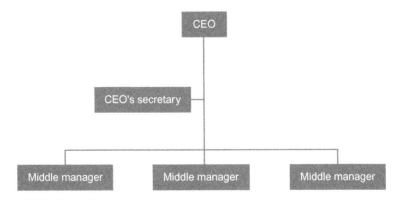

Figure 10.1 A typical organization chart.

more private information about the CEO, and the CEO may trust him or her more.[2] In general, the closer one is to the center of the power, the greater the access to that power and the greater one's influence and position in the organization. During our study of management style in China, we found that in a number of firms, the CEO's secretary was very powerful (Li, 2009b).

Relation-based bosses tend to bypass the middle managers to reach the rank and file employees directly. In our study of a telecom company in China, we found that the CEO maintained such great power distance that she required all employees to address her as "madam." The way she managed the company was to use the rank and file employees as informants to report on their immediate supervisors, and she would in turn use these reports to reward or punish her midlevel managers. Since the middle management was kept in the dark about her intention and policy, they had great fear of her and were constantly guessing and betting on her next move.

10.2.4 Formal Rules in Relation-Based Organizations

It would be a mistake to think that relation-based firms do not have many formal rules. Our research indicates that more often than not, relation-based firms have more formal rules and regulations. However, these rules do not apply to the boss. Our management and leadership survey, conducted in both the United States and China, showed that, compared to the US respondents, a significantly higher percentage of Chinese respondents agreed that "the employees are constantly being checked on for rule violations," and more Chinese respondents agree that "orders and communications are often made in written form" (Li, 2009b). These results are also confirmed by an in-depth interview we conducted in an American-invested firm operating in Shenzhen, China. The human resource director of the firm told us that the firm introduced a set of new regulations intended to increase the fringe benefit for the employees. And to his surprise, many employees looked at the new policy with suspicion and few used it. The reason behind this suspicion is that due to the legacy of a relation-based environment in which firms use formal rules as a tool to constrain workers and not the upper management, employees tend to view any rules categorically negatively.[3] We will further discuss under what conditions relation-based firms tend to erect more formal rules when we discuss the transition of relation-based firms in the concluding chapter of this book.

10.2.5 Lack of Strategic Planning

Our study also revealed that relation-based firms usually lack formal strategic planning. Formal strategic planning requires systematically making strategic choices based on information that is derived from collecting and analyzing codified or quantified data about markets, the competition, and internal operations using statistical models.

Unfortunately, such information is rare in relation-based markets. Annette Kim, who studied the Vietnamese real estate development market, noted that there is an "absence of updated, publicly accessible land use plans, land registration records, industry reports, and comprehensive market studies, reliable information is difficult to obtain" (Kim, 2008).

As a result, in relation-based firms, most competitive intelligence is privately stored and processed in the head of the boss. Such information tends to be nonquantifiable and kept secret by the boss and is therefore not suitable for systematical analysis to aid formal strategic management (Li, Park, & Li, 2004). As Kim wrote about the Vietnamese real estate market: "I found that [the real estate firms] were quite secretive about the way they found land sites. They refused to explain how they found land" (Kim, 2008).

10.2.6 Human Resource Management Practices

The way symphony orchestras recruit music instrument players can perhaps best illustrate the differences between rule-based and relation-based hiring practice. In the United States, most of the professional orchestras use "blind" auditions in their hiring process, in which the candidates sit behind a screen and play, and he or she cannot make any sound that could potentially reveal his or her identity, such as speaking or coughing. Even the candidate's footsteps must be muffled by a rug. The only information that the examiners can use to judge the player is the playing.

In China, it used to be the case that no symphony orchestra used blind auditions. Now, many still don't use it. When I asked a Chinese musician who used to play in an orchestra in China why they did not use it, he told me that the examiners needed to know with whom the candidate studied, among other reasons (Lin, 2009).

The above example and the discussion in the next section "No Exit, No Voice" show that having the right relationship is far more important than professional qualifications in hiring in a relation-based environment. A relationship is one of the rare goods that the older it is, the better it is. This is why we often hear someone boasting that he has known a certain powerful person, such as the President or a CEO, since childhood. Hiring based on relationships is a backward looking philosophy. The employer pays more attention to the past of the prospective employee, making sure he or she has a good reputation in his or her circle. This kind of hiring philosophy is not conducive to taking initiative and making innovation in work, which involves the risk of failure and therefore of damaging one's established relationships or reputation. For example, studies on the Thai culture noted that this philosophy does not encourage Thais to take initiative in organizations (Petison & Johri, 2008).

On the contrary, in a rule-based environment, which, compared to the relation-based hiring philosophy, is more forward looking, firms tend to seek new employees who show good potential for future achievement.

10.2.7 No Exit, No Voice

Having been an executive in both the United States and China gave me the opportunity to observe the supervisor–subordinate relationship first-hand in the two different environments. And being a researcher enables me to make sense out of the patterns I observed. Sitting in a joint business meeting between an American firm and a Chinese firm is quite interesting. On the American side, everyone would compete to speak up, so that they wouldn't be mistaken as timid or shy. And you cannot easily spot who the boss is. On the Chinese side, you can immediately identify who the boss is—he is the one who speaks, while his subordinates sit there in silence. The subordinates only talk when the boss asks them to fill in some details such as a sales figures. (One of my interviewees told me that firms in China are reluctant to hire graduates from Peking University, the most elite school in China, because as rookie members in a firm, instead of sitting quietly in meetings, these graduates would give a summary speech after the boss talked!)

Similar patterns exist in other relation-based societies. Researchers of expatriate manager–local employee relationships found that "Thais have interesting ideas, but may not voice them if the expatriates have presented different ideas" (Petison & Johri, 2008).

Why don't, or shouldn't, subordinates in relation-based firms speak up in meetings, while their counterparts in rule-based firms compete to offer their opinions in front of their superior?

One of the reasons, I would argue, is the structure of the job market. As we discussed in the preceding section, in a rule-based job market, the hiring process is more transparent, impersonal, and merit based.

Job applicants are hired based on their education credentials and abilities. Once hired, the subordinate should show his or her worth by offering his or her knowledge and opinions, which hopefully are new to the boss, and they may even be different from the boss's view. If what they offer is not appreciated by the boss, they should go back to the job market and look for another place where their opinions are more valued.

In a relation-based job market, connections are vitally important. As the cliché goes, "It is not what you know, but *who* you know." A PhD student in our school, who is from China, told me a story that a classmate of hers, who was a below-average student, got a lucrative financial analyst job that had attracted many highly competent applicants. Her classmate just mentioned that her uncle was the CEO of another big bank, and she was hired right on the spot. In such a job market, firms tend to connect to each other and there is an informal guild that controls the market. It is often the case that one needs his or her boss's blessing to find another job.[4] Thus, if someone speaks up in a meeting in a way that offends his or her boss, it would be difficult for this person to find another job in the market. Without the exit option, employees must be extremely careful when voicing their opinions (Fig. 10.2).

Figure 10.2 Relation-based hiring policy.

10.3 WHEN RULES MEET RELATIONS IN THE WORKPLACE: THE FRICTIONS BETWEEN THE TWO SYSTEMS

10.3.1 Talent Flows Between Rule-Based and Relation-Based Societies

Logically, rule-based and relation-based environments attract different types of talents. Here, a personal observation may help illustrate this point. As a Chinese student studying in the United States, I got to know many people with a similar background: coming from a relation-based society to study in a rule-based society. So when they finished their study, they all faced a choice: stay in the United States, or go back to China?

My general observation is that people who have good connections in China or are good at networking and cultivating private relations are more likely to go back to China, and the ones who focus on their specialized knowledge tend to stay in the United States. When I was working at AT&T, I recruited a Chinese man who had just received his PhD in statistics from a prestigious university in the Northeastern region of the United States. He is highly intelligent and specializes in mathematics and statistics, and he does not like the Chinese way of getting ahead using private connections. He has excelled at AT&T. Recently, at a gathering, he told me that he was so glad that he did not go back to China because building personal connections was just not his "cup of tea." Of course, the reader should be cautioned that this is just my observation, not a scientific study.

10.3.2 The Expatriate Failure Issue

In international business operations, one of the major challenges for multinational corporations is how the managers sent from the headquarters manage their foreign subsidiaries effectively and efficiently. Many studies show that these expatriate managers—managers working in a foreign country—have a high failure rate (Black & Gregersen, 1999). Sending expatriates to manage foreign subsidiaries is expensive. The total package of sending a manager abroad for a multinational corporation is usually three times the manager's cost back home. Thus, when an expatriate manager fails to complete his or her assignment, it will cost more for the company since there are the sunk costs of sending the failed manager to the foreign post, such as training, learning, and relocation (Black & Morrison, 1998).

Existing research on expatriate failure has identified the lack of understanding of or the inability to adopt the local culture as the major reason of failure. As a remedy, this stream of research has suggested using cross-cultural training with the prospective expatriate managers. While these cross-culture training efforts may help, they tend to cover mostly cultural norms, such as the "do's and don'ts" in a specific culture, such as presenting your business card with two hands instead of one.

In the early 1990s, when I hosted a Chinese business delegation at AT&T, the head of the delegation, who was the president of a state-owned company in China, would wave his middle finger to make a point in meetings. Naturally, this gesture startled the American attendees in the meeting, but we all realized that his gesture was innocent and due to years of isolation in China, he was not aware of the meaning of waving the middle finger in America. At the end of his visit, AT&T and his firm signed an agreement to form a joint venture. The point I want to make here is that such cultural misunderstandings do not break business deals, as is taught in some cross-culture seminars. There are usually deeper, more fundamental reasons in making or breaking a deal.

One such deeper, more fundamental reason that may significantly affect international business deals and cross-border management is the difference in the governance environment, such as the frictions between rule-based and relation-based systems (Maurer & Li, 2006).

In one of our survey studies of US–Chinese joint venture operations in Shenzhen, China, we asked the Chinese employees about their relationship with the American manager. One of the interviewees, who reported to the manager directly, told us that he thought the manager did not care about him. Why, we asked. He said, "Well, our interaction is only about work; he never asked me personal questions, such as my family background and so on." For him, if the manager does not get personal, it means the manager does not regard him as a valuable employee. We then subtly asked the manager about what he thought of this employee. As it turned out, the manager thought highly of this employee. We then probed him if he chatted with employees about their family and if he made an effort to know their background. "No! As you know very well, I am not supposed to nose around their private lives!" The American manager raised his voice as if we had asked an inappropriate question.[5]

This is a typical misunderstanding between a rule-based managers and relation-based employees. In a rule-based environment, the working relation between the manager and the employee is primarily defined based on the job description, which spells out the responsibility and authorities of each post. The manager assumes the employee is capable (otherwise he would not have been hired in the first place) and expects him to per-form well, unless proven otherwise. The managers should only manage the employee based on job-related information and performance and should not use age, marital status, or any other personal information or traits to reward or punish the employee.

10.3.3 Differences in Working Relationships Between the Two Environments

In a relation-based environment, the manager and the employee tend to spend more time to establish a good relation first. Each party will observe and test the other repeatedly to make sure that the other party is reliable and trustworthy. The manager will not fully trust a new employee unless he has been tested. Such a rationale is the opposite of the norms in rule-based working relationships. In general, the following are some differences in how workers in rule-based and relation-based environment view work-ing relationships (Maurer & Li, 2006):

1. *Scope of Jobs.* Workers in rule-based and relation-based environment have different views on the scope of a job, namely, what duties, respon-sibilities, prerequisites, and benefits are included in a job. In rule-based environment, jobs tend to be defined narrowly in the job description, which must be in accordance with laws and regulations. In a relation-based environment, since the boss has nearly absolute power and thus has a stronger sense of "owning" the employee, the boss may define what the employee should do at his personal preference, and he may even ask the employee to carry out personal errands. The line between work and personal life is blurred, and what is included in the job is more negotiable.

2. *Terms of Working Relationships.* The above leads to a second differ-ence in the working relationship between the two environments: Workers and managers in rule-based and relation-based environment differ in the *precision* of the terms of working relationships. For rule-based managers, the terms of the working relationships should follow the job description and the letter of law and regulations. But for the relation-based workers, since they weigh gaining personal favor from the manager more heavily and emphasize the establishment of a close relationship with the manager, their perception about the terms of the working relationship is beyond work-related issues and may include other activities that may enhance their personal relationship with the boss. Thus they prefer terms of the relationship to be fuzzy.

3. *Expectations of Working Relationships.* Correspondingly, the expectation of the working relationship is different too. Using the example of the US–Chinese joint venture in Shenzhen, while the American manager views the relationship narrowly and as task-oriented and purposely stays out of the employee's personal life, the Chinese employee expects that in order to build a close relationship with the manager, the manager and he should not only develop a good working relationship, but more importantly, they should also develop a good personal friendship that will last beyond the current work assignment. Our interview of managers who worked in relation-based countries, such as Indonesia, Vietnam, and Thailand, told us that they maintained friendship and correspondence with some of their coworkers and employees long after they left the job.

Because of their expectations, relation-based employees tend to take work-related issues personally. As a study on management in Thailand showed, criticism from the expatriate manager may be interpreted by the local employee as a personal attack (Petison & Johri, 2008).

4. *Investments in Working Relationships.* For workers and managers in a relation-based environment, since building a good relationship with coworkers, superiors, and subordinates is very important, they are prepared and willing to invest time and resources to do so. For example, gift giving or gift exchanges are necessary parts of building relationships and tend to involve expensive gifts to show the magnitude of the effort and the commitment the gift giving signals. Invitations to each other's homes may also be used as a necessary and important occasion to build relationships.

On the other hand, to an expatriate manager from a rule-based country who holds a narrow view of the working relationships with the local employees based on job description and regulations, employees getting together at someone's home is just for fun, rather than an investment in building good working relations. Furthermore, many rule-based countries have strict laws regulating gift giving in business dealings. Thus for the expatriate manager, gift giving is at best viewed as ceremonial, which may be unnecessary. Expensive gifts are certainly frowned upon because of the implication of bribery.

5. *Differences in Process Priorities.* In a rule-based environment, there is a high level of generalized trust, and thus people take what they are told by strangers (new employees) more at the face value, such as a person's resume, education background, and work experience. Managers expect the workers to "hit the ground running," and the general attitude toward workers can be summed as "trustworthy unless proven otherwise." Work first, and if work goes well, coworkers, superiors and

subordinates may develop cordial working relationships. In a relation-based society, generalized trust is low. People tend to discount what they hear from someone they have just met, which implies that there may be a lower level of mutual trust between a manager and a new employee than in a rule-based environment. The manager and the employee must test each other in order to establish a level of mutual trust so that they can work together efficiently. Relationships comes first and work follows. The predominant philosophy about interpersonal trust is that anyone is presumed "untrustworthy unless proven otherwise."

Therefore, workers and managers in a relation-based environment are prepared and willing to spend more time to get to know their managers, subordinates, and coworkers, whereas managers from a rule-based country may think it is unnecessary and a waste of time. Table 10.1 summarizes the contrast in the expectations of working relationship formation between rule-based and relation-based workers and managers.

Table 10.1 Expectations of working relationship formation between rule-based and relation-based workers and managers

Dimensions of expectations	Relation-based workers and managers	Rule-based workers and managers
Terms	Vague	Clear
Scope	Wide and deep (it may include all sorts of activities and relationship between an employer and a worker)	Narrow and specific, task-oriented
Duration of the relationship	Long	Short
Views on work-related issues (criticism, discussion)	Take it personal	View it as factual, impersonal
Time needed to develop the working relationship	Long	Short
Costs of developing the relationship	High	Low
Learning curve	Flat, slow learning process, since relations are secretive and particularistic	Steep, fast learning process, since rules are by their nature transparent, public, and general

Source: Adapted from Maurer, S., & Li, S. (2006). Understanding expatriate manager performance: Effects of governance environments on work relationships in relation-based economies. *Human Resource Management Review, 16,* 29–46.

10.3.4 How to Improve Expatriate Performance

Based on the above analyses, we may draw the conclusion that the misunderstandings and mismatches between managers and subordinates in working relationships may be a major reason behind the high failure rate of rule-based expatriate managers working in relation-based environments. In this section we discuss different scenarios of the working relationships to help expatriate managers improve their management efficiency and effectiveness.

There are four combinations of working relationships between expatriate managers and local employees in terms of their expectations and behaviors, as shown in Fig. 10.3.

1. *Both the expatriate manager and local employees are relation-based.* In this case, the expatriate manager completely adopts the local environment and manages the subsidiary the relation-based way. There is minimal confusion and thus the working relationship is harmonious. Both the manager and the local employees take their time to get to know each other and build up their relationships, which implies that the time and resources used in such an effort is relatively high. As we discussed earlier, when the scale and scope of a business is small, the relation-based way can be efficient. However, as the business grows larger, relying on personal relationship will become costly and inefficient. Thus, if the subsidiary has a small number of employees, using the relation-based way to manage can be efficient. Actually it can be more efficient than

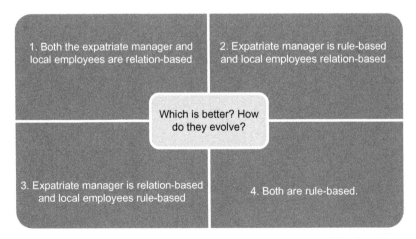

Figure 10.3 Working relationships between expatriate manager and local employees.

the rule-based way, since the manager can manage each employee individually based on the employee's characteristics to fully realize each employee's potential. On the other hand, if the subsidiary has many employees, the relation-based way can be time-consuming and even impossible. Furthermore, if the expatriate manager does not introduce any rule-based management into the organization and maintains the status quo, he or she will hinder the growth and expansion of the subsidiary.

2. *The expatriate manager is rule-based and the local employees are relation-based.* This is the most common scenario for a multinational corporation (MNC) headquartered in a rule-based country and investing in a relation-based country. In general, it is desirable for the MNC expatriate manager to bring a new, rule-based management style to the host country that is relation-based, because, as we discussed earlier, as the scale and scope of the subsidiary grows, or more generally, as the country's economy develops, relation-based governance will become inefficient and must transform to rule-based governance. The caveat is that the expatriate manager must gage the acceptance of rule-based management by the local employees. If the expatriate manager pushes the new management style beyond the ability of acceptability and loses the support of the local employees, then it will backfire and damage the working relationships. In sum, the expatriate should be fully aware of the gap between the rule-based and relation-based expectations of working relationships and should keep a healthy lead in implementing rules in the subsidiary.

3. *The expatriate manager is relation-based and the local employees are rule-based.* It is not unheard of that an MNC headquartered in a rule-based country sends an expatriate manager to a host country that is more local than the local employees. For example, an American firm operating a subsidiary in Indonesia may emphasize the conformity to the local culture and sends a manager who was born in Indonesia. However, this manager's experience about the Indonesian society may be outdated. His or her mentality may be more relation-based than that of the local employees, who may have been exposed to more rule-based practices. In this scenario, the expatriate manager fails to lead the local employees to adopt more rules in the organization. He or she must change or be replaced.

4. *Both are rule-based.* Generally speaking, this is a rare case, but an efficient one, especially if the operation is large and there are many employees.

From a dynamic perspective, it is hoped that the relation-based organizations and societies will eventually migrate to the rule-based environment as they develop and expand. In this sense, it should be the objective of the expatriate manager, who was trained and is experienced in the rule-based environment, to lead the subsidiary and its employees to evolve into a more rule-based operating environment. In order to accomplish this, the expatriate manager should first evaluate the governance environment in the assigned country, study the organizational structure and culture of the subsidiary, and formulate a management strategy that will gradually implement more rule-based management.

QUESTIONS

1. Why do relation-based employees take office parties more seriously than rule-based employees?
2. Compared to the rule-based working relationship, what are the costs and benefits of relation-based working relationship?
3. What can American firms learn from relation-based human resource management?

ENDNOTES

1. Personal interview conducted by author with a JP Morgan executive in Hong Kong in 1994.
2. This may sound contradictory, but it is actually consistent with what we said earlier about the role of a CEO's secretary in relation-based firms. What we mean here is that relative to the managers who are further away from the CEO, the secretary's influence tends to be greater.
3. Personal Interview conducted by author with an American manager in Shenzhen, China, 1999.
4. While similar situations may also occur in more rule-based countries in select industries, it is far more prevalent and severe in relation-based societies.
5. Personal Interview conducted by author with an American manager in Shenzhen, China, 1999.

REFERENCES

Black, J., & Morrison, J. (1998). HCM Beverage Company. Ivey Case 9A98C003, 17. Richard Ivey School of Business.
Black, J. S., & Gregersen, H. B. (1999, March–April). The right way to manage expatriates. *Harvard business Review*, 77, 52–63.

Hiebert, M. (1996). *Chasing the tigers: A portrait of the new Vietnam*. New York, NY: Kodansha International.

Hudong. (2008). Daqiuzhuang. *Hudong*. http://www.hudong.com/wiki/大邱庄.

Kim, A. M. (2008). *Learning to be capitalists*. Oxford: Oxford University Press.

Li, S. (2009a). *Managing international business in relation-based versus rule-based countries*. New York, NY: Business Expert Press.

Li, S. (2009b). *Survey of IT governance and management in China and U.S.*. Norfolk, VA: Old Dominion University.

Li, S., Park, S. H., & Li, S. (2004). The great leap forward: The transition from relation-based governance to rule-based governance. *Organizational Dynamics, 33*(1), 63–78.

Lin, X. (2009). Interview on ochestra recruiting practice. Norfolk, VA.

Maurer, S., & Li, S. (2006). Understanding expatriate manager performance: Effects of governance environments on work relationships in relation-based economies. *Human Resource Management Review, 16*, 29–46.

Petison, P., & Johri, L. M. (2008). Dynamics of the manufacturer-supplier relationships in emerging markets: A case of Thailand. *Asia Pacific Journal of Marketing and Logistics, 20*(1), 76–96.

Shimoni, B. (2008). Separation, emulation, and competition: Hybridization of styles of management cultures in Thailand, Mexico, and Israel. *Journal of Organizational Change Management, 21*(1), 107–199.

CHAPTER 11

Technology and Innovation: Will East Asia Surpass the United States in Innovation?*

The revolution of information technology (IT) that began with the advent of the World Wide Web in the 1990s and culminated in the early 2000s has fundamentally changed the way we live and work. While many people, especially young people, take the use of IT, such as the Internet, for granted without thinking how much efficiency has been gained by using it, they may not realize that merely two decades ago, people would be glued to a large paper map with tiny fonts for hours to plan a trip and would desperately look for a public pay phone on the road if they were lost.

The key to understanding the IT revolution can be simplified to two basic features. The first is **digitization**. Information goods are content that can be digitized into a series of 1s and 0s. If the contents cannot be digitized, such as the mood of a board meeting, then it cannot be called "information goods" in the sense of IT. The second feature is the **dissemination** of information goods. Once the goods is digitized, it can be replicated and transmitted on an extremely large scale with lightning speed virtually without borders and limitations. The technology that enables the production and communication of information is called IT or ICT (information and communications technology); we will use these terms interchangeably in this book.

While the fact that the IT revolution has helped business to drastically improve its efficiency is widely recognized and hardly controversial, many people may not realize that the use of IT in business management and the benefits from using it differ with some interesting pattern across countries. In this chapter, we will examine how the IT revolution affects business and management practices in relation-based societies as opposed to rule-based societies.

---

*This chapter is built on Li, S. (2009). *Managing international business in relation-based versus rule-based countries.* New York, NY: Business Expert Press.

East Asian Business in the New World.

11.1 THE USE OF ICT AND EFFICIENCY

To understand the cost and benefit of using ICT, we can start with look-ing at how a movie is made and distributed. To make a movie is not easy. First, the producer must identify a story, which is often based on a popular novel, acquire the movie rights of the novel, convert it into a movie script, and then shoot the film, which requires a large amount of capital—tens or hundreds of millions of dollars—to hire the actors, rent studios, and so on. Once the movie has been successfully created, making an additional copy of the newly created movie is easy: if you already have a computer, you just need to buy a blank DVD + R, which costs about 25 cents or less; or you can just download it to your device such as an iPad without any hardwire cost. Based on this example, it is easy to see the cost structure of information goods: **they are costly to produce and costless to reproduce**.

From a business management perspective, if a firm wants to use ICT to fulfill its information and communication needs, it must invest resources (financial, human, and technological) to build an IT infrastructure, which may include creating an IT department, purchasing equipment, staffing, and training all the employees to adopt and use IT. Since these expenditures are upfront and do not vary based on how many people will potentially use IT, they can be viewed as fixed costs. If there are few people in the firm who use the newly created IT system to communicate, then the average cost per user will be very high; alternatively, if there is a large number of people in the organization using the new IT infrastructure to communicate, then the average cost of using the IT system will be very low. Thus, the inherent cost structure of ICT (high fixed costs and decreasing marginal cost) implies that large organizations benefit more from the use of ICT than small organizations. In a small organization, the traditional, face-to-face communication is more efficient (see Fig. 11.1) (Liang, Li, & Wu, 2009).

Another feature of ICT that affects its adoption and use is digitization. As we briefly mentioned, only content that can be digitized can be made into information goods. In other words, in order for firms to use ICT in business operations and management, the contents must be able to be dig-itized. If business operations and management rely on the type of information that cannot be digitized, then ICT is not very useful. For instance, an employee comes to work to find that the mood of the office is tense, and the boss seems to be worried by something, or a business owner

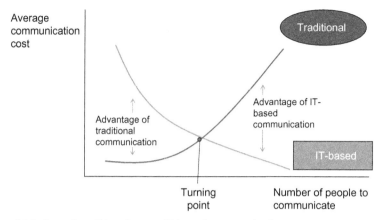

Figure 11.1 Cost of traditional versus IT-based communication.

learns secretly that his rival played golf with a government official, then later sees his government contracts being canceled. This kind of information is difficult to quantify and thus may not be used in decision-making models. This discussion leads to our view that **the use of ICT is more congruent with business operations and management that rely on formal decision-making processes based on quantifiable and publically available information.**

11.2 THE INTERNET AND THE RELATION-BASED SOCIETIES

If we compare the Internet (which is like the air and water for ICT) and the governance environment of the relation-based societies, we will find some very interesting contrasts (see Fig. 11.2) (Li, 2005). First, the Internet is a network without a center. The network consists of millions of servers that directly or indirectly link to each other. It is a decentralized network; no one—neither a country nor a firm or person—controls it. A relation-based society tends to be highly hierarchical, or centralized. Most are controlled by a dictator or a strong ruling circle. Second, the structure of the Internet is based on a universal platform on which different software and programs may communicate with each other through commonly recognizable protocols. A relation-based society, on the contrary, tends to maintain its own proprietary system that is not compatible with others. Third, information is free on the Internet. The very premise of the Internet is that it serves as a huge depository for all sorts of information for people to

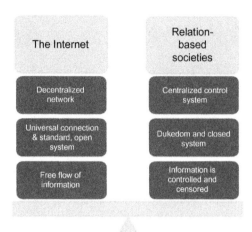

Figure 11.2 Contrasting features of the Internet and relation-based societies.

access, mostly free. In relation-based societies, much information is controlled by the state and labeled as "state secrets."

These three major differences put the Internet and the government of relation-based societies at odds, and it is not surprising that most relation-based societies try to limit the use of the Internet by citizens and firms. In their book entitled *Open Networks, Closed Regimes: The Impact of the Internet on Authoritarian Rule*, the authors discussed eight governments that severely limited the use of the Internet in their countries (Kalathil & Boas, 2003). They include China, Cuba, Singapore, Vietnam, Burma (Myanmar), United Arab Emirates, Saudi Arabia, and Egypt. As can be seen, they all are nonrule-based, with perhaps Singapore being slightly more rule-based than the others, whereas China and Vietnam are among the most relation-based. The fundamental question the book's authors asked is whether the Internet will help to push these closed regimes open. They concluded that the rise of the Internet poses great challenges to these authoritarian (nonrule-based) regimes, but it alone cannot end authoritarian regimes. They noted that "authoritarian regions can guide the development of the Internet so that it serves state-defined goals and priorities." As for the reaction of the citizens and firms to the state control and censorship of the Internet, they observed that "Internet users may back away from politically sensitive material on the web…and entrepreneurs may find it more profitable to cooperate with authorities than to challenge their censorship" (Kalathil & Boas, 2003).

Figure 11.3 Inside and outside the great (fire) wall (photo collage).[1]

11.2.1 Yahoo!'s Dilemma in China

In 2004, the Chinese authorities asked the Hong Kong subsidiary of Yahoo!, a US-based company, to submit the private e-mail records of Shi Tao, a Chinese journalist. Yahoo! obliged. The Chinese authorities used the records to sentence Shi Tao a 10-year imprisonment for "endangering state security." Yahoo!'s compliance with the Chinese authorities was heavily criticized back home in the United States. During a Congressional hearing in which Yahoo! executives testified, Tom Lantos, the late US congressman, blasted Yahoo!'s CEO Jerry Yang and company lawyer Michael Callahan: "Technically and financially, you are giants, but morally, you are pygmies" (Li & Gaur, 2014). In his Congressional testimony, Yahoo! CEO Yang hinted that his company was in no position to defy such an order from the Chinese authorities (Yang, 2007, November 6).

There are many similar cases in which firms or citizens have been accused by a relation-based regime of using the Internet to commit crimes that "endanger state security" (Reporters Without Borders, 2003–2009) (Fig. 11.3).

In addition to the clash between ICT and relation-based government at the societal level due to the three fundamental differences, the use of ICT at the firm level in relation-based societies also encounters some resistance due to the incompatibilities between ICT and the organizational culture and structure.

11.3 THE INTERFACE BETWEEN GOVERNANCE AND ICT IN RELATION-BASED ORGANIZATIONS

11.3.1 Cultural Compatibility

As we discussed earlier in this book, culture can be defined and analyzed from many different angles. We focus on a dimension that is most relevant to the rule-based versus relation-based comparison: the **low context** versus **high context** communications. Low context communication refers to the style of communication that is direct, explicit, and verbal, as opposed to high context communication that relies on the implicitly shared references between the parties and indirect, nonverbal expressions. It is well known that the Chinese culture emphasizes the high context communication style whereas Americans prefer a more direct style of communication (Gao & Ting-Toomey, 1998). In their book on Chinese communication style, Gao and Ting-Toomey cited an interesting example to illustrate the difference between the American and Chinese ways of communication, which I paraphrase here:

Scenario 1. Conversation between a Chinese man (C1) and another Chinese friend (C2):

C1: I am flying to New York for a vacation tomorrow! (I hope he will give me a ride to the airport.)

C2: That sounds fun! (He may need me to drive him to the airport.) Do you have someone to drive you to the airport? I can give you a ride.

Scenario 2. Conversion between an American (A1) and another American friend (A2):

A1: I am flying to New York for a vacation tomorrow! Can you give me a lift to the airport?

A2: That sounds fun! Of course, what time should I pick you up?

Scenario 3. Conversion between a Chinese (C1) and another American friend (A2):

C1: I am flying to New York for a vacation tomorrow! (I hope he will give me a ride to the airport.)

A2: That sounds fun! Have a good time! (If he needs a ride, he will ask me.)

As we discussed earlier, the contents of ICT must be the information that can be digitized. Many types of high context information, such as hints, shared past experiences, or the mood of the message, cannot be digitized and thus cannot be stored and transmitted through ICT, limiting the use of ICT in a relation-based organization. Below we discuss some specific issues that relation-based firms face in adopting ICT in their management and operations.

11.3.2 Informational Compatibility

A management information system, or MIS, is an ICT-based internal control tool that integrates and analyzes business operation and management-related information to aid strategy formulation and decision making in an organization. For MIS to function, it must rely on and can only process digitized and codified information. However, a great deal of information within an organization that is vital for strategy formulation and decision making, such as the mood in the factory, gossip, rumors, or the conflict between two managers, cannot be digitized, as Mintzberg noted (Mintzberg, 1979).

An encounter between a researcher with a local business leader in Vietnam may illustrate informal and yet efficient information gathering:

"I know where you were this morning," the leader of one of the largest land development companies in HCMC [Ho Chi Minh City] told me. I was startled by this revelation, since I had not told him I had been interviewing another company that morning. I was not aware of any connection between the two companies because I had been introduced to them through different people (Kim, 2008).

Later on the researcher learned that leader had an informal network that extended to the other company she interviewed.

The rumor that a firm's major client was seen having a long conversation with a competitor of the firm at an industry gathering cannot be verified or quantified for entry into the MIS database to be analyzed. But several months later the MIS database showed that a contract with the client was not renewed. In a relation-based environment, this type of information is more important than in a rule-based environment for business intelligence and decision making, as most deals are based on private relationships. So, due to the lack of informational compatibility, the use of MIS in relation-based firms is more limited.

11.3.3 Decision Mode Compatibility

The decision mode of relation-based firms does not have a high compatibility with MIS aided by ICT for the following reasons.

First, MIS is most efficient in disseminating a large amounts of information to many users. With the aid of ICT and MIS, an entry-level manager may have access to as much information about the market competition and firm's operation as the firm's CEO (of course, excluding confidential information, such as board meetings or other information on a need-to-know basis). This democratization of information access has greatly empowered the rank and file staff members and managers to make decisions on their own and has consequently made the modern organizations more flat and flexible in terms of decision making. Of course, the above scenario is only possible if the vital information, such as market intelligence and intra-organizational information can be digitized, which tends to be more the case in rule-based rather than relation-based firms.

Second, for relation-based firms, most vital information for decision making is secretive (as private relationships tend to be secretive and exclusive) and controlled by the head of the firm. The reasons for this are that first, private relationships are hard to delegate, so the big boss must tend to them in person; second, due to the lack of exit options for the subordinates in a relation-based firm (see chapter: Why Some East Asia Countries Thrive Despite Corruption), they are unlikely to voice their honest opinions and take responsibilities to make decisions, which in turn makes centralizing decision making a necessity, and the boss usually relies on his gut feeling about the market (which lacks publicly verifiable information) and his private relationships with other key players in the market, nullifying the use of MIS for decision making.

11.3.4 Mode of Vertical Communications

In our survey on IT governance and usage in American and Chinese firms, we found an interesting difference between American and Chinese managers and professional staff. We asked both American and Chinese respondents to what degree they use ICT to communicate (1) with their supervisors and (2) with their subordinates. We found that Americans reported that they use ICT to communicate with their subordinates and bosses more or less equally (with the use of ICT for upward communication being slightly higher), and the Chinese managers indicated that they use more ICT to communicate with their subordinates than with their bosses. What can we make out of this difference?

As we just discussed, people in a rule-based environment tend to use low context information, which can be more easily digitized and transmitted by ICT. Furthermore, in a rule-based environment, rules tend to be equally applied to everybody, including both the supervisor and subordinates, so there should not be a systematic difference in using ICT for upward or downward communications. In a relation-based environment, in addition to the fact that high context communication is often used, which is difficult to be conveyed via ICT, the relationship between a supervisor and a subordinate is more unequal than in a rule-based environment. In other words, using culture scholar Hofstede's term, there is a greater **power distance** in relation-based organizations (Hofstede & Hofstede, 2005). Digitized information, such as e-mail, is viewed as cold, faceless, and certainly not something that can be used to cultivate cordial, personal relationships. In a relation-based setting, the subordinates tend to have a strong motivation to cultivate a warm, individual relationship with the boss. And understandably, the motivation to have a good relationship with a boss is expectedly stronger than in rule-based environments. Thus our survey results may reflect the fact that while bosses may use ICT to reach down, most people prefer the more personalized mode, such as face-to-face, when communicating with their superiors in relation-based countries like China.

11.3.5 The Commitment Problem

Adopting IT in operation and management may jeopardize existing relationships, including relationships within a firm between manager and staff, and relationships between firms. The reason for this is that IT, especially the Internet, drastically reduces the search cost for market information and new partners, making long-term commitment to relationships, such as a supplier relationships or any employment relationship, harder to maintain. For example, a story told by Guo Fansheng, the CEO of Huicong Company in China, vividly illustrates the conflict between the introduction of IT and the reliance on relations. As all executives know, a major headache in most purchase departments is that the purchasing manager may take kickbacks, which are difficult to verify and punish. So when Guo selected a purchasing manager, he would put paramount importance on the loyalty and integrity of the candidate and test and retest to make sure he or she was trustworthy so that he could make a long-term commitment to this relationship. Such a relation-based arrangement worked fine until the Internet arrived. Once his firm needed to make a major purchase, he ordered his purchasing manager to get bids and the manager presented the best bid to Guo. Out of curiosity, Guo put an anonymous message on a purchasing Website to solicit bids. Many bids came in and, not surprisingly, some of them were lower than the best bid his manager presented to him. The difference was as wide as over 1 million yuan (US$140,000 in 2008). Guo was furious. He called the manager in, showed him the lower bids he got from the Web, and asked him if he had taken any kickback. The manager adamantly rejected his accusation. Guo said, "Then you must be grossly incompetent, and either way, you're fired" (Guo, 2008).

Did Guo do the right thing to fire the manager? He hinted that it may not be a well-thought-out decision, since it is very likely that with an opening bid on the Internet, it is almost certain that he will find a lower bid than his manager can get through his own established personal network. The conclusion Guo drew was to open the purchasing process to the Internet. Of course, in doing so, he may have lost some capable purchasing staff members, who may feel that their expertise—cultivating long-term relationships with suppliers—is threatened.

11.3.6 How ICT Affects Corporate Governance

From our analysis above, while firms in the rule-based environment have substantially improved their efficiency through the use of ICT and MIS in operation management and strategic decision making, it is clear that due to its culture, information and communication mode, and decision mode, **the use of ICT and MIS in relation-based firms is more limited to processes that can be easily digitized**, such as processing paychecks, automating production, and bookkeeping (the use of MIS in accounting may be limited as relation-based firms manipulate accounting information more heavily, as we showed in chapter: Political and Economic Systems in East Asia). The conventional wisdom predicts that with the adoption of ICT, which puts all firms on an equal footing, firms in developing countries will leapfrog to catch up to the firms in the developed world in productivity and efficiency. Based on our analysis, this may not be the case if the firms in developing countries are relation-based and limit their use of ICT only to simple processes. Their gains in efficiency from the use of ICT may not be as big as that of their counterparts in rule-based environments. Thus it is possible that the gap in ICT-based efficiency gain may be widening instead of narrowing. On the other hand, in the increasingly globalized market, **the competitive pressure from the rule-based firms that have made substantial gains from fuller adoption of ICT will force relation-based firms to transform themselves into more rule-based firms so that they can become more competitive as they grow and expand beyond their traditional domain.** And, indeed, a greater effort to realize the potential from the adoption of ICT in true decision making will help them in the process.

11.4 INNOVATION AND CREATIVITY IN EAST ASIA

While conclusive evidence is still lacking, studies and anecdotal evidence paint a paradoxical picture of innovation in East Asia. For example, according to a 2015 study by Thomas Reuters, East Asia is well represented in "Top 100 Global Innovators" and yet, China, the world's second largest economy, is conspicuously missing there (Thomas Reuters, 2015) (Table 11.1).

And the paradox does not stop there. On the one hand, we see greater efforts by the governments in East Asia to heavily invest in education, science, and technological innovations, and on the other hand, we see young people are trained to memorize outdated materials in order to pass the standard test to get into elite schools, which are ruled by the old elite professors whose knowledge is also outdated. We see stronger risk-taking spirit and energy in entrepreneurs in creating new products and services in the rapidly expanding markets, and we also see rampant fraud and violation of intellectual property rights that discourage innovation. In this section, we will sort out these confusing observations and identify patterns behind them.

Table 11.1 Top 100 global innovators, 2015

Country	Firms	Leading sectors
Japan	40	Chemicals & Cosmetics, Manufacturing & Medical
United States	35	Hardware & Electronics, Software, Pharmaceuticals, Aerospace & Defense
France	10	Institution & Government Research, Aerospace & Defense
Germany	4	Pharmaceuticals
Korea (S)	3	Hardware & Electronics
Switzerland	3	Pharmaceuticals
Belgium	1	Chemicals & Cosmetics
Canada	1	Telecommunications
Netherland	1	Household Goods
Sweden	1	Telecommunications
Taiwan	1	Hardware & Electronics
China	0	
Total	100	

Source: Thomas Reuters. (2015). Top 100 global innovators. *Thomas Reuters.* http://top100innovators. stateofinnovation.thomsonreuters.com/.

11.4.1 A Cultural Explanation

Previous research comparing creativity in East and West come primarily from a cultural perspective to explain why they differ (see Zhou and Su, 2010; and Morris and Leung, 2010 for review). The main findings from this genre are the following: The Western culture encourages creativities that are **novel and original**, while the Eastern culture emphasizes finding **useful and practical** solutions in creative quests. The emphasis in individualism in the West encourages people to express themselves in their creativity, while the orientation toward collectivism in the East urges people to adhere to a collectively recognized model. Historically, the fact that the Eastern languages (such as Chinese) were ideographic and did not use alphabetic symbols hindered the ability of abstract thinking, which is the basis for mathematics, and therefore slowed the development of modern sciences in the East (Morris & Leung, 2010).

11.4.2 Political and Economic Factors

The cultural explanation has its limits. First, it failed to explain what is behind culture. For example, why does the East emphasize useful and practical innovation rather than novel and original creativity? It also failed to explain the great leap forward in the output of scientific research in East Asia in recent years while the culture did not undergo drastic changes. I think we must consider the political and economic factors in explaining innovation and creativity in East Asia.

A main feature is that the governments of East Asia countries play a more active role in promoting innovation and creativity. These governments are not only more authoritarian in pushing their pro-education and pro-technology policies, but also more resourceful in funding education and research and development. Under such a push, the major East Asian countries have substantially increased their research output. Table 11.2 presents the number of publications in research journals in 2014 and the increase in the number from 1996. Of all countries in the table, China had the greatest increase from 1996: its number of publications in 2014 is nearly 16 times that in 1996. South Korea and Taiwan also made impressive increases. Japan's increase is smaller than that of the United States. The quality of research can be measured by the number of citations per publication. The United States has the highest citation rate, whereas China has the lowest. In terms of per capita publication, China is still the lowest.

Table 11.2 Number of publications in research journals, 2014

Country	Number of publications 2014	Increase in publications from 1996	Citations per publication	Publication per 1000 people
United States	552,690	1.67	0.64	1.75
China	452,877	15.78	0.34	0.32
Japan	114,999	1.35	0.45	0.91
South Korea	72,269	7.15	0.43	1.45
Taiwan	37,966	3.67	0.38	1.65

Source: SCImago. (2015). *SJR—SCImago Journal & Country Rank.* http://www.scimagojr.com (SCImago, 2015).

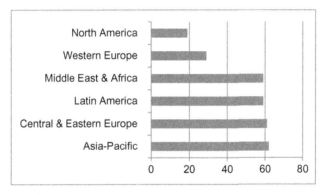

Figure 11.4 Average rate of unlicensed software use (%). *BSA/The Software Alliance. (2014). The compliance gap: BSA global software survey. www.bsa.org.*

Another feature is that the legal protection of intellectual property rights is relatively weak in East Asia, especially in China. As can be seen from Fig. 11.4, the Asia–Pacific region has the highest software piracy rate in the world. China is among the worst offenders, with 74% unlicensed software use (BSA/The Software Alliance, 2014). Studies show that there is a negative correlation between software piracy and the development of the software industry in a country (BSA & IDC, 2009). Therefore, due to high piracy the software industry is adversely affected in East Asia, especially China.

A third feature is that there is a strong economic force for innovation which is fueled partly by the unmet demands due to government monopolies and restrictions, and partly by freedom resulting from the lack of rules governing innovation and new markets. For example, China is a pioneer in online payment usage with facial recognition technology. It is estimated that nearly a quarter of China's population made payments online, totaling $213 billion, which is much higher than that in the United States (Wong & Osawa, 2015, December 29). A driver of the boom in online payment development is the dominance of the state in banking and financial services that discriminates against private businesses, which has made them slow to develop new services. At the same time, the lack of regulation on online payment allowed entrepreneurs to create their own standards and solutions. A Chinese finance executive commented that "you can be very creative, do whatever you want" in this "big gray area." The "wild west" market environment has made China "far ahead of the rest of the world" in internet finance and also a hotbed for fraud. "The opportunities and the risks of Internet finance are proportional, which means they are both immense," commented Joe Ngai, an executive in Hong Kong (Wong & Osawa, 2015, December 29).

11.4.3 The Effect of the Relation-Based System on Innovation

Compared with their counterparts in rule-based economies, firms in relation-based economies lack incentives to adopt new technologies for three main reasons. First, new technology may lead to a faster depreciation of their sunk investment in relations (see earlier discussion in this chapter). Second, in relation-based industries, competition is restrained by incumbent firms and government regulatory agencies. Since new technology tends to stimulate competition, the incumbent relation-based firms tend to be more resistant to adopting new technology. A third reason is that by their nature, established relationships, the main asset of these firms, have the tendency of being backward looking. There is a saying in Chinese that "friendship is like a ceramic vase, the older it is, the better it is." On the contrary, technological innovation is forward looking (see our earlier discussion on similar practices in human resource management).

Based on our discussion on the nature of relation-based system and the anecdotal observations, I think innovative activities in relation-based societies have the following characteristics:

1. Product and service innovations that are tangible with simple property rights structures can be more effectively and efficiently protected in a relation-based environment, due to the savings on the cost of setting up a sophisticated and comprehensive legal infrastructure required for more complicated property rights protection. For example, the

manufacturing industry, including garments, furniture, and toys etc., are well-developed in the relation-based countries such as China.

2. Product and service innovations that require cross-border collaborations, (infrequent) arm's length deals, complicated property rights that can be qualified and qualified by a third party, and written into a contract, are more effectively and efficiently protected by rule-based systems. For example, financial products, software, and movies are better protected in mature, rule-based economies such as the United States and Western Europe.

3. Product and service innovations that are tacit, intangible, difficult to qualify and quantify, difficult to share with a third party, require frequent face to face interactions, and hard to specify in contracts, are more effectively and efficiently protected in a relation-based environment. Examples of such innovations may include one of a kind products and services between two private parties (personal guards, drunk driver service, congestion driving service, rent-a-fiancée/fiancé service, sauna, foot-massage, karaoke, etc.).[2]

In summary, the market for and development of creativity and innovation in East Asia shows great potential and high uncertainty and risk. The market is shaped by the political and economic systems, culture, and the governance environment. While the government is actively promoting and investing in education and scientific and technological research, the rampant violation of intellectual property rights deters entrepreneurial creativity and innovation. In addition, the relation-based governance is not congruent with technological innovation. With East Asian countries' efforts to adopt more public rules and to improve intellectual property protection, their pace of creativity and innovation will accelerate.

QUESTIONS

1. What are the basic features of information goods?
2. Which societies can more fully utilize ICT to improve efficiency, rule-based or relation-based? Why?
3. Identify factors (both positive and negative) that will affect China's effort to become a technology superpower.

ENDNOTES

1. In this collage, the great wall is made of Chinese yuan in 50 cents notes. The Chinese government uses informants to post pro-government messages on the internet and rewards them 50 cents per posting. The two cartoon characters are the Internet police

created by the government. The sky is filled with barred words by the Chinese government (including the author's name) that are to be kept out by the wall. Inside the wall, people are enjoying life as long as they don't criticize the government.

2. For example, in China, if one drinks in a party and cannot drive, he can call someone to come to drive his car and him home. If one is stuck in traffic, he can call for a service that will send two people by a moped: one will drive his car to be stuck in traffic and the other will speed him away on the moped. One can also hire a fiancée to visit his parents.

REFERENCES

BSA, & IDC. (2009). *Sixth annual BSA-IDC global software 08 piracy study.* www.bsa.org.

BSA/The Software Alliance. (2014). *The compliance gap: BSA global software survey.* www.bsa.org.

Gao, G., & Ting-Toomey, S. (1998). *Communicating effectively with the Chinese.* Thousand Oaks, CA: Sage Publications.

Guo, F. (2008). *The China model: Guide for family business Growth.* Beijing: Peking University Press.

Hofstede, G., & Hofstede, G. J. (2005). *Cultures and organizations: Software of the mind.* New York, NY: McGraw-Hill.

Kalathil, S., & Boas, T. (2003). *Open networks, closed regimes: The impact of the Internet on authoritarian rule.* Washington, DC: Carnegie Endowment for International Peace.

Kim, A. M. (2008). *Learning to be capitalists.* Oxford: Oxford University Press.

Li, S. (2005). The impact of information and communication technology on relation-based governance system. *Journal of Information Technology for Development, 11*(2), 105–122.

Li, S. (2009). *Managing international business in relation-based versus rule-based countries.* New York, NY: Business Expert Press.

Li, S., & Gaur, A. (2014). Financial giants and moral pygmies? Multinational corporations and human rights in emerging markets. *International Journal of Emerging Markets, 9*(1), 11–32.

Liang, T. P., Li, S., & Wu, S. P. J. (2009). *The effect of national governance environment on firm IT governance and performance.* Paper presented at the frontier in IT research, National Sun Yat-Sen University, Kaohsiung, Taiwan.

Mintzberg, H. (1979). *The structure of organization.* New York, NY: Prentice-Hall.

Morris, M., & Leung, K. (2010). Creativity East and West: Perspectives and parallels. *Management and Organization Review, 6*(3), 313–327.

Reporters Without Borders. (2003–2009). Press freedom index.

SCImago. (2015). *SJR—SCImago Journal & Country Rank.* http://www.scimagojr.com.

Thomas Reuters. (2015). Top 100 global innovators. *Thomas Reuters.* http://top100innovators.stateofinnovation.thomsonreuters.com/.

Wong, G., & Osawa, J. (2015, December 29). China moves to cool off web finance. *The Wall Street Journal, 2.*

Yang, J. (2007, November 6). Testimony before the Committee on Foreign Affairs, U.S. House of Representatives, *Committee on Foreign Affairs.* Washington, DC.

Zhou, J., & Su, Y. (2010). A missing piece of the puzzle: The organizational context in cultural patterns of creativity. *Management and Organization Review, 6*(3), 391–413.

CHAPTER 12

The Transition From Relation-Based to Rule-Based Governance in East Asia*

12.1 THE PUZZLE SOLVED: TOGETHER OR SEPARATE CHECKS?

In their book on the Chinese style of communication, Gao and Ting-Toomey provided the following observation: the Chinese way of communication "can create enormous difficulty for Chinese in interactions with strangers (outsiders) because most Chinese do not feel comfortable or knowledgeable about dealing with strangers" (Gao & Ting-Toomey, 1998). A similar observation is made by Wallach and Metcalf in how Americans perceive the Asians' attitude and behavior:

> They [Americans] interact with Asians socially as well as at work and find them to be among the kindest, most considerate, and polite people they have ever met. Then, they meet other Asians in a public situation (on a bus, driving in traffic, in the market) and see them as rude, impolite, and inconsiderate. They wonder how people from the same culture can behave so differently.

Wallach and Metcalf's observation is similar to one of the puzzles we posed in the introduction—why Americans greet strangers on street and the Chinese don't (Wallach & Metcalf, 1995).

While these observations are quite accurate and even insightful, they do not explain what the root cause for such attitude and behavior is. With our analysis of rule-based versus relation-based systems, it is now clear that a major cause of Chinese clearly distinguishing "insiders" from "outsiders"

---

* Parts of this chapter are adopted from Li, S. (2009). *Managing international business in relation-based versus rule-based countries.* New York, NY: Business Expert Press., and from Li, S., & Park, S. H. (2015). The transition from relation-based to rule-based governance in East Asia: theories, evidence, and challenges: 27: Old Dominion University.

is that **in a relation-based governance environment, people do not
need to deal with strangers.**

What is behind the culture of excluding and thus ignoring strangers
are the political and economic institutions that forced people and firms to
rely on other people and firms with whom they have a close relationship
to overcome the "institutional holes" in the legal system. When the state
cannot enforce public rules impartially, people invest in private relationships and rely on them for protection.

Coming back to the puzzle of why Chinese compete to pay for group
meals while Americans ask for separate checks, we can now explain it with
a clear logic: in a relation-based society, people tend to deal only with
people they know very well. They have close ties and interact on a frequent basis. It is feasible that every member of the close-knit group can
take turns to pay for the group meal rather than calculating each member's
share every time. But more importantly, it creates a familial, altogether
warm feeling within the group. It is a bonding effort (or "team building"
in modern management jargon). What if there is someone who always
evades paying? In a small group with repeated interaction, a freeloader will
be kicked out of the group. In a relation-based society, being shunned by
a group is a signal that someone is not a good prospect for business or
any partnership, which is essentially a death sentence as far as this person's
career is concerned. So any rational person will avoid such a perception at
any cost. And this is why the relation-based culture places loyalty, honor,
and reciprocity as paramount in its value system.

12.2 THE CHALLENGE FACING EAST ASIA: THE TRANSITION FROM RELATION-BASED TO RULE-BASED GOVERNANCE

As shown in this book, the relation-based governance has helped East Asian countries to achieve rapid economic growth. Now, as the scale and scope of their economies expand globally, continuing to rely on the relation-based way will hinder their further development and globalization effort. In order to overcome the bottleneck, East Asian countries must make the leap to transform their relation-based system into the rule-based system. There is strong evidence that such a transition has occurred among East Asian countries.

12.2.1 Different Stages of Transition in Major East Asia Countries

12.2.1.1 Japan

World Bank Aggregate Worldwide Governance Indicator (WGI) (2014): 8.3 (ranging from −12.5 (worst) to 12.5 (best)), WGI percentile rank: 88% (100% = highest) (World Bank, 2015b) (Fig. 12.1).

ICC Open Markets Index (2015): 3.6 (Average openness), rank: 44 (1 = most open). Improvement from 2011: 10% (International Chamber of Commerce, 2015).

In terms of the overall governance environment, Japan has made the greatest change from traditionally relying on relation-based governance to rule-based governance. Its overall Worldwide Governance Indicator (WGI) is 8.3 and it is ranked in 88% in the world. The transformation is especially advanced in the government system, as shown in the high

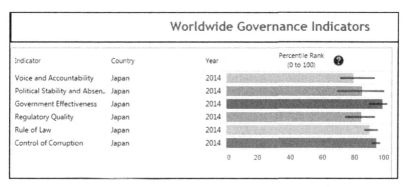

Figure 12.1 Percentile rank of Worldwide Governance Indicators of Japan, 2014. *World Bank. (2015b). Worldwide Governance Indicators. In W. Bank (Ed.). http://info.worldbank. org/governance/wgi/index.aspx#reports.*

percentile rank of "Government Effectiveness." This achievement has greatly benefited from two reforms. The first was the Meiji Restoration in the late 1860s when Japan decided to open its country and economy, and adopt modern Western rules and governance. The second is the American occupation after its defeat in World War II, when democratization along with the establishment of the rule of law were pushed by the US government. Now, Japan is a mature democracy with a fair, effective, and efficient legal system, which is the necessary condition for the rule-based governance (see chapters: Western Rules Versus Eastern Relations: A Fundamental Framework to Understand East Asia and Political and Economic Systems in East Asia).

However, compared to its achievement in the political system, the transformation toward rule-based government in the economic and business sphere is less advanced. According to the ICC Open Markets Index study that classify all countries in the five groups based on market openness ranging from "most open," "above average openness," "average openness," "below average openness," and "very weak," Japan belongs to the 3rd group (average openness), lower than South Korea and Taiwan (see below). Studies show that the relation-based way of doing business in Japan is still strong, and it is still difficult for foreign companies to enter the market (Hill, 2005; Japanstrategy, 2013–2014; Li, 1999).

12.2.1.2 South Korea

World Bank Aggregate Worldwide Governance Indicator (WGI) (2014): 4.6 (ranging from −12.5 (worst) to 12.5 (best)), WGI percentile rank: 74% (100% = highest) (World Bank, 2015b).

ICC Open Markets Index (2015): 3.8 (Average openness), rank: 41 (1 = most open). Improvement from 2011: 12% (International Chamber of Commerce, 2015) (Fig. 12.2).

Like the rest of East Asia, South Korea has been a relation-based society in which informal networks among big businesses and between big businesses and governments were extensive, strong, and exclusive. The unique Korean organization that best symbolized the relation-based way of doing business is *chaebol* (재벌), which literally indicates a clan that owns wealth or property. It is a South Korean-style of a business conglomerate with the following characteristics. Typically, it is a holding (controlling, or parent) company that owns numerous enterprises that operate globally. The head of the holding/controlling company, usually the head of the family that founded the conglomerate, controls all operations. Informal

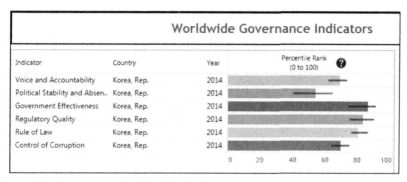

Figure 12.2 Percentile rank of Worldwide Governance Indicators of South Korea, 2014.

collusion among the *chaebols* is believed to be widespread. The controlling families of chaebols maintain their close relationships with each other through marriages and through industrial associations, such as the Federation of Korean Industry.

The close relationship between the chaebols and the government can be viewed as mutually beneficial: businesses were backed by the government to grow and go abroad, and government used chaebols to develop the country's economy (Huang & O'Neil-Massaro, 2001). From the 1960s to the 1980s, the Korean economy took off rapidly and by the late 1980s, it had become an industrialized nation with a per capita income of $8600 (1990s purchase power parity adjusted) (World Bank, 2015a). With the scale and scope of its economy greatly expanded into the world market, there was a need for Korea to move away from the relation-based system. Since the late 1980s, Korea has steadily transforming its governance system toward a more rule-based system by opening up its economy. During this period, two major events accelerated the process. One is the democratization in the late 1980s and early 1990s, which we reviewed in Chapter 3, Political and Economic Systems in East Asia, and the other is the 1997 Asian Financial Crisis.

The 1997 Asian Financial Crisis hit South Korea extremely hard due to the vulnerability of the economy resulting from the cozy relationship between the chaebols, the government, and the banks (which were used by the government to finance chaebols aggressive expansions). Korea's stock market crashed, the currency fell by more than half of its value to the US dollar (from 800 won/$1 to 1700 won/$1), further exacerbating Korea's ability to service its foreign debt, and, as a result, Korea more than doubled its national debt-to-GDP ratio from approximately 13–30% (Wikipedia, 2015).

Responding to the crisis, the government, led by the newly elected president Kim Dae Jung, made a sweeping structural reform that fundamentally changed the governance environment of Korea, and greatly contributed to its transition from relation-based to rule-based governance. These reforms include the labor reform that broke the relation-based, rigid employment practices; the financial reform that increased transparency, accountability, and sound management, and deregulation and liberalization; corporate reform that specifically targeted the chaebols with five principles of corporate restructuring, which are essentially rule-based governance; and economic liberalization in general that opened the banking and other sectors to foreign competition (Moon & Mo, 2015).

Now Korea's overall WGI is 4.6, which is much higher than China's (see below), but lower than those of Japan and Taiwan (see below). Among the six individual WGI, its Government Effectiveness is the highest. Compared with Japan, Taiwan, and China, Korea's Open Markets Index has achieved the biggest improvement from 2011 to 2015. Its markets are more open (3.8) than Japan's (3.6).

12.2.1.3 Taiwan

World Bank Aggregate Worldwide Governance Indicator (WGI) (2014): 6.4 (ranging from −12.5 (worst) to 12.5 (best)), WGI percentile rank: 81% (100% = highest) (World Bank, 2015b).

ICC Open Markets Index (2015): 4.1 (Above average openness), rank: 28 (1 = most open). Improvement from 2011: 8% (International Chamber of Commerce, 2015).

The political and economic environment of Taiwan since the 1950s was similar to that of South Korea's in that it was under authoritarian rule with a pro-business economic policy (see chapter: Political and Economic Systems in East Asia). The business-government relationship was close, and family businesses dominated the economy (Lien, Lau, & Li, In press). From the 1950s to the 1980s, Taiwan enjoyed fast economic growth and become one of the four tigers that created the Asian Miracle (see chapter: Political and Economic Systems in East Asia).

In the late 1980s, Taiwan's democratization accelerated. In 1986, the first opposition party, the Democratic Progressive Party, was founded. Instead of dismantling it, the ruling party under Chiang Ching-kuo allowed and recognized it, marking the beginning of the rapid democratization. In 1987, Chiang ended the martial law and restored constitutional rule. In 2000 the opposition party won the presidential election, which successfully and peacefully ended the one-party rule in Taiwan.

At the same time, Taiwan has made strides in corporate governance reform. Until the late 1990s, the business environment of Taiwan could have been characterized as informal and family-based, with modern, rule-based corporate governance virtually missing (Lien et al., In press). The 1997 Asian Financial Crisis adversely impacted Taiwan's economy.

In the aftermath of the crisis, from 2001 and 2003, the Taiwanese government embarked upon a series of reforms to introduce more rule-based corporate governance. These include amending the Company Law to require companies to disclose cross-holding information, directing the Taiwan Stock Exchange (TSE) to establish an online system of information disclosure for all of Taiwan's listed firms, and promulgating a set of new regulations to improve the quality of information disclosure. In addition, the TSE began in 2003 to conduct annual reviews and evaluations of the quality of firms' information disclosures, and the results were published online as a reference for all investors. Since 2003, to ensure board independence, the TSE has also required newly listed firms to reserve at least two seats for independent directors. These measures have greatly facilitated the transition of Taiwan's governance system from relation-based to rule-based (Lien et al., In press).

In 2014 Taiwan's overall WGI was 6.4, which is very close to those of the advanced rule-based countries such as the United States (7.3). As can be seen from Fig. 12.3, its "Government Effectiveness" and "Regulatory Quality" are particularly high: ranked around 88% and 89% in the world, respectively.

Taiwan's achievement in market openness is the most impressive. It ranks higher than Japan, South Korea, and China, and is the only one among them in the "Above average openness" group. (The only

Figure 12.3 Percentile rank of Worldwide Governance Indicators of Taiwan, 2014.

countries/regions in Asia that have higher rankings than Taiwan are Singapore (5.5) and Hong Kong (5.5), which are ranked 1 and 2 in the world in the "Most open" group, respectively (International Chamber of Commerce, 2015)).

12.2.1.4 China

World Bank Aggregate Worldwide Governance Indicator (WGI) (2014): −2.6 (ranging from −12.5 (worst) to 12.5 (best)), WGI percentile rank: 39% (100% = highest) (World Bank, 2015b) (Fig. 12.4).

ICC Open Markets Index (2015): 3.0 (Average openness), rank: 59 (1 = most open). Improvement from 2011: 7%. (International Chamber of Commerce, 2015).

Different from the above three countries, China was a communist country from 1949 when Mao seized power until 1976 when Mao died. In the late 1970s the Chinese government started an economic reform which aimed at introducing market forces, establishing new economic laws and regulations that aimed to more clearly demarcate and protect property rights, and gradually divesting the government from businesses. The reform has substantially changed the economic system, which can be gauged by examining the changes in the Economic Freedom Index (EFI). In 1980, China's EFI was 3.64. By 2010, it was much higher: 6.37.[1]

The reform has released a tremendous force of productivity in the Chinese that was suppressed under Mao's ultra-leftist policy. The Chinese economy took off and has witnessed double-digit growth for decades, creating the world's second largest economy (see chapter: Political and Economic Systems in East Asia).

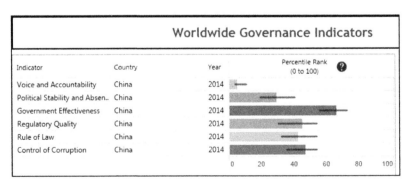

Figure 12.4 Percentile rank of Worldwide Governance Indicators of China, 2014.

From the governance perspective, all the reform efforts are aiming to shift away from the old relation-based way of governing economic activities and to establish more effective public rules (Li, 2013). In this sense, the economic reform is an attempt to transition from relation-based system to rule-based system. In the late 1990s, the government called for banking reforms to make bank financing based more on the market rather than relation-based to disfavor state firms and well-connected firms. The government also announced its intention to clean up smuggling, which is essentially relation-based trading in which the well-connected firms can import without paying tariffs, and to wean government organizations from conducting business, thus reducing the opportunities in which officials and their relatives can enter restricted and lucrative industries (Hofman & Wu, 2009).

Further evidence of the transition comes from China's attempt to adopt international standards governing trade and finance. In 2000, China entered the World Trade Organization. Six years later, China made an effort to converge to the International Financial Report Standard, or IFRS. Based on Li's Governance Environment Index, the quality of accounting is an important part of rule-based governance (Li, 2009). The fact that China has (at least partially) adopted IFRS, which provides more stringent standards and open criteria for the public to access and evaluate firm's financial information, a vital element of a rule-based system, shows the Chinese government efforts to become a member of the international, more rule-based community. Research shows that investors of the Chinese stock market increasingly relied on publicly released financial information after China's convergence toward IFRS (Qu, Fong, & Oliver, 2012).

China's overall WGI is −2.6, which is low and the lowest among the major East Asian countries discussed here. A further review on the six individual indicators of China's WGI in 2014 revealed mixed results of the transition toward rule-based governance. The indicator that has achieved the most improvement is "Government Effectiveness," while the two indicators measuring political rights and freedom of press ("Political Stability and Absence of Violence" and "Voice and Accountability") have lagged behind, with the latter being particularly low.

In terms of market openness, China is the lowest of the four countries discussed here. Moreover, its improvement rate is also the slowest: a merely 7% from 2011 to 2015.

Summarizing the above discussion and observations, we can see that over a 30-year span since China started economic reform, its economic institutions have moved substantially toward being more rule-based (as evidenced in the change of the Economic Freedom Index from 1980 to 2010); however, we also notice that in terms of the transition toward a rule-based governance environment, China's progress is slow, which is especially the case in the freedom of expression and political rights. Market openness is also still very low. China has a long way to go in the transition, which leads us to the discussion on the difficulty of the transition.

12.2.2 The Difficulty of the Transition

The transition is not easy. Powerful groups that have invested heavily in private relationships and exclusive networks for a long time will fight very hard to keep the relation-based way of doing business and resist the change. However, the change is inevitable and will occur and when it does, old relationships will begin to crack and, realizing the return from the investment in private relationship will diminish, people will cease to make new investment into it and stop the upkeep of the relationship. When the old relationship is in decline and the new public rules are not effective yet, there will be a governance vacuum and confusion. In many ways, the 1997 Asian financial crisis was triggered by the transition in several Asian countries, such as South Korea, Thailand, and Indonesia. China started its transition in the late 1970s and is still in the process after nearly four decades. Japan, one of the wealthiest countries in the world, still relies heavily on the relation-based way compared to other wealthy nations (as shown in its low Open Markets Index) (International Chamber of Commerce, 2015; Li, 1999). Below we will discuss a unique difficulty during China's transition. In a later section, we will discuss the difficulties during the transition that are particularly relevant to foreign firms doing business in East Asia.

12.2.3 A Unique Challenge in China: Mao + Deng = ?

The transformation from a relation-based to a rule-based governance environment is a comprehensive social change that includes different dimensions ranging from political, economic, legal, and cultural institutions (systems). The speed of change varies widely among different dimensions. The "hard" (or formal) institutions, such as laws, political and economic regulations and policies, can be changed rather quickly by government decrees, which can be as fast as overnight in some instances. Change to culture, the "soft" or informal institutions, usually takes a long time, sometimes several generations (North, 1990). In this regard government decrees do not really work—they simply cannot order people to change the way they think.

Without the corresponding change in the legal culture, any new laws will not be effectively and efficiently implemented and enforced. Take the case of the product quality and safety problem in China that has brought worldwide attention in recent years. Ever since China became the world's factory for consumer and industrial products, harmful or illegal materials have been a problem in many products ranging from toys, animal feed, human food, to home construction products. Perhaps the most well-known incident is the tainted milk case, in which several Chinese diary firms added an industrial chemical called melamine, which is used for making plastics and glues, to make the milk appear as if it contained more protein in lab tests, thus cutting the production cost. The additive severely affected human kidneys and caused more than 51,900 children to be hospitalized and six deaths due to kidney failure. Worldwide, numerous products in many countries were contaminated by melamine originating in China (WHO (World Health Organization), 2008).

When the tainted milk news broke, people were outraged. People inside and outside China asked how such a practice could have existed for years, and how could it be prevented from happening in the future. The culture change perspective may provide an answer.

A brief review of China's business ethics history will tell us that this is not surprising at all. This is a product of the culture of Mao and Deng, the two most prominent figures that define China today (Li, 2004).

Mao Zedong ruled China from 1949 to 1976. His China was characterized by its extreme radical communism and absolute poverty. Being rich was shameful, Mao told his subjects. The less property one had, the more glorious one became. Private property was not respected or protected. In order to achieve our revolutionary goals, we must break the laws, the Great Helmsman taught the masses. Mao proudly called himself "lawless." Net result: little respect for property rights, and the end justifies any means.

Mao's death in 1976 brought an end to his ultra-leftist rule. Beginning in 1978, China began its "reform." Deng Xiaoping, who ruled for the next 20 years, was a pragmatic man with a vision of making China prosperous. One of his most famous sayings was a 180 degree reversal from Mao: "getting rich is glorious." The Chinese people took him seriously. They began to get rich. But neither Deng nor his successors realized that to emulate the success of the advanced economies, China needed not only written laws that protect property rights but also a culture that encourages trust and honesty. Needless to say, neither Deng nor his successors have had any success in nurturing such a business culture.

Thus the combination of Mao's lawless legacy and Deng's call for "getting rich" has mutated into a unique capitalism with Chinese characteristics in which people can get rich by any means—even if it means cutting corners in product quality or using poisonous additives. Thus we observe simultaneously the booming of moneymaking activities and the poisonous baby formula in China.

Will China's capitalism ever evolve into a stage in which we can fully trust the safety of its products (ie, a more rule-based stage)? No doubt the Chinese government is making a great effort to reduce fake and problem products by promulgating many laws and punishing many corrupt officials. However, as we have just discussed, while laws can be made overnight, culture changes slowly. Mao's influence on Chinese business culture and practice will be there for a long time. As long as the CEOs of dairy product companies in China can sleep soundly knowing that their products are killing babies, the practice will continue. Under the combination of Mao and Deng, the world should be prepared to see more fake and unsafe products from China.

12.2.4 The Role of Government in the Transition

The role of the government in a society undergoing the transition from a relation-based to a rule-based governance environment is several-fold. First, assuming that the government is actively pushing through the transition, it should effectively and efficiently deal with the opposition forces, which are the vested interest groups that have deeply entrenched positions in the relation-based system. The government must be able to design and implement incentives for them to support the transition. In other words, the government needs to use its power and resources to compensate the vested interest groups so that they can part with their sunk capital in the established relations without strong resistance.

Second, the government should make great efforts to minimize the social disruption associated with the transition. A radical transition that dismantles the old relation-based way almost overnight tends to cause great social upheaval and dislocation of social groups and segments and makes the government unable to effectively and efficiently govern the society. However, there is always a tradeoff between the speed of the transition and the stability during the transition. The Russian model of transforming from Communism (a relation-based system) toward a more rule-based system is characterized by a revolutionary change, or what is commonly known as the "big bang" approach, or "shock therapy." The intent is to give the old communism a strong electrical shock to knock it out; when the society wakes up, it is capitalistic!

On the other hand, the Chinese model of transition is slow and steady, while the Communist Party keeps an absolute power, a strategy termed by the party as "feeling the stones when crossing the river."

While there is a heated debate on the pros and cons of each model with no consensus; many cannot even agree on what criteria should be used to evaluate the success of the transition. Some put political freedom above everything else, while others emphasize political stability, and there are people whose sole measure of success is economic development. However, the following facts are commonly recognized: China has had faster economic growth in the past three decades with greater political stability, whereas Russia has established an infant democracy with greater political freedom.

12.3 OPPORTUNITIES AND CHALLENGES FOR MULTINATIONAL CORPORATIONS DOING BUSINESS IN EAST ASIA DURING THE TRANSITION

12.3.1 Opportunities for Multinational Corporations During the Transition

Whilst the East Asian countries, especially China, are undergoing the transition, there are new opportunities for multinational corporations (MNCs) from the rule-based countries. These opportunities include three types: (1) the new demands for products and services that are needed for doing business in a more rule-based environment, such as the legal profession, accounting and auditing services, and credit and business rating services; (2) products and services that are needed during the transition such as consulting services to help the government to formulate policies that can make the transition efficient and smooth or facilitate firms to make the transition successfully to avoid organizational breakdown or business interruption; and (3) products and services that are difficult to protect in the relation-based environment, including complicated financial products and services, product and services that have high contents of intellectual properties, the licensing and franchising industries, and the medical and pharmaceutical industries.

12.3.2 The Challenges Facing Multinational Corporations During the Transition

In order to realize the opportunities opened by the transition, MNCs must have a good understanding of the challenges and risks arising from the transition.

The Danger of a Governance Vacuum. During a transition from relation-based to rule-based governance, the old relation-based way declines, and realizing it, people and firms begin to reduce their investment in establishing new relationships and try to get as much from established relationships since the investment in them is sunk, encouraging opportunistic behaviors. At the same time, newly established public rules and laws may not be functioning well because for any law and public regulation to be effectively and efficiently enforced, there must be a stronger moral code and legal culture that respects the law and encourages self-discipline; for without such a culture, laws and regulations are nothing more than ink on paper. The combination of the decline of the relation-based way and the ineffective infancy of a rule-based system may create a governance vacuum that makes the society unstable and business activities vulnerable to organized crime. Furthermore, businesses may suffer from a worsening of bureaucracy resulting from the mushrooming of numerous independent regulatory agencies when a dictatorship collapses (Shleifer & Vishny, 1993). For example, after the fall of the dictator Suharto in Indonesia, corruption got worse because there was no one to keep a rein on the government bureaucracy to make sure that the demand for bribes by each government department was optimized so that the dictator could maximize his total bribe income and deliver the pubic goods that the briber asked for. After he was gone, there emerged many semi-independent politicians who acted like dukes controlling one segment of the government bureaucracy and demanding much higher amounts for bribes (Kuncoro, 2009).

The Tendency to Overregulate During the Transition. An intriguing phenomenon in societies undergoing rapid transition from relation-based governance to rule-based governance is that transitioning societies tend to implement and enforce more formal rules, even more than rule-based countries. Two examples from Taiwan, a society undergoing rapid transition from a relation-based to a rule-based governance environment, vividly illustrate this tendency.[2]

The first example regards the changes in Taiwan's primary and secondary education. Before Taiwan's democratization, the hiring of teachers was made by school principals. Although it used certain rules, such as requiring a degree from an accredited teacher's college, the process tended to be tainted by powerful politicians. During the democratization process (which may be viewed as an effort to transform from a relation-based to a rule-based governance system), reformers tried to eliminate the corruption in the teacher hiring process. In doing so, the reformers seemed to have overdone it. They essentially took the hiring power away from the principal and made the hiring solely reliant on a very clearly defined, easily measured, and strictly enforced rule: a nationwide teachers test. Anyone who scored high on the test would be hired. Needless to say, the ones with the highest scores may not necessarily be the best candidates for the job.

Another example regards the tenure and promotion process in universities in Taiwan. In order to eliminate corruption and political influence, the reformers instituted a points system that cumulates points based on teaching, research, and services. In so doing, they have essentially made administrators (president, provost, dean, and chairs) powerless in the process.

These two examples suggest that in the process of moving away from the traditional relation-based governance system and embracing the new rule-based way of governance, a society tends to go overboard, nullifying human authorities out of the fear that people at the top will abuse their power as in the old relation-based system.

The main reason for such an overreaction to limit authority's discretion in favor of strict formal rules is the long duration of authoritarian rule in which power has been abused for personal gains. Such abuses have left a deep indelible scar on the society and the people so that they would rather take away any discretional power from the authorities and completely rely on formal, objective rules. The lack of trust in government, public officials, or anyone in power is the fundamental cause of this overregulation.

While such measures may successfully curtail the abuse of power common in the old relation-based setting, the cost of doing so for the society and business can be quite high. The discretion of authorities to make decisions is necessary in any organization or society. Indeed, if formal rules can take care of every contingency, then officials and managers are not necessary. There must be a certain amount of trust in the people who are in power for an organization or society to run efficiently. **The challenge to societies undergoing the transition from a relation-based to a rule-based governance environment is how to nurture and establish public trust in general and confidence in the government in particular.**

12.3.3 Strategic Implications for Doing Business in Relation-Based Societies Undergoing the Transition

While being fully aware that each business situation is different, and the application of what we have discussed in this book has to be made by the business executive in the situation, I have tried to highlight several general points that may help both business executives and policy makers in dealing with relation-based societies and the transition from relation-based to rule-based governance.

Relying on Relationships Can Be a Double-Edged Sword. It is vital for a foreign player entering into a relation-based market to invest in establishing reliable relationships in the local market. In doing so, the foreign player should realize two caveats. First, using relations to circumvent formal rules may be illegal, even in a relation-based society. Second, when the foreign player uses relations to gain advantage in the local market, its partners and competitors also use relations to try to outcompete it. And local partners or competitors may have stronger relationships within the power circle. In the early 1990s, McDonalds obtained a prime location in Beijing through *guanxi*, only to find that a Hong Kong businessman, Li Ka-shing, who had a stronger *guanxi* had McDonalds evicted for Li's real estate development project (Economist, 1994).

Beware of the Governance Vacuum During the Transition. The vacuum created by the transition is especially dangerous for foreign investors and firms in a sense that as outsiders, they see new investment and business opportunities created by the newly promulgated laws and regulations and rush in to do business without realizing that the laws and regulations are routinely ignored and that the insiders see the vacuum created by the transition as an opportunity to loot (Li, 1999).

What to Do With Rigid and Many Formal Rules During the Transition. Even in a business environment characterized by numerous stifling formal rules that make doing business difficult and costly, there are booming businesses and some firms seem to be doing well, so there must be hidden ways to get around the rules to get things done. If a new foreign firm enters such a market, the first thing to do is to get a proper introduction to the insiders in the industry and learn from them. A common error is to totally rely on financial incentives or to pay a high fee to hire the most influential local player to help you. As mentioned by a seasoned businessman we interviewed in Asia,

> It is not as simple as paying money or bribing....If you just offer money to someone to get his business or his help, he will look down on you and will not take it. You have to show that you are resourceful in some ways and can help him to get things that he otherwise cannot get.

A foreign player entering into a new, relation-based market must be able to bring unique competences or resources that are valued highly by the local market in order to "earn" a proper introduction and respect.

At the very least, the foreign player should try to use old relations to establish new relations. As the small world network theory stated, most strangers can be connected by no more than six existing links (Gurevich, 1961). Quite often, the foreign firm is able to find someone in its firm that either directly or indirectly knows a local player. As we showed in Chapter 2, Western Rules Versus Eastern Relations: A Fundamental Framework to Understand East Asia, introduction by a mutual friend in this way is more effective and may earn some instant credit rather than using a local consultant who is hired by the foreign player without any existing relationships.

Once the foreign firm becomes a new insider, it should quickly learn the hidden informal rules of the game to overcome the obstacles erected by the formal rules. At this stage, local partners or consultants are very useful in helping to navigate through the maze of bureaucracy and protectionism.

QUESTIONS

1. Why is the transition from relation-based to rule-based governance so difficult for China?
2. Will the East Asian countries be able to get rid of relation-based business practice altogether? Why or why not?
3. What are the risks arising from the transition for foreign firms doing business in East Asia?
4. What do the MNCs from rule-based countries need to prepare in order to succeed in relation-based countries in transition?

ENDNOTES

1. The EFI "measures the degree to which the policies and institutions of countries are supportive of economic freedom." It is based on 42 variables to measure the degree of economic freedom in five broad areas: (1) size of government, (2) legal system and property rights, (3) sound money, (4) freedom to trade internationally, and (5) regulation. As can be seen, three areas (2, 4, and 5) are pertinent to a sound rule-based governance system, and we thus can use it as a proxy to examine China's transition toward a rule-based system. The EFI has a range from 1 (least free) to 10 (most free) Gwartney, J., & Lawson, R. (2012). *Economic freedom of the world: 2012 annual report.* Toronto, ON: The Fraser Institute.
2. I benefited from the discussions with Dr. Kuang S. Yeh of National Sun Yat-sen University in Kaohsiung, Taiwan during my visits from 2007 to 2009.

REFERENCES

Economist, (1994). The ultimate takeaway. *The Economist*, 36.
Gao, G., & Ting-Toomey, S. (1998). *Communicating effectively with the Chinese.* Thousand Oaks, CA: Sage Publications.
Gurevich, M. (1961). *The social structure of acquaintanceship networks.* Cambridge, MA: MIT Press.
Gwartney, J., & Lawson, R. (2012). *Economic freedom of the world: 2012 annual report.* Toronto, ON: The Fraser Institute.
Hill, C. (2005). *International business: Competing in the global marketplace* (5th ed.). New York, NY: McGraw-Hill.

Hofman, B., & Wu, J. (2009). *Explaining China's development and reform*. Washington, DC: World Bank.

Huang, Y., & O'Neil-Massaro, K. J. (2001). *Korea first bank (A) and (B)*. Boston, MA: Harvard Business School Case.

International Chamber of Commerce, (2015). *ICC open markets index* (3rd Edition 2015). Paris, France: International Chamber of Commerce.

Japanstrategy. (2013–2014). *Japan market entry: Why is business in Japan so difficult?* Japanstrategy. com, http://www.japanstrategy.com/business-in-japan/.

Kuncoro, A. (2009). Corruption Inc, *Insider Indonesia*. www.insideindonesia.org: 4.

Li, S. (1999). Relation-based versus rule-based governance: an explanation of the East Asian miracle and Asian crisis. *Paper presented at the American Economic Association Annual Meeting in New York,* January. Listed on the Social Science Research Network (<http://papers.ssrn.com/paper.taf?abstract_id=200208>), 2000. Reprinted in *Review of International Economics, 2003, 11(4),* 651–73, *American Economic Association Annual Meeting in New York*. New York.

Li, S. (2004). Why is property right protection lacking in China? An institutional explanation. *California Management Review, 46*(3), 100–115.

Li, S. (2009). *Managing international business in relation-based versus rule-based countries*. New York, NY: Business Expert Press.

Li, S. (2013). China's (painful) transition from relation-based to rule-based governance: When and how, not If and why. *Corporate Governance: An International Review, 21*(6), 567–576.

Li, S., & Park, S.H. (2015). The transition from relation-based to rule-based governance in East Asia: Theories, evidence, and challenges: 27: Old Dominion University.

Lien, Y., Lau, C., & Li, S. (In press). Institutional reforms and the effects of family control on corporate governance. *Family Business Review*.

Moon, C. -I., & Mo, J. (2015). *Economic crisis and structural reforms in South Korea*. Washington, DC: Economic Strategy Institute.

North, D. (1990). *Institutions, institutional change, and economic performance*. Cambridge: Cambridge University Press.

Qu, W., Fong, M., & Oliver, J. (2012). Does IFRS convergence improve quality of accounting information? Evidence from the Chinese stock market. *Corporate Ownership & Control, 9*(4), 1–10.

Shleifer, A., & Vishny, R. (1993). Corruption. *Quarterly Journal of Economics, 108*(3), 599–617.

Wallach, J., & Metcalf, G. (1995). *A practical guide for Asians on how to succeed with U.S. managers*. Singapore: McGraw-Hill.

WHO (World Health Organization). (2008). *Melamine-contamination event, China, 2008*. http://www.who.int/foodsafety/fs_management/infosan_events/en/index.html.

Wikipedia. (2015). *1997 Asian financial crisis*. https://en.wikipedia.org/ wiki/1997_Asian_financial_crisis#South_Korea.

World Bank, (2015a). *World development indicators*. Washington, DC: World Bank.

World Bank, (2015b). *Worldwide Governance Indicators*. In W. Bank (Ed.). http://info.world-bank.org/governance/wgi/index.aspx#reports.

CHAPTER 13

Conclusion: What Can We Learn From East Asia?

Facing the globalizing world and the rise of East Asia, America as a nation and Americans as individuals need to get ready to compete. In this book, we have reviewed the way that East Asian countries view business, politics, and society, and how their views contribute to their economic development and competitiveness. Concluding the book, we will discuss what the United States can learn from the experience of East Asia to improve its competitiveness.

13.1 A COMPARISON BETWEEN EAST ASIA AND THE UNITED STATES

A few years ago I met a Chinese scholar who was visiting the United States and he made a simple and obvious observation: "there is a 12-hour time difference between China and the United States!" While deceptively simple, the comment is profound. There is a day-and-night difference between the two: what is bright in one country is dark in the other. American culture worships individualism, Chinese frown upon it; in the United States, manpower is expensive and things are relatively cheap and in China it is the opposite; Americans criticize and make fun of politicians all the time, in China people are locked up for doing it. But more theoretically, I argue that the following differences are primarily responsible in defining the competitiveness of each country, or between the East and West in general.

In the Eastern political and social philosophy, family in its traditional form—a married couple with their natural children, grandchildren, and greatgrandchildren—is the most important unit. From an economic development perspective, such traditional families are conducive to the development of the hard-working attitude, which in turn helps to improve productivity, facilitating the transfer of such an attitude from generation to generation, and helping to preserve the wealth created by the family within the family (Li, Park, & Selover, 2015). In this regard, the strong traditional family values gives East Asia an edge over the United States for economic development.

However, beyond the family as an unit in the social structure is where the East Asian philosophy gets into a problem: they do not care about the community and social associations. The Eastern philosophy views the family not only as a unit for the individuals but also as the ruling unit of the state. The Chinese word for state or government is a two-character word "guo-jia" 国家. "Guo" (国) means a country, whereas "jia" (家) means the family. For Chinese, state, country, and the family are intertwined and inseparable. A well-known Chinese wisdom is "qijia zhiguo" (齐家治国) meaning "manage one's family well then one can rule the country." Here is a quantum leap: from family directly to the state without the middle organization, the community. In the traditional Chinese society, people maintain the interior of their home so well as if it is a palace but do not care much about the outside of the home, leaving streets and the neighborhood littered with garbage. The lack of community development in East Asia hinders the development of social capital, which is an important source for the development of a civil society and a well-functioned democratic system (Putnam, 1993). Thus as far as the development of community is concerned, the East Asian societies are weak.

Interestingly, such a weakness may be compensated by the strong state in East Asia. Compared to their Western counterparts, East Asians have high respect for state leaders and follow government orders closely without many questions or challenges. As we have seen from the WGIs of the major East Asian countries, they all have high "Government Effectiveness" score.

In contrast to the Eastern philosophy, the Western values, represented by the American culture, treasures people as individuals and encourages people to freely express themselves and be different. Extending this much emphasized individualism into the view on the family, the American culture views the family as an extension of the individual and serves the need of the individual who wants to form a family. So the form of the family is not important and constant; it changes according to the changing needs of the individual who forms it. As a result, the nontraditional family forms are much more tolerated and accepted than they are in East Asia, such as families with same-sex parents, single parents, unmarried parents, and children without blood ties to parents. From the economic development perspective, the absence of the traditional family structure hinders the formation of productive attitudes, savings, and the preservation of culture between generations (Li et al., 2015).

Table 12.1 Political and economic views and practice, East versus West

Political and economic views and practice	Emphasis on individualism	Emphasis on traditional family value	Emphasis on social institutions and communities	Emphasis on the power of the state (government)
East Asia	Weak	Strong	Weak	Strong
Western Europe and the United States	Strong	Weak	Strong	Weak

However, the West makes up for its weakness in traditional family with its strong tradition in emphasizing the development of social institutions and communities, which are the backbone of the civil society and a well-functioning democracy (Tocqueville, 1835–1840).

Compared to East Asia, the West views the government with deep suspicion and caution, and wants to keep it in check with many constraints. As succinctly put by one of the founding fathers of the United States, Thomas Paine, "Government, even in its best state, is but a necessary evil; in its worst state, an intolerable one" (Paine, 1776). Thus governments in the West have less power than their counterparts in East Asia (Table 12.1).

13.2 WHAT CAN WE LEARN FROM THE RELATION-BASED WAY?[1]

From the perspective of the rule of law, using the relation-based way to obtain public goods and services controlled by the government is illegal. It usually involves bribing the official in power to get the goods or services one otherwise cannot get through legal channels. (Of course, it can be argued that the reason one circumvents the legal channels to obtain the public goods illegally through private relations is that the legal way of distributing the goods and services is not fair, and the government is monopolizing too many resources at the cost of social equity and efficiency.) As a general principle, we are not encouraging people and firms to break the law, even if the law is not fair.

13.2.1 The Advantage of Relation-Based Interfirm Collaboration

In Chapter 2, Western Rules Versus Eastern Relations: A Fundamental Framework to Understand East Asia, we explained that in contract fulfillment and enforcement, the relation-based way can be more complete than the rule-based way because the latter can only fulfill and enforce what is written, whereas the former can go beyond it and follow the mutual feeling and the common spirit between two parties. This is an advantage of the relation-based way of doing business.

In research on the interfirm relationship in Vietnam, the authors used cases to illustrate this point very convincingly (Nguyen, Weinstein, & Meyer, 2005). In one case, a manager of a subcontracting firm located in a remote place asked the manager of the client firm for help to deal with government bureaucracy (because the client was in the capital city and was more experienced) on an order unrelated to the client firm. The manager at the client firm analyzed the order and pointed out that it was not efficient for the subcontractor to do it in-house and helped the subcontractor to outsource it. In another example, a contractor received an export order unrelated to the client. But the contractor did not have the export license, which the client had. To help the contractor, the client purchased the order at cost and handled the export process on the contractor's behalf (Nguyen et al., 2005).

Certainly, those mutual assistances were not in their contractual relationship. In fact it is virtually impossible to specify these kinds of situations in a written contract. This cooperation is based on the general spirit of long-term collaboration and mutual help without calculating financial gains or losses each time, but in the long run, both partners benefit from the savings in transaction costs.[2]

13.2.2 Making Nonfamily Business a Family Business

From a business operation perspective, there is much to discover and learn from the relation-based way. Guo Fansheng, the successful entrepreneur in China we quoted earlier in the book, is an enthusiast of relation-based management, which he calls *qin-qing* management. *Qin-qing* is the Chinese phrase for the affection, emotion, and love that exist among family members, which can be roughly translated into "family-feeling." He strongly believes that the best way to manage an enterprise is to run it like a family using the "family-feeling" management style, which, if used artfully, can make employees view the firm as their own family and wholeheartedly put their maximum effort into their work. So instead of repudiating family business as old-fashioned, he calls for nonfamily firms to be run like a family firm (Guo, 2008).

From a different perspective, economists George Akerlof and Robert Shiller have argued the same underlying theme when comparing the success of Toyota in Japan and the failure of Kaiser, a car company in Argentina. They showed that trust is one of the major factors that explains their difference in success and failure (Akerlof & Shiller, 2009). From the perspective of our discussion, Japan is traditionally a relation-based society with a high level of trust, whereas the trust level in Argentina is low (see chapter: Western Rules Versus Eastern Relations: A Fundamental Framework to Understand East Asia). The relation-based way has enabled Toyota to build close working relationships between managers and workers and be run more like a family business.

How can such an organizational culture be nurtured in large corporations, especially in a rule-based environment where most transactions are kept at an arm's length, and work and family are more clearly demarcated? In this book, we have been arguing that the "family-feeling" style (the relation-based way) is only practical when an organization is small. How can the CEO of a large company give personal treatment to thousands of employees?

While this is a new subject that needs to be studied, here are some preliminary observations that may give us some ideas. Guo has the following advice based on his experience. When his firm was small and private, he would approve a company loan for his managers when they wanted to buy a house. That was okay, Guo said, since the company was his and he treated his managers as family members. When his firm grew big and received outside investment, it became inappropriate for him to dole out company loans to his managers. So in order to preserve the family feeling among his senior managers, he loaned his personal money to a senior manager to buy a house. "When your company grew big, you must institutionalize the "family feeling." To do it, you have to cough up your own money; you can't use the company's money anymore," advised Guo (Guo, 2008). This is quite an extreme case. But the point is clearly made.

The second piece of advice Guo gave was that in order to institutionalize the family feeling in the company when it becomes big, the founder(s) must make a clear policy that bars family members from working in the company. "In order to make all nonfamily members feel that you [the boss] treat them like a family, you must first stop giving favors to your own family," Guo explained (Guo, 2008).

To create the "family-feeling," companies should consider giving more in-kind benefits rather than simple cash compensation. They also should offer more family-friendly and family-style activities. We have begun to see this trend in some successful companies in the West.

Ever since the sociologist Max Weber first proclaimed that in order to modernize, leaders of organizations must change from relying on personal charisma to following bureaucratic rules, seeking a charismatic leader for an organization has been viewed as old-fashioned and thus frowned upon (Weber, 1958 (1904–1905)). Now it is time to rethink this philosophy: if rule-based firms can add more "family-feeling" to their organizational culture, they will be more competitive. In this sense, it is to the firm's advantage to have a charismatic leader—someone who has the ability to earn trust, who has good interpersonal skills and is good at cultivating relations, and who is generous in his or her treatment of friends. Thus, in sum, the emphasis in relation-based culture—loyalty, generosity toward friends, reciprocity, the "family-feeling"—is certainly something executives and managers in rule-based market should begin to pay more attention to in order to stay competitive in the increasingly globalized market.

13.3 WHAT CAN WE LEARN FROM EAST ASIA?

13.3.1 Restoring the Hard Working Culture

The success of the American economy has been built by Americans with a strong hard-working culture. As the country has become affluent leading to changes in the political landscape and economic policies, that hard-working culture has been gradually weakened. Without such a hard-working culture, United States cannot keep its competitive edge, and will eventually lose its leading position in the increasingly globalized world, in which the rapidly rising economies, such as China, are powered by a workforce with a strong hard-working culture. As a country, the United States must find its way to restore the hard working culture, which is not easy given the rigidity of political and economic institutions of the United States. As individuals, we can learn habits that are conducive to efficiency and productivity, adopt lifestyles that help us to delay gratification and invest in the future.

In our chapter on the role of culture in economic development (see chapter: The Role of Culture in Economic Development: Does Culture Give East Asia an Edge Over America in Economic Competition?), we cited a study that identified some cultural traits that are positively associated with high productivity. Among these traits are the dissatisfaction with one's economic situation (which gives motivation to improve it), self-reliance, obeyance of authority, and preservation of the traditional family structure.

In 2015, the Japanese government made a push to reintroduce the teaching of the traditional values that have gradually been undermined in the course of modernization (Obe, 2015, December 28). Among the traditional values are "be filial to your parents," "bear yourself in modesty and moderation," "devote yourself to learning and gain an occupation," "acquire knowledge and develop your talent," and "work to promote public good."

13.3.2 Improving Government Effectiveness

We should learn from East Asia to make our government more effective in governing. This is a hard sell to Americans since we hold such a low opinion of government. However, recognizing that the government is a "necessary evil" and making it effective and efficient do not have to contradict each other. Since we will be stuck with a government anyway, we should make it do good for the society and the economy. For it to do so, we must respect it and give it enough power to act. The widely held view in the West, especially in America, that government cannot be trusted and is always wasteful may help the people to better safeguard citizens' rights and stop officials abusing power, but it is not conducive to making the government more effective.

Another reason that American governments are weak is because of the high degree of autonomy of local governments and the highly decentralized governing structure in the United States. Under the federal system, the state governments do not take orders from the federal government in most economic and business-related policies and decisions and, likewise, the local governments do not have to listen to the state government when they decide on local business matters. While the system has many obvious advantages, there are costs. One of them is the lack of coordination in the global competition. For instance, in the region where I live, Hampton Roads, Southeast Virginia, a one-million population metropolitan region consisting of many cities including the big cities of Chesapeake, Norfolk, and Virginia Beach, there is a need to construct an integrated transportation infrastructure such as a light rail system and to construct a conference center to attract professional and business travelers. However, instead of coordinating these efforts, each major city independently decides whether and how to build its own light rail and each wants to build its own conference center. As a result, Norfolk built its light rail that goes nowhere, since Virginia Beach has not decided whether to build its light rail to connect with Norfolk's. Currently, several cities are increasing their conference and hotel facilities simultaneously, which will lead to overcapacity in the region. When Norfolk plans to build a mega factory outlet mall that will benefit the whole region including Virginia Beach, the latter refuses to let the mall developer build an access road that will go through Virginia Beach. These coordination issues can be resolved more effectively and efficiently for the benefit of all cities involved if the government above them, namely Virginia State, has more authority to coordinate.

13.4 GET READY TO COMPETE

When I teach an international business class in the United States, I ask the students if they know the names of Chinese and Russian presidents. Many do not. If I ask who the American president was in a class in East Asia, all students would know it with intimate details about the president. It is fair to say that Americans are the least globalized. Why is that?

In 1960, the US accounted for 40% of the world's total output (World Bank, 2015). In other words, America was nearly half of the world: the rest of the world—some 300 countries—together only produced a slightly more than half. So America was the center of the world. Other countries had to follow the terms that the US set, and they had to speak the language that the Americans spoke. The need for Americans to learn about the rest of the world was not warranted, since the other countries were so small, economically and militarily.

In 2014, the share of the US economy in the world dropped to 22% (World Bank, 2015). While still big, the United States is no longer as dominant as it used to be. Furthermore, the emerging economies such as China are rapidly catching up. As the newly emerging countries are challenging US dominance, the United States must learn from these countries in order to compete with them. American students must know who the leaders in these countries are.

Ultimately, competition is primarily determined at the atom level, which is us, the individuals who constitute the country and the economy. We must take actions to improve our ability to compete in the globalizing world. I hope that this book helps us to better understand East Asia and the relation-based system, and thus helps us to better prepare ourselves for the competition and then win it.

QUESTIONS

1. What do you think we (the government, firms, and people) should do to improve the country's competitiveness in the world?
2. What do you think are the concrete measures that the governments in the United States can do to restore and develop the hard-working culture?
3. What do you think you need to do to get ready to compete in the increasingly globalized world?

ENDNOTES

1. Adopted from Li, S. (2009). *Managing international business in relation-based versus rule-based countries.* New York, NY: Business Expert Press.
2. While this kind of cooperation also exists in rule-based countries, it is more prevalent in relation-based countries.

REFERENCES

Akerlof, G. A., & Shiller, R. J. (2009). *Animal spirits: How human psychology drives the economy, and why it matters for global capitalism.* Princeton, NJ: Princeton University Press.

Guo, F. (2008). *The China model: Guide for family business growth.* Beijing: Peking University Press.

Li, S. (2009). *Managing international business in relation-based versus rule-based countries.* New York, NY: Business Expert Press.

Li, S., Park, S.H., & Selover, D. (2015). Cultural dividend: A hidden source of economic growth in emerging countries: Old Dominion University.

Nguyen, T., Weinstein, M., & Meyer, A. D. (2005). Development of trust: A study of interfirm relationships in Vietnam. *Asia Pacific Journal of Management, 22,* 211–235.

Obe, M. (2015, December 28). In Japan, ethics lessons spur debate. *The Wall Street Journal, 1.*

Paine, T. (1776). *Common Sense.* Philadelphia, PA: Printed and Sold by W. and T. Bradford.

Putnam, R. (1993). *Making democracy work: Civic traditions in modern Italy.* Princeton, NJ: Princeton University Press.

Tocqueville, A. D. (1835–1840). *Democracy in America.* London: Saunders and Otley.

Weber, M. (1958 (1904–1905)). *The protestant ethics and the spirit of capitalism.* New York, NY: Charles Scribner's Sons.

World Bank, (2015). *World development indicators.* Washington, DC: World Bank.

INDEX

Note: Page numbers followed by "*f*" and "*t*" refer to figures and tables, respectively.

A

Address
  differences between East and West, 60–62
Adversarial tradition, 47
Amazon.com, 4
America
  cultural revolution, need for, 68–69
  inner-city schools in, 55–56
Apple, 5, 109–110
ASEAN (Association of Southeast Asian Nations), 1
Asian Financial Crisis 1997, 173, 175
Asian Miracle, 174
Asian tigers, 38
Authoritarianism, 18–19, 50
  neo-authoritarianism, 49–50
Authority, 62–63
Automation, 114, 115*f*

B

Bao Gong, 46, 47*f*
Barriers
  to investment, 5–6
  to market entry, 124–125
  to market exit, 125–126
"Beggar thy neighbor", 100, 100*f*
Bribery-corruption relationship, 76–81, 83*f*
Bush administration, 50
Business
  groups, in relation-based markets, 126–127
  relation-based market structure, 120–122
Business strategies
  automation, 114, 115*f*
  considerations for, 116–117
  cost reduction, pressure for, 107, 108*f*
  in East Asia, 105
  global standardization strategy, 109–110, 109*f*
  hybrid strategy, 109*f*, 110

international, 105–111
  localization strategy, 109*f*, 110, 113–114
  local responsiveness, pressure for, 108, 108*f*
  low cost production, 111–113, 112*f*, 112*t*
  mass customization, 115–116
  profiting from global expansion, 105–106
  traditional strategy, 109, 109*f*
Business transactions, in relation-based governance, 22–25

C

Callahan, Michael, 157
Cambodia
  political economic system, 44
Capital, sunk, 124
Capitalism, 34
  elements of, 34*f*
Capitalist society, customer service quality in, 119–120
Carrefour, 114
Chaebols, 39, 172–173
Chen Shui-bian, 85, 92
Chiang Ching-kuo, 17–18, 40, 174
Chiang Kai Shek, 17–18, 40
Chief executive officers (CEOs), 135–136
  private relations, 137–138
China
  China Natural Petroleum, 120–121
  Chinese Communist Party, 42, 44, 78–79, 86, 90
  corruption in, 78–81, 79*t*
  counterfeit goods, 131–132
  culture's role in economic growth, 65–66
  information management, 86–88
  Maotanchang, 9
  political economic system, 42–44
  relation-based market structure, 122–123
  relation-based ways of financing, 89
  Yahoo!'s dilemma in, 157–158

Commitment problem, in information and
    communication technology, 161–162
Communist party, organizational structure
    of, 42–43
Communist societies, customer service
    quality in, 119
Confucianism, 57, 65–66
Confucius, 57
Conjuangco, Manuel, 81
Constitutional monarchy, 37
Consumers
    effect of globalization, 8
Core competencies, leveraging, 106
Corporate governance
    information and communication
        technology, effect of, 162
Corruption, 71
    in China, 78–81, 79t
    and economic efficiency, 74–75, 75f
    and economic growth, 71–76
    efficiency-enhancing, 76–78, 82–83
    by government officials, 71–73
    in Philippines, 79t, 81–82
    by society as a whole, 71–73
    trust and, 76–78
    worldwide, 73, 73f, 82–83
Corruption Perception Index (CPI), 73, 74f
Cost
    economies, realizing, 106
    low cost production, 111–113, 112f, 112t
    reduction, pressure for, 107, 108f
Counterfeit goods, 131–132, 132t
Creativity, 163–167
    cultural explanation, 164
    political and economic factors, 164–166,
        165f, 165t
    relation-based system, effect of, 166–167
Cultural change, 66–67
Cultural compatibility, of information and
    communication technology, 158–159
Cultural Index, 63, 63f
Cultural revolution, need for, 68–69
Culture, 55
    defined, 56
    effect on economic performance, 62–66
    Hofstede's cultural dimensions, 58–60
    triple package argument, 64–65, 68

Customer service quality, 119–120
    in capitalist society, 119–120
    in communist societies, 119

D

Daqiuzhuang, 135–136
Decision mode compatibility, of
    information and communication
    technology, 159–160
Delayed gratification, 64
Dell, 114
Democracy, representative, 33, 34t
Democratic People's Republic of Korea, 45
Democratic Progressive Party, 174
Deng Xiaoping, 42–43, 65–66, 138, 178–180
Developed countries
    effect of globalization, 8
Dictatorship, 33–34
Digitization, 153
Direct investment, 90–93, 93f
Dissemination, of information goods, 153

E

Earnings management, 87–88, 94
East Asia, 1–3
    business strategies in, 105
    compared with United States, 189–191,
        191t
    counterfeit goods in, 131–132, 132t
    creativity in, 163–167
    customer service quality in, 120
    economic growth of, 2–3, 3t
    economic miracle, 17–20
    exchange-rate regimes of, 101–102
    government effectiveness, improving,
        195–196
    hard-working culture, restoring, 194–195
    human resource management, 135
    income per capita of, 2
    information and communication
        technology, 153
    innovation in, 163–167
    market structures in, 119
    population of, 2
    South, 2f
Economic efficiency, corruption and,
    74–75, 75f

Economic Freedom Index (EFI), 37–42, 44–45, 176–178, 186
Economic growth, corruption and, 71–83
Economic performance
    culture's effect on, 62–66
    religious and ethical systems role in, 56–57
Economy
    market, 34
    nonmarket, 34–35
Efficiency-enhancing corruption, 76–78, 82–83
Electrolux, 113
Ethical systems
    role in economic performance, 56–57
Ex ante monitoring capability, 23–24, 26–27, 48, 48f, 89
Exchange-rate regimes
    of East Asia, 101–102
    in worldwide, 99–100
Exchange rates, 97, 99
Ex nunc monitoring capability. *See* Interim monitoring capability
Expatriate managers, 143–145
    performance, improving, 148–150, 148f
Ex post monitoring capability, 24, 26–27, 49, 49f, 89

F
Family value, 63
Feng Lun, 122
Financial situation, people's perception about, 62
Financing, relation-based ways of, 89
Firms
    business strategies, 105
    information management by, 87–88, 88f
    profiting from global expansion, 105–106
Fisher Effect, 99
Fixed exchange-rate regimes, 100
Float exchange-rate regimes, 100
Foreign exchange
    market, 97–98
    risk, 97
Foreign investment flows, 89–90
Formal rules, in relation-based organizations, 139

Forward exchange rate, 97
Freedom, 62–63
Free market, 34

G
Geopolitical issues, of business strategies, 116
Global competition, 9, 195–196
Globalization, 3–7
    defined, 3
    drivers of, 5–7
    gains and losses in, 7–8
    of markets, 4
    of production, 5
Global standardization business strategy, 109–110, 109f
Governance
    defined, 19
    environment, 19, 20f
    modes of, 94–95
    relation-based, 20–22
    rule-based, 20–22
    vacuum, 182–185
Governance Environment Index (GEI), 74, 74f, 92–93, 93f, 177
Government
    effectiveness, improving, 195–196
    relation-based market structure, 120–122
    role in transition from relation-based to rule-based governance, 180–181
Gross domestic product (GDP), 3t

H
Hard-working culture, restoring, 194–195
Hofstede, Geert
    cultural dimensions, 58–60
Honda, 114
Hong Kong
    business groups, in relation-based markets, 127
    counterfeit goods, 131–132
    political economic system, 41–42
Huang Mengfu, 122
Human resource management, 135
    practices, 140–141
    right relationship, 140–141, 142f
Hybrid business strategy, 109f, 110

I

Impulse control, 64–65
Independent Commission Against
    Corruption (ICAC), 41
Indirect (portfolio) investment, 90–93, 93*f*
Individualism, 58
Indulgence, 60
Industrial and Commercial Bank of China,
    120–121
Information, in relation-based societies,
    85–86
Informational compatibility, of information
    and communication technology, 159
Information and communication
    technology (ICT), 153
  advancement in, 6
  commitment problem, 161–162
  cultural compatibility, 158–159
  decision mode compatibility, 159–160
  digitization, 153
  dissemination, 153
  distinguished from traditional
    communication, 154, 155*f*
  effect on corporate governance, 162
  informational compatibility, 159
  Internet, 155–158, 157*f*
  mode of vertical communications,
    160–161
  use of, and efficiency, 154–155
Information management
  by firms, 87–88, 88*f*
  by relation-based government, 86–87
Inner-city schools, in America, 55–56
Innovation, 163–167, 163*t*
  cultural explanation, 164
  political and economic factors, 164–166,
    165*f*, 165*t*
  relation-based system, effect of, 166–167
Inquisitorial tradition, 47
Insecurity, 64
Interest rates, 99
Interim monitoring capability, 24, 26–27,
    48, 48*f*, 89
International business strategy, 105–111
International Financial Report Standard
    (IFRS), 177
International Fisher Effect, 99

Internet, 6, 7*f*, 155–158
  contrasting features of, 157*f*
  Yahoo!'s dilemma, in China, 157–158
Investment
  barriers, 5–6
  direct, 90–93, 93*f*
  foreign, flows of, 89–90
  indirect (portfolio), 90–93, 93*f*
  protection, 93*f*
  types of, 91–95

J

Japan
  business groups, in relation-based
    markets, 127
  political economic system, 37–38
  transition from relation-based to rule-
    based governance, 171–172, 171*f*
Japan Airlines (JAL), 97–99
J. P. Morgan, 138

K

KFC, 106, 113
Kim Dae Jung, 174
Kim Il-sung, 45
Kim Jong-il, 45
Kim Jong-un, 45
Kuomintang (KMT), 39

L

Lantos, Tom, 157
Laos
  political economic system, 44
Lee Kuan Yew, 40–41
Legal system, 46–47
Lenin, Vladimir, 42–43
Leninist parties, 43
Levi, 116
Li Jiange, 91–92
Li Ka-shing, 184
Lincoln, President, 33
Local employees–expatriate manager
    relationship, 148–149, 148*f*
Localization business strategy, 109*f*, 110,
    113–114
Local responsiveness, pressure for, 108, 108*f*
Location economies, achieving, 105–106

Long-term orientation, 60
L'Oreal, 113
Low cost production, 111–113, 112*f*, 112*t*

M
Maoist, 6
Maotanchang, education at, 9, 10*f*, 11*f*
Mao Zedong, 2–3, 42–43, 65–66, 78–79,
    86, 176, 178–180
Marcos, Ferdinand, 81–82
Market(s)
    economy, 34
    free, 34
    foreign exchange, 97–98
    globalization of, 4
    structures. *See* Market structures
Market structures, 119
    counterfeit goods, 131–132, 132*t*
    customer service quality, 119–120
    relation-based market structure, salient
        features of, 120–127
    trade flows, between rule-based and
        relation-based countries, 127–131,
        129*f*
Martin, Lockheed, 116
Martin, Raytheon, 116
Marxist–Leninist, 6
Masculinity, 60
Mass customization, 115–116
McDonalds, 184
Meiji Restoration, 37, 171–172
Microprocessors, 6
Microsoft, 109
Modes of governance, 94–95
    implications of, 95
Multinational corporations, during
        transition from relation-based to rule-
        based governance, 181–186
    challenges to, 182–184
    opportunities for, 181–182
Myanmar
    political economic system, 44

N
Names
    differences between East and West, 60–62
National Day, 22–23

Nationalism, rise of, of business strategies,
    116–117
Neo-authoritarianism, 49–50
Nixon, Richard, 86
Nonmarket economy, 34–35
North Korea
    political economic system, 45

O
Obama administration, 50
O'Neill, Liz, 116
Open Markets Index, 171–172, 174, 176,
    178
Opium War, 41
Ordering, 19–20
    private, 19
    public, 19
Organizational structure, 136–137, 138*f*

P
Park Chung Hee, 17–18, 38–39
Pegged exchange-rate regimes, 100
Philippines
    corruption in, 79*t*, 81–82
    Philippine Tobacco Filters Corporation,
        81–82
Policy considerations, 67–68
Political economic system, 17, 33, 35–45,
    35*f*
    Cambodia, 44
    China, 42–44
    Hong Kong, 41–42
    Japan, 37–38
    Laos, 44
    Myanmar, 44
    North Korea, 45
    Singapore, 40–41
    South Korea, 38–39
    Taiwan, 39–40
    Vietnam, 44
Political Freedom Index, 37–42, 44–45
Power distance, 58, 160–161
Private ordering, 19
Private relations, 137–138
Procter & Gamble (P&G), 106, 113
Producers
    effect of globalization, 8

Production, productivity, 62–64, 66–69
    globalization of, 5
Profiting from global expansion,
    109–110
Protestant work ethics, 56–57
Public ordering, 19
Purchasing power parity (PPP), 98

Q

Quantitative easing (QE), 102–103

R

Relation-based governance, 20–22. *See also*
    Transition from relation-based to rule-
    based governance
    business transactions in, 22–25
    costs and benefits of, 25–30, 28*f*
    distinguished from rule-based
        governance, 29*t*, 30–31
    types of, 29*t*
Relation-based market structure, salient
    features of, 120–127
    barriers to entry, 124–125
    barriers to exit, 125–126
    business groups, 126–127
    government and business, 120–122
    tendency of, 122–124
Relation-based organizations
    formal rules in, 139
    lack of strategic planning, 140
Relation-based relationship management,
    137–138
Relation-based societies, 191–194
    advantage of, 191–192
    information in, 85–86
    information management by, 86–87
    Internet, 155–158
    nonfamily business into family business,
        making, 192–194
    talent flows in, 143
    working relationships, 145–147, 147*t*
Religious systems
    role in economic performance, 56–57
Representative democracy, 33, 34*t*
Return on assets (ROA), 88, 88*f*
Right relationship, and human resource
    management, 140–141, 142*f*

Rule-based governance, 20–22. *See also*
    Transition from relation-based to rule-
    based governance
    distinguished from relation-based
        governance, 29*t*, 30–31
    types of, 29*t*
Rule-based society
    talent flows in, 143
    working relationships, 145–147, 147*t*
Rule of law, 19

S

Salim Group, 127
Secret society, 22
Shi Tao, 157
Singapore
    counterfeit goods, 131–132
    political economic system, 40–41
Sinopec, 120–121
South East Asia, 2*f*
South Korea
    business groups, in relation-based
        markets, 127
    political economic system, 38–39
    transition from relation-based to rule-
        based governance, 172–174, 173*f*
Spot exchange rate, 97
Stalin, Joseph, 86
Starbuck's, 117
State
    role of, 49–52
    security, 42–43
State Grid Corp, 120–121
Strategic management, 105
Strategic planning
    lack of, in relation-based organizations,
        140
Subsidiary skills, leveraging, 106
Sunk capital, 124
Superiority complex, 64–65

T

Taiwan
    Democratic Progressive Party, 174
    political economic system, 39–40
    transition from relation-based to rule-
        based governance, 174–176, 175*f*

Taiwan Stock Exchange (TSE), 175
Talent flows, between rule-based and
    relation-based societies, 143
Technologies
    advancements in, 6–7
    telecommunication, 6
Telecommunication technologies, 6
Thailand
    business groups, in relation-based
        markets, 127
    relation-based market structure, 121,
        123–124
Three monitoring mechanisms, 48–49
Tiange Technology, 91–92
Titles, 138–139
Totalitarianism, 33–34
Trade, falling, 5–6
Trade flows, between rule-based and
    relation-based countries, 127–131,
    129f
    policy and strategic implications, 131
Traditional business strategy, 109, 109f
Transition from relation-based to rule-
    based governance, 169
    challenges to, 178–180
    communication, 169–170
    difficulty of, 178
    government, role of, 180–181
    multinational corporations, role of. See
        Multinational corporations, during
        transition from relation-based to rule-
        based governance
    stages of, 171–178
    strategic implications for doing business,
        184–186
Transparency International (TI), 73
Transportation technology, advancement
    in, 6
Triple package argument, 64–65, 68
Trust, and corruption, 76–78

U
Uber, 4, 5f
Uncertainty avoidance, 60
United States
    compared with East Asia,
        189–191, 191t
    customer service quality in, 119
    effect of globalization, 8
    US Federal Reserve, 102–103

V
Vertical communications, mode of,
    160–161
Vietnam
    political economic system, 44
    relation-based market structure, 123

W
Weber, Max, 56–57
Western Goddess of Justice, 45, 46f
Working relationships, 145–147, 147t
    differences in process priorities,
        146–147
    expectations of, 146
    investments in, 146
    scope of jobs, 145
    terms of, 145
World Trade Organization, 177
World Value Survey, 63
Worldwide Governance Indicator (WGI),
    171–172, 171f, 173f, 174–177, 175f,
    176f, 190

X
Xi Jinping, 114

Y
Yahoo!'s dilemma, in China, 157–158
Yuandan, 131
Yu Zuomin, 135–136

Printed in the United States
By Bookmasters